Reviews of the first edition

"This readable account displays the main strands of the thick skein of human head counts unusually well."

– Scientific American

"Livi-Bacci marshals an impressive array of evidence to describe large-scale population changes in human history and their future implications."

– Choice

"This is a bold and intelligent book . . . providing a coherent overview of an enormous topic. Livi-Bacci is a thoughtful, incisive, and wide-ranging guide into a vast terrain. . . . Readers will not get lost."

– Journal of Interdisciplinary History

"This is a work that repays reading, and I hope it will find a wide audience. Anthropologists who do not normally pay much attention to demographic matters may discover here that there is a potentially much wider disciplinary audience for their research than they had realized."

– Current Anthropology

"Authoritative, succinct and readable."

– Ansley J. Coale, Princeton University

"Graceful and wide-ranging. . . . The story is fascinating, and told with style and enthusiasm."

– Sam Preston, University of Pennsylvania.

This publication was made possible through the cooperation of Biblioteca Italia, a Giovanni Agnelli Foundation programme for the diffusion of Italian culture.

A CONCISE HISTORY OF WORLD POPULATION

Second Edition

Massimo Livi-Bacci

translated by Carl Ipsen

First published in Italy as *Storia minima della popolazione del mondo*,
copyright © Loescher – Ottobre 1989

Copyright © Massimo Livi-Bacci 1992, 1997

The right of Massimo Livi-Bacci to be identified as author of this work has been
asserted in accordance with the Copyright, Designs and Patents Act 1988.

First published in Italian 1989
English translation first published 1992; reprinted 1993, 1994 (twice), 1995.
Second edition published 1997
2 4 6 8 10 9 7 5 3 1

Blackwell Publishers Inc.
350 Main Street
Malden, MA 02148, USA

Blackwell Publishers Ltd
108 Cowley Road
Oxford OX4 1JF, UK

Library of Congress Cataloging-in-Publication Data
Livi-Bacci, Massimo.
   [Storia minima della popolazione del mondo. English]
   A concise history of world population / Massimo Livi-Bacci;
translated by Carl Ipsen. — 2nd ed.
     p. cm.
   Includes bibliographical references and index.
   ISBN 0–631–20454–7. — ISBN 0–631–20455–5 (pbk.)
   1. Population – History.   I. Title.
HB871.L56513   1997
304.6—dc20   96–34353
                                         CIP

British Library Cataloguing in Publication Data
A CIP catalogue record for this book is available from the British Library

Typeset in 10½ on 13pt Garamond by Words & Graphics Ltd, Anstey, Leicester
Printed in Great Britain by Hartnolls Limited, Bodmin, Cornwall

This book is printed on acid-free paper

Table of Contents

List of Figures

List of Tables

Introduction

Why is the present population of the world just over five billion[1] and not several orders of magnitude greater or smaller? For thousands of years prior to the invention of agriculture the human species must have numbered a thousandth part of what it does today; and there are those who maintain that our planet, given the available resources, could comfortably accommodate a population ten times larger than it does at present. What are the factors that through the ages determine demographic growth? How is the difficult balance with resources and environment maintained? These are fairly old questions, confronted for the first time in a modern form by Malthus, who, not by accident, inspired the work of Darwin.

In the pages of this "concise history" I intend to address these fundamental questions, discussing the underlying suppositions, the proposed solutions, the points already clarified and those still requiring investigation. The reader will find here a general discussion of demographic development and, I hope, a guide to understanding the mechanisms which through the ages have determined population growth, stagnation, or decline.

Since the invention of fire the human species has sought to modify the environment and enrich the resources it provides. In the very long run (millennia), humanity has grown numerically in relative harmony with available resources. Certainly the system of hunting and gathering could not have allowed the survival of many more than several million people, just as the European system of agriculture could only with great difficulty have supported more than the hundred million inhabitants who lived on the continent prior to the Industrial Revolution. However, in shorter spans of time (centuries or generations) this equilibrium is not so obvious for two fundamental reasons. The first is the recurrent action of catastrophic events – epidemics, climatic or natural disasters – which alter radically one term of the population–resources equation. The second lies in the fact that the demographic mechanisms that determine reproductive intensity, and

---

[1] Throughout I use the US billion = 1,000,000,000.

so demographic growth, change slowly and do not "adapt" easily to rapidly evolving environmental conditions. It is frequently claimed that the human species is equipped with "self-regulating" mechanisms that allow for the speedy re-establishment of the balance between numbers and resources. This is, however, only partially true, as these mechanisms when they do work, are imperfect (and of varying efficiency from population to population and from one age to another), so much so that entire populations have disappeared – a clear sign of the failure of all attempts at regulation.

In the following pages I devote a great deal of attention to the functioning, in various contexts and periods, of the mechanisms that determine the always precarious balance between population and resources. In order to do this I have had to enlarge my plan of attack to include problems and topics rarely touched upon in demographic works – from biology to economics – and so have been haunted by the constant fear of losing the depth of this study for the breadth of its extension. This is, however, a calculated and consciously accepted risk. Given the frequent setbacks suffered by attempts at interdisciplinarity, the temptation to take shelter within safe disciplinary boundaries is great; but problems remain complex and in order to resolve them it is not sufficient that they be individually identified and isolated. Now and then it is worth making an attempt at reconstruction.

1

The Space and Strategy of Demographic Growth

1   Humans and Animals

Throughout human history population has been synonymous with prosperity, stability, and security. A valley or plain teeming with houses, farms,
and villages has always been a sign of well-being. Traveling from Verona
to Vicenza, Goethe remarked with pleasure: "One sees a continuous range
of foothills . . . dotted with villages, castles and isolated houses . . . we
drove on a wide, straight and well-kept road through fertile fields . . . The
road is much used and by every sort of person."[1] The effects of a long
history of good government were evident, much as in the ordered Sienese
fourteenth-century landscapes of the Lorenzetti brothers. Similarly, Cortés
was unable to restrain his enthusiasm when he gazed over the valley of
Mexico and saw the lagoons bordered by villages and trafficked by canoes;
the great city; and the market (in a square more than double the size of
the entire city of Salamanca) that "accommodated every day more than
sixty thousand individuals who bought and sold every imaginable sort of
merchandise."[2]

This should come as no surprise. A densely populated region is implicit
proof of a stable social order, of nonprecarious human relations, and of well-
utilized natural resources. Only a large population can mobilize the human
resources necessary to build houses, cities, roads, bridges, ports, and canals.
If anything, it is abandonment and desertion rather than abundant population that has historically dismayed the traveler.

Population, then, might be seen as a crude index of prosperity. The

---

[1]   J. W. Goethe, *Italian Journey*, tr. W. H. Auden and Elizabeth Mayer (North Point
Press, San Francisco, 1982), p. 46.
[2]   H. Cortés, *Cartas de relación* (Editorial Porrua, Mexico, 1976), p. 62.

1 million inhabitants of the Paleolithic Age, the 10 million of the Neolithic, the 100 million of the Bronze, the 1 billion of the Industrial Revolution, or the 10 billion that we shall doubtless attain in the course of the coming century certainly represent more than simple demographic growth. Even these few figures tell us that demographic growth has not been uniform over time. Periods of expansion have alternated with others of stagnation and even decline; and the interpretation of these, even for relatively recent historical periods, is not an easy task. We must answer questions that are as straightforward in appearance as they are complex in substance: Why are we 5 billion today and not more or less, say 100 billion or 100 million? Why has demographic growth, from prehistoric times to the present, followed a particular path rather than any of numerous other possibilities? These questions are difficult but worth considering, since the numerical progress of population has been, if not dictated, at least constrained by many forces and obstacles which have determined the general direction of that path. To begin with, we can categorize these forces and obstacles as biological and environmental. The former are linked to the laws of mortality and reproduction which determine the rate of demographic growth; the latter determine the resistance which these laws encounter and further regulate the rate of growth. Moreover, biological and environmental factors affect one another reciprocally and so are not independent of one another.

Every living collectivity develops particular strategies of survival and reproduction which translate into potential and effective growth rates of varying velocity. A brief analysis of these strategies will serve as the best introduction to consideration of the specific case of the human species. Biologists have identified two large categories of vital strategies, called r and K, which actually represent simplifications of a continuum.[3] Insects, fish, and some small mammals practice an r-strategy: these organisms live in generally unstable environments and take advantage of favorable periods (annually or seasonally) to reproduce prolifically, even though the probability

---

[3]   For the discussion that follows I have followed the lead provided by R. M. May and D. I. Rubinstein in their "Reproductive Strategies," in *Reproductive Fitness*, ed. C. R. Austin and R. V. Short (Cambridge University Press, London, 1984), pp. 1–23. See also R. V. Short, "Species Differences in Reproductive Mechanisms," in the same volume, pp. 24–61. An essay of broader scope is that of S. C. Stearns, "Life History Tactics: A Review of the Ideas," *The Quarterly Review of Biology*, 51 (1976), pp. 3–47. The relevance of r and K strategies to demography is supported by A. J. Coale in the first chapter of A. J. Coale and S. Cotts Watkins, eds, *The Decline of Fertility in Europe* (Princeton University Press, Princeton, 1986), p. 7.

of offspring survival is small. It is just because of this environmental instability, however, that they must depend upon large numbers, because "life is a lottery and it makes sense simply to buy many tickets."[4] *r*-strategy organisms go through many violent cycles with phases of rapid increase and decrease.

A much different strategy is that practiced by *K*-type organisms – mammals, particularly medium and large size, and some birds – who colonize relatively stable environments, albeit populated with competitors, predators, and parasites. *K*-strategy organisms are forced by selective and environmental pressure to compete for survival, which in turn requires considerable investment of time and energy for the raising of offspring. This investment is only possible if the number of offspring is small.

r and *K* strategies characterize two well-differentiated groups of organisms (figure 1.1). The first are suited to small animals having a short life span, minimal intervals between generations, brief gestation periods, short intervals between births, and large litters. *K* strategies, on the other hand, are associated with larger animals, long life spans, long intervals between generations and between births, and single births.

Figure 1.2 records the relation between body size (length) and the interval between successive generations for a wide array of living organisms: as the first increases so does the second. It can also be demonstrated that the rate of growth of various species (limiting ourselves to mammals) varies more or less inversely with the length of generation and so with body size.[5] At an admittedly macroscopic level of generalization, the lower potential for demographic growth of the larger animals can be linked to their lower vulnerability to environmental fluctuations and this too is related to their larger body size. Because their life is not a lottery and their chances of survival are better, the larger animals do not need to entrust the perpetuation of the species to high levels of reproduction. The latter, in fact, would detract from those investments of protection and care required to ensure the offspring's reduced vulnerability and keep mortality low.

---

[4] May and Rubinstein, "Reproductive Strategies," p. 2.

[5] May and Rubinstein, in the article cited above, note that for mammals there exists a close relationship between body weight and age of sexual maturity. As we shall see below, the rate of growth of a population can be derived from Lotka's equation, $r = lnR_0/T$, where T is the average length of generation and R_0 is the average number of daughters per woman after mortality (net reproduction rate). It follows that r is reasonably sensitive to changes in T (closely linked to the age of sexual maturity) and less sensitive to changes in R_0, as it is directly linked to lnR_0. Changes in the value of T, then, from species to species, have a strong influence on the value of r.

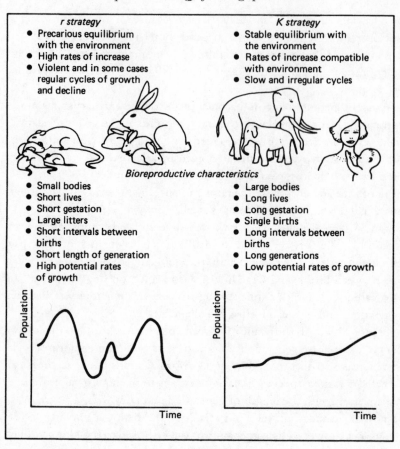

Figure 1.1   r strategy and *K* strategy

These ideas have been well known at least since the time of Darwin and Wallace, founders of the theory of natural selection. Nonetheless, they provide a useful introduction to discussion of the factors of human increase. Our species obviously practices a *K* strategy, in that it has successfully controlled the fluctuating environment and invests heavily in the raising of its young.

Two principles will be particularly helpful for the purpose of confronting the arguments of the following pages. The first concerns the relation between population and environment and should be understood broadly to include all the factors – physical environment, climate, availability of food, and so on – that determine survival. The second concerns the relation between

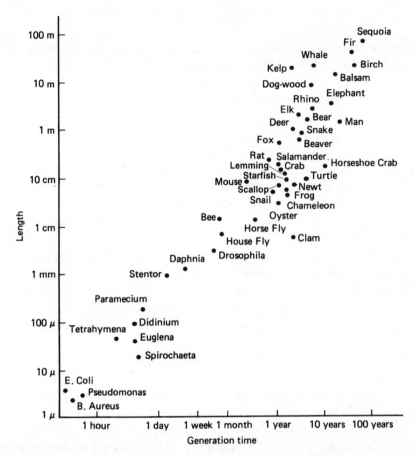

Figure 1.2 The length of an organism at the time of reproduction in relation to the generation time, plotted on a logarithmic scale
Source: J. T. Bonner, *Size and Cycle: an Essay on the Structure of Biology* (Princeton University Press, Princeton, 1965), p. 17.

reproduction and mortality insofar as the latter is a function of parental investment, which in turn relates inversely to reproductive intensity.

2   Divide and Multiply

Many animal species are subject to rapid and violent cycles which increase or decrease their numbers by factors of 100, 1,000, 10,000, or even more in a brief period. The 4-year cycle of the Scandinavian lemming is well known, as are those of the Canadian predators (10 years) and many infesting insects of temperate woods and forests (4 to 12 years). In Australia, "in certain years the introduced domestic mouse multiplies enormously. The mice swarm in crops and haystacks, and literal bucketfuls can be caught in a single night. Hawks, owls and cats flourish at their expense . . . but all these enemies have little effect in reducing the numbers. As a rule the plague ends rather suddenly. A few dead mice are found on the ground and the numbers dwindle rapidly to, or below, normal."[6] Other species maintain an equilibrium. Gilbert White observed two centuries ago that eight pairs of swallows flew round the belfry of the church in the village of Selborne, just as is the case today.[7] There are, then, both populations in rapid growth or decline and populations that are more or less stable.

The human species varies relatively slowly in time. Nonetheless, as we shall see below, long cycles of growth do alternate with others of decline, and the latter have even led to extinction for certain groups. For example, the population of Meosamerica was reduced to a fraction of its original size (one-fifth, one-tenth?) during the century that followed the Spanish conquest (initiated at the beginning of the sixteenth century), while that of the conquering Spaniards grew by half. Other populations have disappeared entirely or almost entirely – the population of Santo Domingo after the landing of Columbus or that of Tasmania following contact with the first explorers and settlers – while at the same time others nearby have continued to increase and prosper. In more recent times, the population of England and Wales multiplied sixfold between 1750 and 1900, while that of France in the same period increased by barely 50 percent. According to probable projections, Kenya's population will have increased tenfold between 1950 and 2010, while in the same period that of Germany by a mere 10 percent.

These few examples should suffice to demonstrate at what different rates the human species can grow even in similar situations (France and England) and over long periods. It should also be clear that here lies the heart of demography as a science: to measure growth, analyze mechanisms, and understand causes.

Population growth (whether positive or negative, rapid or slow) can be described by a simple calculation. In any interval of time a population (P) varies numerically as a result of renewal or arrivals (births B and immigration I) and elimination or departures (deaths D and emigration E).

---

[6] F. MacFarlane Burnet, *Natural History of Infectious Diseases* (Cambridge University Press, London, 1962), p. 14.

[7] May and Rubinstein, "Reproductive Strategies," p. 1.

Leaving aside migration (considering the population "closed," as is that of the entire planet), the variation of the population dP in any interval of time t – by convention and for convenience demographers use years – is given by the following:

$$dP = B - D,$$

and so the rate of growth r (where $r = dP/P$) will be equal to the difference between the birth rate b (where $b = B/P$) and the death rate d (where $d = D/P$):

$$r = dP/P = b - d$$

The range of variation of the birth and death rates is fairly wide. Minimum values are 5 to 10 per thousand (possible today with mortality and fertility under control) and maximum 40 to 50 per thousand. As mortality and fertility are not independent, it is unlikely that opposite extremes should coexist. Over long periods growth rates vary in practice between −1 and 3 percent per year.

For most of human history fertility and mortality must have remained in virtual equilibrium, as the rate of population growth was very low. If we accept the estimates of 252 million for the world population at the beginning of the present era (0 AD) and 771 million in 1750 (table 1.2), at the beginning of the Industrial Revolution, then we can calculate the average annual growth rate for the period as 0.06 percent. If we imagine that mortality averaged 40 per thousand, then fertility must have been 40.6 per thousand, just 1.5 percent greater than mortality. The past 30 years have witnessed a much different situation, as fertility has exceeded mortality by 200 percent.

Fertility and mortality rates are numerical calculations with little in the way of conceptual content, and as such are not well adapted to the description of the phenomena of reproduction and survival on which demographic growth depends.

3 *Jacopo Bichi and Domenica Del Buono, Jean Guyon and Mathurine Robin*

Jacopo Bichi was a humble sharecropper from Fiesole (near Florence).[8] On November 12, 1667 he wed Domenica Del Buono. Their marriage, although

---

[8] I am indebted to Carlo Corsini for having supplied me with the following examples taken from family reconstructions for the diocese of Fiesole.

soon ended by the death of Jacopo, nonetheless produced three children: Andrea, Filippo, and Maria Maddalena. The latter died when only a few months old, but Andrea and Filippo survived and married. In a sense, Jacopo and Domenica paid off their demographic debt: the care received from their parents, and their own resistance and luck succeeded in bringing them to reproductive age. They in turn bore and raised two children who also arrived to the same stage of maturity (reproductive age and marriage) and who, in a sense, replaced them exactly in the generational chain of life. Continuing the story of this family, Andrea married Caterina Fossi, and together they had four children, two of whom wed. Andrea and Caterina also paid their debt. Such was not the case for Filippo, who married Maddalena Cari. Maddalena died shortly afterward, having borne a daughter who in turn died at a young age. The two surviving sons of Andrea constitute the third generation: Giovan Battista married Caterina Angiola and had six children, all but one of whom died before marrying. Jacopo married Rosa, who bore eight children, four of whom married. Let us stop here and summarize the results of these five weddings (and ten spouses):

Two couples (Jacopo and Domenica, Andrea and Caterina) paid their debt, each couple bringing two children to matrimony.
One couple (Jacopo and Rosa) paid their debt with interest, as the two of them produced four wedded offspring.
One couple (Giovan Battista and Caterina Angiola) finished partially in debt in spite of the fact that they produced six children; only one wed.
One couple (Filippo and Maddalena) was completely insolvent, as no offspring survived to marry.

In three generations, five couples (ten spouses) produced nine wedded children in all. In biological terms, ten breeders brought nine offspring to the reproductive phase, a 10 percent decline which, if repeated for an extended period, would lead to the family's extinction.

A population, however, is made up of many families and many histories, each different from the others. In this same period, and applying the same logic, six couples of the Patriarchi family married off 15 children, while five Palagi couples did so with 10. The Patriarchi paid with interest, while the Palagi just fulfilled their obligation. The combination of these individual experiences, whether the balance is positive, negative, or even, determines the growth, decline, or stagnation of a population in the long run.

In 1608 Québec was founded and the French inhabitation of the Saint

Lawrence Valley, virtually abandoned by the Iroquois, had begun.[9] During the following century, approximately 15,000 immigrants arrived in these virgin lands from Normandy, from the area around Paris, and from central western France. Two-thirds of these returned to France after stays of varying lengths. The current population of 6 million French Canadians descends, for the most part, from those 5,000 immigrants who remained, as subsequent immigration contributed little to population growth. Thanks to a genealogicodemographic reconstruction carried out by a group of Canadian scholars, a considerable amount of information relating to demographic events is known about this population. For example, two pioneers, Jean Guyon and Mathurine Robin, had 2,150 descendants by 1730. Naturally, subsequent generations, including wives and husbands from other genealogical lines, contributed to this figure, which in and of itself has little demographic significance. On the other hand, the fate of another pioneer, the famous explorer Samuel de Champlain, was very different, and he left no descendants at all. The extraordinary Canadian material also provides measures of significant demographic interest. For example, the 905 pioneers (men and women) who were born in France, migrated to Canada before 1660, and both married and died in Canada produced on average 4.2 married off-spring (figure 1.3), a level of fertility which corresponds to a doubling of the original population in a single generation (from two spouses, four married children). The exceptionally high reproductive capacity of the settlers of French Canada was the result of an extraordinary combination of circum-stances: the physical selection of the immigrants, their high fertility and low mortality, ample available space, low density, and the absence of epidemics.

We have unknowingly touched the heart of the mechanisms of population growth. As we have seen, a population grows (or declines or remains stationary) from one generation to the next if those who gain access to reproduction (here defined by the act of marriage) are in turn successful in bringing a larger (or smaller or equal) number of individuals to marriage. The end result, whatever it might be, is basically determined by two factors: the number of children each individual, or each couple, succeeds in producing – due to biological capability, desire, age at marriage, length of cohabitation, and other factors – and the intensity of mortality from birth until the end of the reproductive period. A familiarity with these mechanisms, which I shall

---

[9]   The discussion that follows is derived from H. Charbonneau et al., *Naissance d'une population. Les Français établis au Canada au XVIIe siècle* (Presses de la Université de Montréal, Montréal, 1987).

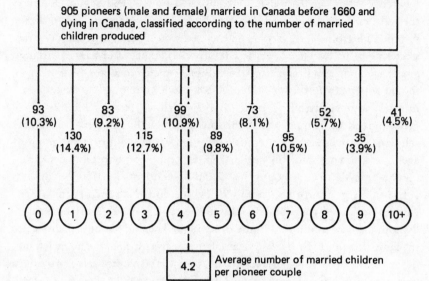

Figure 1.3   Growth of the French Canadian population (seventeenth century): pioneers and their children

discuss in the following section, is essential for understanding the factors of demographic change.

4   Reproduction and Survival

The growth potential of a population may be expressed as the function of two measures, whose significance should be intuitive: (1) the number of births, or children, per woman, and (2) life expectancy at birth. These are synthetic measures of, respectively, reproduction and survival. The first describes the average number of children produced by a generation of women during the course of their reproductive lives and in the hypothetical absence of mortality.[10] Below we shall consider the biological, social and cultural factors which determine the level of this measure. The second, life expectancy at birth, describes the average duration of life (or average number

---

[10]   The average number of children per woman, or total fertility rate (TFR), is the sum of age-specific fertility rates for women between the minimum and maximum ages of reproduction, $f_x = B_x/P_x$. B_x is the number of births to woman age x and P_x is the female population age x.

of years lived) for a generation of newborns and is a function of the force of mortality at the various ages, mortality which in turn is determined by the species' biological characteristics and relationship with the surrounding environment. In the primarily rural societies of past centuries, which lacked modern birth control and effective medical knowledge, both of these measures might vary considerably. The number of children per woman ranged from less than five to more than eight (though today, in some Western societies characterized by high levels of birth control, it has declined below one), and life expectancy at birth ranged from 20 to 40 years (today it is approaching 80 in some countries).

The number of children per woman depends, as has been said, on biological and social factors which determine: (1) the frequency of births during a woman's fecund period, and (2) the portion of the fecund period – between puberty and menopause – effectively utilized for reproduction.[11]

The frequency of births

This is an inverse function of the interval between births. Given the condition of natural fertility – a term used by demographers to describe those premodern societies which did not practice intentional contraception for the purpose of controlling either the number of births or their timing – the interval between births may be divided into 4 parts:

1 A period of infertility after every birth, as ovulation does not recommence for a couple of months. However, this anovulatory period, during which it is impossible to conceive, increases with the duration of breast-feeding, which is often continued until the second, and in some cases even third, year of the child's life. The duration of breast-feeding, however, varies considerably from one culture to another, so much so that the minimum and maximum limits for the infertility period fall between 3 and 24 months.

2 The waiting time, which consists of the average number of months that pass between the resumption of normal ovulation and conception. It is possible that some women, either for accidental or

[11] The discussion that follows owes a heavy debt to the work of J. Bongaarts and J. Menken, "The Supply of Children: A Critical Essay," in *Determinants of Fertility in Developing Countries*, ed. R. A. Bulatao and R. B. Lee (Academic Press, New York, 1983), vol. 1, pp. 27–60. The evaluation of the components of fertility is based on the assumption that all births are the products of stable unions (marriage), an hypothesis close to reality for many cultures and periods.

natural reasons, may conceive during the first ovulatory cycle, while others, even given regular sexual relations, may not do so for many cycles. We can take five and ten months as our upper and lower limits.

3 The average length of pregnancy, which as everyone knows is about nine months.

4 Fetal mortality. About one out of every five recognized pregnancies does not come to term because of miscarriage. According to the few studies available, this seems to be a frequency which does not vary much from population to population. After a miscarriage, a new conception can take place after the normal waiting period (five to ten months). As only one in five conceptions contributes to this component of the birth interval, the average addition is one to two months.

Summing the minimum and maximum values of 1, 2, 3, and 4, we find that the interval between births ranges from 18 to 45 months (or approximately 1.5 to 3.5 years), but, as a combination either of maxima or minima is improbable, this interval usually falls between two and three years. The above analysis holds true for a population characterized by uncontrolled, natural fertility. Of course, if birth control is introduced the reproductive life span without children may be expanded at will.

The fecund period used for reproduction

The factors that determine the age of access to reproduction, or the establishment of a stable union for the purpose of reproduction (marriage), are primarily cultural, while those that determine the age at which the reproductive period ends are primarily biological.

1 The age at marriage may vary between a minimum close to the age of puberty – let us say 15 years – and a maximum which in many European societies has exceeded 25.

2 The age at the end of the fecund period may be as high as 50, but on average is much lower. We can take as a good indicator the average age of mothers at the birth of the last child in populations that do not practice birth control. This figure is fairly stable and varies between 38 and 41.

We can say then – again combining minima and maxima and rounding – that the average length of a union for reproductive purposes, barring death or divorce, may vary between 15 and 25 years.

Simplifying still more, we can estimate what the minimum and maximum levels of procreation might be in hypothetical populations not subject to mortality. To obtain the minimum we combine the minimum reproductive period (15 years) with the maximum birth interval (3.5 years).

$$\frac{15\text{-year reproductive period}}{3.5\text{-year birth interval}} = 4.3 \text{ children}$$

To obtain the maximum level we instead combine the maximum reproductive period (25 years) with the minimum birth interval (1.5 years):

$$\frac{25\text{-year reproductive period}}{1.5\text{-year birth interval}} = 16.7 \text{ children}$$

These combinations of extremes (especially the latter) are of course impossible, as the various components are not independent from one another. The repeated childbearing which follows early marriage, for example, can create pathological conditions which lower fecundability or else lead to an early decline in sexual activity and so increase the birth interval. In stable historical situations, average levels of under five or over eight children per woman are rare.

The number of children per woman depends primarily upon the age at marriage (the principal factor determining the length of the reproductive period) and the duration of breast-feeding (the principal component determining the birth interval). Figure 1.4, borrowed from the Bongaarts and Menken article on which this discussion is based, shows how the average number of children per woman can vary as a result of the variation (between maximum and minimum values) of each component. We take as a standard seven children, obtained by combining average values of the various components. As one component varies the others remain fixed.[12]

In figure 1.5 the above model is applied to several historical (and theoretical) examples. In addition to the biological maximum (1), there is: a

---

[12] These various hypotheses fit into the Bongaarts and Menken model. In fact, the number of children (TFR, so ignoring mortality) is obtained by dividing the length of the reproductive period (age at the birth of the last child minus the average age at marriage) by the birth interval. In the model the age at marriage is made to vary between 15 and 27.5 years (22.5 in the standard model) and the average age at the birth of the last child varies between 38.5 and 41 (40 in the standard). For calculating the birth interval, the minimum, maximum, and standard values (in years) for the components are the infecund postpartum anovulatory period (0.25, 2.0, 1.0) the waiting period (0.4, 0.85, 0.6), and fetal mortality (0.1, 0.2, 0.15).

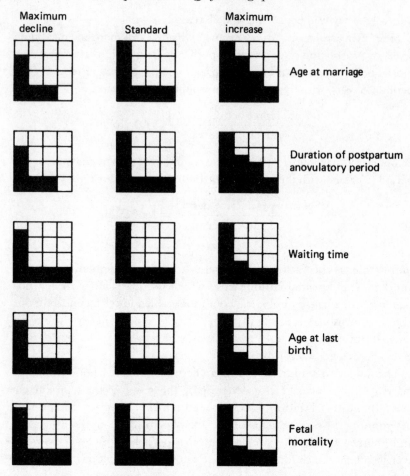

Figure 1.4   Effect on the average number of children per woman of maximum variations of the components of fertility above and below the standard (1 square = 1 birth)

possible maximum (2) resulting from a combination of early marriage (at age 18) and short birth intervals (due to early weaning); a possible minimum in the absence of birth control (6) resulting from late marriage (at age 25) and prolonged breast-feeding; three intermediate levels (3), (4), and (5); and finally, examples of medium and very high levels of birth control, (7) and (8), yielding respectively three and one children. These examples should not be considered to represent a chronological or evolutionary sequence, as almost all can be found in populations living in the same historical periods (except for the last two, characterized by strongly controlled fertility, which

Children per woman (*TFR*)	Reproductive space utilized	Characteristics	Populations	Historical example (populations)
(1) 16		Biological maximum	Theoretical	None Individual cases only
(2) 11.4		Very early unions Minimum intervals	Select groups	French Canadians born before 1660
(3) 9		Late unions Minimum intervals	Select groups	Canadian Hutterites, 1926–30 = 8.5
(4) 7.5		Early unions Long intervals	Many developing populations	Egypt, 1960–65 = 7.1
(5) 7		Standard		
(6) 5		Late unions Long intervals	Many European populations (18th - 19th century)	England, 1751–1800 = 5.1
(7) 3		Voluntary birth control (medium diffusion)	Europe (first half 20th century)	Italy, 1937 = 3.0
(8) 1	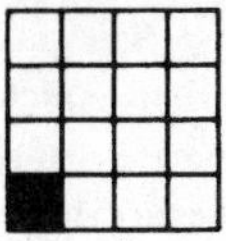	Voluntary birth control (high diffusion)	Several present-day European populations	Liguria (Italy) 1990 = 1.0

Figure 1.5 Fertility models

can only be found in modern populations).

In addition to the biosocial components determining fertility, human reproductivity must also contend with the hard check of mortality, a factor that we have ignored up to this point. Reproductivity and mortality are not independent of one another for any living species, including humans. When the number of offspring is very large, the risk of death in early infancy increases and the competition for resources within the family can lower resistance at all ages. On the other hand, high fertility is in the long run incompatible with low, or recently lowered, mortality, given the resultant excessive population growth. Nonetheless, mortality is to a large degree rooted in human biology and so is independent of fertility levels.

A fairly simple way to describe human mortality is provided by the survivorship function, 1_x, which traces the progressive elimination of a generation of 10^n individuals from birth to the age at which the last member dies.[13] Figure 1.6 shows three survivorship curves. The lower curve corresponds to a life expectancy at birth (e_0) of 20 years. This is a very low figure, near to the minimum compatible with the continued survival of a population, and might characterize a primitive population living in a hostile environment. The upper curve corresponds to an e_0 of 80 years, a level that

---

[13]   I shall make frequent reference to the life table, and so it will be useful at this point to briefly illustrate its workings, referring the reader to specialized publications for a more in-depth treatment. A life table describes the gradual extinction of a generation of newborns (or hypothetical cohort) with the passage of time. This cohort conventionally consists of 10^n individuals; let us use 1,000.

The values of 1_x, where x represents age, describe the number of survivors of the initial 1,000 at each birthday up until the complete extinction of the generation. Another fundamental function of the life table is q_x (conventionally expressed per 1,000 or other power of 10), which represents the probability that the survivors at birthday x will die before birthday $x + 1$. These probabilities can refer to periods longer than a year, and the prefixes 1, 4, 5 (or other values) indicate the age intervals to which the probability refers. Another frequently used function is life expectancy, or e_x (where x again refers to a specific birthday), which indicates on average the number of years of life remaining to those who have survived to age x (1_x), given the mortality levels listed in the life table. "Life expectancy at birth" is expressed by e_0. Here there is an apparent paradox: in life tables that reflect the high mortality of historical demographic regimes, life expectancy increases for several years after birth ($e_0 < e_1 < \ldots < e_5$ and even beyond). This is due to the fact that in the first years of life large numbers of babies are eliminated who contribute little to the sum of years left to live for the generation and so lower the average value represented by life expectancy. Once this effect has ceased, after a few years depending upon mortality levels, life expectancy begins its natural decline with age. Keep in mind, however, that in high-mortality regimes, e_{20}, for example, can be higher than e_0.

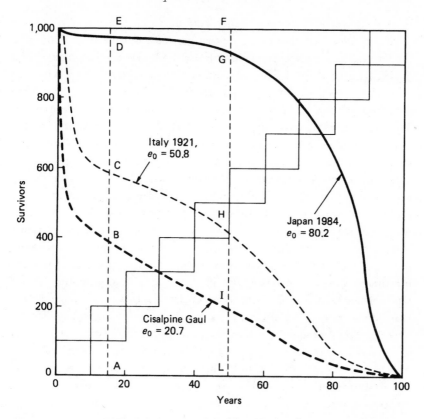

Figure 1.6 Survival curves for three female populations characterized by low, medium, and high life expectancy at birth. Survival curves trace the numerical decline with age of a generation of 1,000 births. Life expectancy at birth is equal to the number of boxes filling the space bounded by the ordinate, the abscissa and the survival curve. The area AEFL, equal to 35 squares (35 years), describes the length of the reproductive period. The areas ADGL, ACHL and ABIL describe the average effective reproduction lives for the three generations of 1,000 newborn girls equal 34.4, 24.8 and 10.2 years. The ratios ADGL/AEFL, ACHL/AEFL, and ABIL/AEFL are, respectively, 98.2, 70.8 and 29.2% and represent the average part of the reproductive period lived by the three generations.

the more developed countries are about to reach. The third, intermediate curve ($e_0 = 50$) is typical of those countries that have benefited from a limited degree of modern medical progress. In figure 1.6 I have chosen as the maximum age, in all three cases, 100 years, assuming that this is the limit of human longevity. This assumption is not far from the truth, as considerably less than 1 percent of the initial generation survives to this age.[14] Continuing to refer to figure 1.6, if we imagine that no one dies until their hundredth birthday, at which age everyone dies, then the 1_x curve will be rectangular (it will be parallel to the abscissa until age 100, at which point it will drop vertically to 0) and e_0 will be equal to 100. The life expectancies at birth described by the other curves are proportional to the areas under those curves. The shape of the survivorship curves depends upon the force of mortality at the various ages. In human population there is a period of high mortality immediately after birth and during early infancy, the result of fragility in the face of the external environment. Mortality risk reaches a minimum during late infancy or adolescence and then, from maturity, rises exponentially as a function of the gradual weakening of the organism. In high-mortality regimes (see the $e_0 = 20$ curve) the curve tends to be concave up. As mortality improves, infant mortality becomes less of a factor and the curve becomes more and more concave down. From a strictly genetic point of view – the hereditary genetic transmission of characteristics – survival beyond the reproductive years (for simplicity, say 50 years of age) is of course irrelevant. However high or low it might be, the rate of mortality beyond age 50 will have no effect on the genetic patrimony of a population. Before and during the reproductive years, on the other hand, the higher the level of mortality the stronger the selective effect as individuals possessing characteristics unfavorable to survival are eliminated and so do not pass on these characteristics to subsequent generations.

Nonetheless, increased survival beyond the reproductive ages may have indirect biological effects, as older adults contribute to the accumulation, organization, and transmission of knowledge, while also favoring parental investments and so can contribute to the improved survival of new generations.

Figure 1.7 shows two survivorship models typical of other species, together with high- and low-mortality human models. Model A typifies those species that are subject to the relatively constant mortality risk presented by other predatory species, while model B is typical of those (r-strategy) species that depend upon prolific reproduction for survival and

---

[14] In the last quarter century, the decline of mortality at very-old ages (over 80) in low-mortality countries has accelerated (1–2 percent per year). If this trend should continue, the proportion surviving to the age of 100 could become significant, and the hypothesis of the "rectangularization" of the survival curve becomes unlikely as the entire 1_x curve would gradually shift to the right. See V. Kannisto, J. Lauritsen, A. R. Thatcher, J. W. Vaupel, "Reductions in Mortality at Advanced Ages: Several Decades of Evidence from 27 Countries," *Population and Development Review*, 20, 4 (1994).

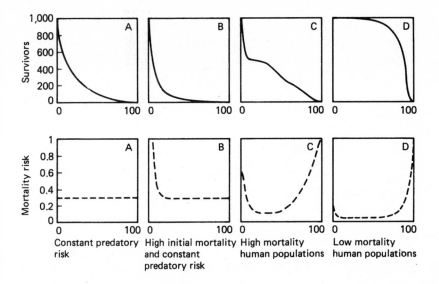

Figure 1.7 Survival models

are subject to very high postnatal mortality.

Let us return to the human species. In order to appreciate its reproductive capacity, we must understand the laws governing its survival until the end of the reproductive period. Afterward, whether or not an individual survives is theoretically unimportant.[15] From figure 1.6 we can see that, with life expectancy at birth equal to 20 years, only 29.2 percent of the potential fecund life of a generation is actually lived due to the decimation caused by high mortality. This proportion increases gradually with increasing life expectancy (and the elevation of the l_x curve). In the examples given, it is 70.8 percent when e_0 equals 50 and 98.2 percent when e_0 equals 80.

It should be clear now that the reproductive success of a population – and so its growth – depends upon the number of children born to those women who survive to reproductive age. If we imagine a level of six children per woman in the absence of mortality, then in that case where only 30 percent of the reproductive space is used ($e_0 = 20$) the number of children born per woman is $6 \times 0.3 = 1.8$. When $e_0 = 50$ and 70 percent of the reproductive space is used, the number or children is $6 \times 0.7 = 4.2$; and when 98 percent is used

---

[15]   This is theoretical because, while the survival of an individual beyond the reproductive period may not contribute directly to reproduction, it may nonetheless improve the chances for survival of the children.

($e_0 = 80$), the total is $6 \times 0.98 = 5.88$. Since there are two parents for every child, each hypothetical couple pays its demographic debt (and the number of parents and children is about equal) if our calculation above yields a level of two. A number larger than two implies growth. If the number of surviving children is four, then the population will double in the course of a single generation (about 30 years) and the average annual growth rate will be 2.3 percent.[16]

[16] The preceding discussion includes in a simplified form several fundamental demographic relationships which it may be useful to explain more fully. In a stable population (one subject to levels of mortality and fertility that are unchanging in time) the age structure and rate of growth are also fixed according to the following equation:

$$R_0 = e^{rT}$$

where R_0 is the net reproduction rate, or the number of daughters that each woman on average produces during the entire reproductive period. It may also be expressed as:

$$R_0 = \Sigma f_x 1_x$$

where f_x is the age-specific fertility rate, or the number of daughters born per woman at age x, and 1_x is a survivorship function (the ratio between the survivors at age x and the size of the generation at birth). Returning to the first equation, T is the average length of generation, which is fairly well approximated by the average age of childbearing, and varies for human populations within a narrow interval (27–33 years); r is the rate of growth for a stable population. In this ideal stable population, the rate of growth r varies directly with R_0, the number of daughters per woman, and inversely with T. It should be added that the net reproduction rate bears a close relationship to the gross reproduction rate R, which is the sum of the f_x and describes the number of daughters per woman in the absence of mortality. The relationship between R_0 and r is well approximated by the equation $R_0 = R1_a$, where 1_a is the probability of survival from birth to the average age of childbearing a. The initial equation may be rewritten as:

$$R1_a = e^{rT}$$

If we imagine T constant (in fact it varies little), then the rate of growth r can be expressed as a function of 1_a, an index of mortality, and R, an index of fertility. It can be demonstrated that 1_a is very nearly equal to the values calculated in figure 1.6 for the percentage of the reproductive life utilized. Furthermore, 1_a is strongly correlated with e_0, or life expectancy at birth, so r may be expressed as a function of R and e_0. Finally, there is a close relationship between R and TFR (average number of children per woman in the absence of mortality): one simply multiplies R by 2.06 (a constant representing the ratio between total births and female births) to obtain TFR. In figure 1.8, r is expressed as a function of TFR and e_0, using a value of T equal to 29 years.

5   *The Space of Growth*

Fertility and mortality, acting in tandem, impose objective limits on the pattern of growth of human populations. If we imagine that in a certain population these remain fixed for a long period of time, then, by resorting to a few simplifying hypotheses,[17] we can express the rate of growth as a function of the number or children per woman (*TFR*) and life expectancy at birth (e_0).

Figure 1.8a shows several "isogrowth" curves. Each curve is the locus of those points that combine life expectancy (the abscissa) and number of children per woman (the ordinate) to give the same rate of growth *r*. Included on this graph are points corresponding to historical and contemporary populations. For the former, life expectancy is neither below 15, as this would be incompatible with the continued survival of the population, nor above 45, as no historical population ever achieved a higher figure. For similar reasons the number of children per woman falls between eight (almost never exceeded in normally constituted populations) and four

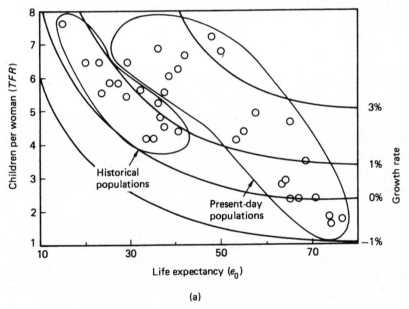

(a)

Figure 1.8a   Relation between the average number of children per woman (*TFR*) and life expectancy (e_0) in historical and present-day populations

---

[17]   See previous note.

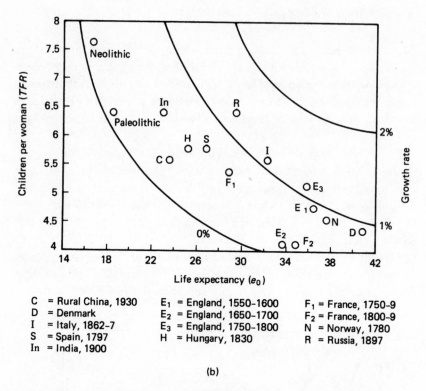

C = Rural China, 1930 E_1 = England, 1550-1600 F_1 = France, 1750-9
D = Denmark E_2 = England, 1650-1700 F_2 = France, 1800-9
I = Italy, 1862-7 E_3 = England, 1750-1800   N = Norway, 1780
S = Spain, 1797   H = Hungary, 1830   R = Russia, 1897
In = India, 1900

(b)

Figure 1. 8b   Relation between *TFR* and e_0 in historical populations

(recall that these are populations not practicing birth control). For the present-day populations included in figure 1.8a, control of fertility and mortality make possible e_0 values of 80 and *TFR* of 1. Figure 1.8b identifies specific examples within the more restricted boundaries of historical populations. These examples have varying degrees of precision, being in some cases based on direct and dependable observation, in others on estimates drawn from indirect and incomplete indicators, and in others on pure conjecture. Nonetheless, most of these populations fall within a band that extends from growth rates of 0 to 1 percent, a space of growth typical of historical populations. Within this narrow band, however, the fertility and mortality combinations vary widely. Denmark at the end of the eighteenth century and India at the beginning of the twentieth, for example, have similar growth rates, but these are achieved at distant points in the strategic space described: the former example combines high life expectancy (about 40 years) and a small number of children (just over four), while in the latter case low life expectancy (about 25 years) is paired with many children (just under seven).

Although their growth rates must have been similar, the points for Paleolithic and Neolithic populations are assumed to have been far apart. According to a well-accepted opinion (see chapter 2), the Paleolithic, a hunting and gathering population, was characterized by lower mortality, due to its low density, a factor that prevented infectious diseases from taking hold and spreading, and moderate fertility, compatible with its nomadic behavior. For the Neolithic, a sedentary and agricultural population, both mortality and fertility were higher as a result of higher density and lower mobility.

Figure 1.8c includes points for some of the most populous countries of the world since 1950. The strategic space utilized, previously restricted to a narrow band, has expanded dramatically. Medical and sanitary progress has shifted the upper limit of life expectancy from the historical level of about 40 years to the present level of about 80, while the introduction of birth control

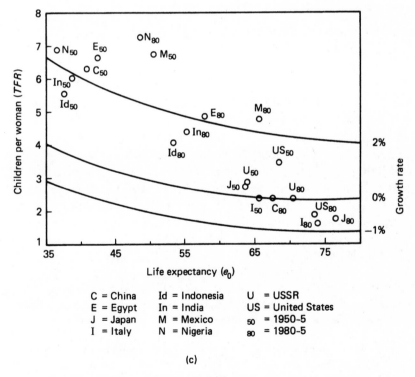

C = China   Id = Indonesia   U = USSR
E = Egypt   In = India   US = United States
J = Japan   M = Mexico   50 = 1950-5
I = Italy   N = Nigeria   80 = 1980-5

(c)

Figure 1.8c   Relation between TFR and e_0 in present-day populations

has reduced the lower limit of fertility to a level of about one child per woman. In this much-expanded space the populations listed vary between a maximum annual potential growth rate of 4 percent (many developing countries have a growth rate of over 3 percent) and a minimum of −1 percent (which will, for example, be realized by Italy should the current fertility and mortality levels remain unchanged). We are able to recognize the exceptional nature of the current situation if we keep in mind that a population growing at an annual rate of 4 percent will double in about 18 years, while another declining by 1 percent per year will halve in 70.[18] Two populations of equal size experiencing these different growth rates will find themselves after 28 years (barely a generation) in a numerical ratio of four-to-one!

The two situations described in figures 1.8b and 1.8c differ not only in the strategic space they occupy, but also, and especially, in their permanence. The first of the two figures represents a situation of great duration, while the second is certainly unstable and destined to change rapidly, since it implies a rate of growth that cannot in the long run be sustained.

6   Environmental Constraints

Although the strategic space of growth is large, only a small portion of it can be permanently occupied by a population. Sustained decline is obviously incompatible with the survival of a human group, while sustained growth can in the long run be incompatible with the resources available. The mechanisms of growth, therefore, must continually adjust to environmental conditions (which we might call environmental friction), conditions with which they interact but which also present obstacles to growth, as attested to by the millennia during which the population growth rate has been very low. For the moment I shall limit myself to the macroscopic aspects of these obstacles to demographic growth, saving for later a more detailed discussion of their operation.

In a justly famous essay, Carlo Cipolla wrote: "It is safe to say that until the Industrial Revolution man continued to rely mainly on plants and animals

---

[18]   It may be useful to recall a mnemonic device for the calculation of population doubling times. These can be approximated by dividing 70 by the annual growth rate (expressed as a percentage): a growth rate of 1% implies a doubling time of 70 years, of 2% 35 years, of 3% 23 years. Similarly, if the growth rate is negative, the population halving time is obtained by the same method: if the population is declining by 1% per year, it will halve in 70 years, if by 2% in 35, and so on.

for energy – plants for food and fuel, and animals for food and mechanical energy."[19] It is this subordination to the natural environment and the resources it provides that constituted a check to population increase, a situation particularly evident for a hunting and gathering society. Imagine a population that utilizes a habitat extending only to those places that can be reached, and returned from, in a single day's walk. The abundance of available food depends upon the ecology of the area, the accessibility of resources, and the related costs (so to speak) of extraction and utilization, and this in turn places a check on the number of inhabitants. In the simplest terms, vegetal biomass production (primary productivity) per unit area is a function of precipitation, and animal biomass production (of herbivores and carnivores – secondary productivity) is in turn a function of the vegetal biomass, so that precipitation is the principal factor limiting both the resources available to hunters and gatherers and their numerical growth.[20] Figure 1.9 shows the relation between vegetal biomass and precipitation in

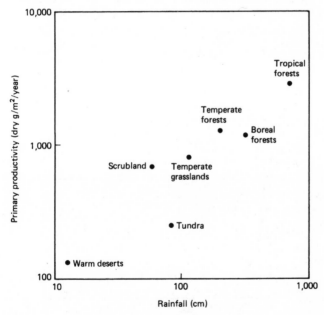

Figure 1.9 Relationship between rainfall and primary productivity for world biomes

Source: F. A. Hassan, *Demographic Archaeology* (Academic Press, New York, 1981), p. 12

[19] C. M. Cipolla, *The Economic History of World Population* (Penguin Books, Harmondsworth, 1962), pp. 45–6.

[20] F. A. Hassan, *Demographic Archaeology* (Academic Press, New York, 1981), pp. 7–12.

various parts of the world, while figure 1.10 charts the dependence of Australian Aboriginal population density on the intensity of rainfall.

Table 1.1 reports possible values for the population density of hunter-gatherer societies in different ecological systems, according to certain hypotheses regarding biomass and precipitation. This is, of course, only a model, but one that effectively describes a double check on population increase. The first check is imposed by natural limits of vegetal and animal production which define the maximum number of individuals that can be fed. In an area 10 kilometers in diameter, the sustainable population ranges from 3 for an arctic area to 136 for subtropical savannah. The second check relates to the incompatibility of very low population density (arctic and semi-desert areas, for example) with the survival of a stable population group. In order to ensure a reasonable choice of partners and to survive catastrophic events these groups must not be too small.

Archaeological and contemporary observations have placed the density of hunter-gatherer populations at between 0.1 and 1 per square kilometer.[21] Higher densities may be encountered near seas, lakes, and streams, where fishing can effectively supplement the products of the earth. Clearly the limiting factors at this cultural level are essentially precipitation and the availability and accessibility of land.

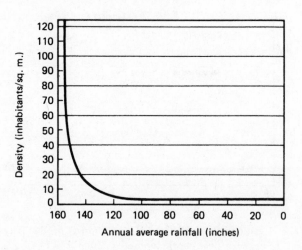

Figure 1.10   Relation between annual precipitation and population
density (Australian Aborigines)

[21]   Ibid., p. 7.

Table 1.1 Estimated population density and size for catchment territory of 314 km² in different world biomes

Biome	Biomass (kg/km²)	Population density (persons/km²)	Number of persons
Arctic	200	0.0086	3
Subtropical savanna	10,000	0.43	136
Grassland	4,000	0.17	54
Semidesert	800	0.035	11

Source: F. A. Hassan, *Demographic Archaeology* (Academic Press, New York, 1981), p. 57

The Neolithic transition to stable cultivation of the land and raising of livestock certainly represented a dramatic expansion of productive capacity. This transition, which many call a "revolution," developed and spread slowly over millennia in a variety of ways and forms. The progress of cultivation techniques, from slash and burn to triannual rotations (which have coexisted in different cultures up to the present day); the selection of better and better seeds; the domestication of new plants and animals; and the use of animal, air, and water power have all enormously increased the availability of food and energy.[22] Population density as a result also grew; that of major European countries (France, Italy, Germany, England, the Low Countries) in the mid-eighteenth century was about 40–60 persons per square kilometer, 100 times greater than that of the hunters and gatherers. Naturally, productive capacity varied greatly in different epochs as a function of technological and social evolution, a point easily demonstrated by comparing the agriculture of the Po Valley or the Low Countries with the fairly primitive methods used in some parts of the continent. Throughout the globe, innovation has allowed for the notable expansion of productivity per unit of energy invested. It appears, for example, that productivity per hectare tripled in Teotihuacán (Mexico) between the third and second millennia BC due to the introduction of new varieties of corn;[23] and in various zones of Europe during the modern era the ratio of agricultural production to seed increased thanks to new grains.[24]

Nonetheless, success in mastering the environment has always been dependent upon the availability of energy. As Cipolla observed, "the fact that

[22] V. G. Childe, *Man Makes Himself* (Mentor, New York, 1951).
[23] Hassan, *Demographic Archaeology*, p. 42.
[24] B. H. Slicher van Bath, *The Agrarian History of Western Europe. A.D. 500–1850* (Edward Arnold, London, 1963), app.

the main sources of energy other than man's muscular work remained basically plants and animals must have set a limit to the possible expansion of the energy supply in any given agricultural society of the past. The limiting factor in this regard is ultimately the supply of land."[25] In preindustrial Europe, populations seem to have approached with some frequency the limits allowed by the environment and available technology. These limits may be expressed by the per capita availability of energy and, again following Cipolla, must have been below 15,000 calories, or perhaps even 10,000, per day (a level which the richest countries today exceed by a factor of 20 or 30), the majority of which were dedicated to nutrition and heating.[26]

The environmental limits to demographic expansion were again shattered by the enormous increase in available energy that resulted from the industrial and technological revolution of the second half of the eighteenth century and the invention of efficient machines for the conversion of inanimate materials into energy. World production of coal increased tenfold between 1820 and 1860 and again between 1860 and 1950. It has been calculated that worldwide energy availability increased sixfold between 1820 and 1950 (while population in the same period doubled).[27] During this century (between 1900 and 1990), total world energy consumption has increased by a factor of almost 16 and per capita consumption fivefold. The dependency of energy availability on land availability was again (and perhaps definitively) broken and the principal obstacle to the numerical growth of population removed.

Figure 1.11, taken from Deevey,[28] describes schematically (on a double logarithmic scale and simplifying drastically the complexities of history) the evolution of population as a function of the three great technological-cultural phases described above: the hunter-gatherer (until the Paleolithic Age), the agricultural (from the Neolithic), and the industrial (since the Industrial Revolution). During these three phases (the last of which we are still in the midst of) population has increased by increments which become progressively smaller with the passage of time, as the limits of growth are approached. This outline is simply the application of that concept, common to both animal biology and Malthusian demography, according to which the

[25]　Cipolla, *Economic History*, p. 46.

[26]　Ibid., p. 47.

[27]　W. S. Woytinsky and E. S. Woytinsky, *World Population and Production. Trends and Outlook* (The Twentieth Century Fund, New York, 1953), pp. 924–30; J. H. Gibbons, P. D. Blair, and H. L. Gwin, "Strategies for Energy Use," *Scientific American*, Sept. 1988, p. 86.

[28]　E. S. Deevey, Jr., "The Human Population," *Scientific American*, Sept. 1960, pp. 194–204.

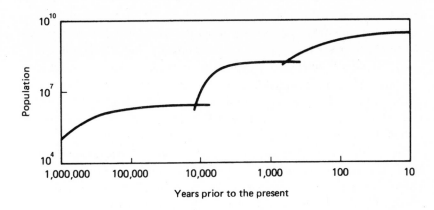

Figure 1.11 Cycles of demographic growth

growth of a species (gnat, mouse, human or elephant) in a restricted environment varies inversely with its density. This comes to pass because the available resources are considered fixed and so population growth creates its own checks. For the human species, of course, the environment, and so the available resources, has never been fixed but continually expands due to innovation. In the Deevey outline, demographic growth in the first long period of human history, which continued up until 10,000 years ago, was limited by the biomass available for nutrition and heating at a rate of several thousand calories per day per person. In the second phase, from the Neolithic to the Industrial Revolution, limits were imposed by the availability of land and the limited energy provided by plants, animals, water, and wind. In the present phase, the limits to growth are not so well defined, but may be connected to the adverse environmental effects of combined demographic and technological growth and the attendant cultural choices.

7 *A Few Figures*

In July 1990, the People's Republic of China carried out its fourth census since the revolution and, with the help of seven million carefully trained census takers, counted 1.134 billion inhabitants. It was the largest social investigation ever undertaken. Until the middle of this century there were still quite a few areas of the less-developed world for which there existed at best fragmentary and incomplete demographic estimates. In Western countries the modern statistical era began in the nineteenth century, when the practice of taking censuses of the population at regular intervals, begun by some countries in the preceding century, became general. The 10.4 million persons counted in the Kingdom of Spain in the summer of 1787 by order of Charles III's prime minister, Floridablanca, or the 3.9 million counted in the United States in 1790 as instructed by the first article of the constitution approved three years earlier in Phildelphia, are the first examples of modern censuses in large countries.[29] In previous centuries there were, of course, head counts and estimates – often serving fiscal purposes – for limited areas and often of limited coverage. Included among the latter are the family lists from the Han to the Ching dynasties in China (covering a period of almost two millennia ending in the previous century).[30] For the evaluation of these the work of the statistician must be complemented by that of the historian, who is able to evaluate, integrate, and interpret the sources. In many parts of the world before this century, in Europe prior to the late Middle Ages or in China before the present era, one can only estimate population size on the basis of qualitative information – the existence or extension of cities, villages, or other settlements, the extension of cultivated land – or on the basis of calculations of the possible population density in relation to the ecosystem, the level of technology, or social organization. The contributions of paleontologists, archaeologists, and anthropologists are all needed.

The data on world demographic growth in tables 1.2 and 1.3 are largely based on conjectures and inferences drawn from non-quantitative information. Table 1.2 presents a synthesis of these trends. The long-term rates of growth are, of course, an abstraction, as they imply a constant variation of demographic forces in each period, while in reality population evolves cyclically. Following Biraben's hypothesis, according to which human population prior to the High Paleolithic era (30,000–35,000 BC) did not exceed several hundred thousand, growth during the 30,000 years leading up to the Neolithic era averaged less than 0.1 per 1,000 per year, an almost imperceptible level consistent with a doubling

[29]   M. Livi-Bacci, "Il censimento di Floridablanca nel contesto dei censimenti europei," *Genus*, 43 (1987), nn.3–4.
[30]   J. Lee, C. Campbell, and Wang Feng, "The Last Emperors: An Introduction to the Demography of the Qing Imperial Lineage," in *Old and New Methods in Historical Demography*, ed. R. Schofield and D. Reher (Oxford University Press, Oxford, 1993).

Table 1.2 Population, total births, and years lived (10,000 BC to AD 2000)

Demographic index	10,000 BC	0	1750	1950	2000
Population (millions)	6	252	771	2530	6235
Annual growth (%)	0.008	0.037	0.064	0.596	1.812
Doubling time (years)	8369	1854	1083	116	38
Births (billions)	9.29	33.6	22.64	10.42	6.25
Births (%)	11.3	40.9	27.5	12.7	7.6
Life expectancy (e_0)	20	22	27	35	58
Years lived (billions)	185.8	739.2	611.3	364.7	362.5
Years lived (%)	8.2	32.7	27.0	16.1	16.0

For births, life expectancy, and years lived, the data refer to interval between the date at the head of the column and that of the preceding column (for the first column the interval runs from the hypothetical origin of the human species to 10,000 BC).

Table 1.3 Continental populations (400 BC to AD 2000, data in millions)

Year	Asia	Europe	USSR[a]	Africa	America	Oceania	World
400 BC	95	19	13	17	8	1	153
0	170	31	12	26	12	1	252
200	158	44	13	30	11	1	257
600	134	22	11	24	16	1	208
1000	152	30	13	39	18	1	253
1200	258	49	17	48	26	2	400
1340	238	74	16	80	32	2	442
1400	201	52	13	68	39	2	375
1500	245	67	17	87	42	3	461
1600	338	89	22	113	13	3	578
1700	433	95	30	107	12	3	680
1750	500	111	35	104	18	3	771
1800	631	146	49	102	24	2	954
1850	790	209	79	102	59	2	1,241
1900	903	295	127	138	165	6	1,634
1950	1,376	393	182	224	332	13	2,520
2000	3,736	511	296	832	830	31	6,236
0–1750	0.06	0.07	0.06	0.08	0.02	0.06	0.06
1750–1950	0.51	0.63	0.82	0.38	1.46	0.74	0.59
1950–2000	2.00	0.53	0.97	2.62	1.83	1.74	1.81

[a] 2000: territories of former USSR.

Sources: J. N. Biraben, "Essai sur l'évolution du nombre des hommes," *Population*, 34 (1979), p. 16. For 1950 and 2000: United Nations, *World Population Prospects: The 1994 Revision* (New York, 1995).

time of 8,000–9,000 years.[31] In the 10,000 years prior to the birth of Christ, during which Neolithic civilization spread from the Near East and Upper Egypt, the rate increased to 0.4 per 1,000 (which implies a doubling in less than 2,000 years) and population grew from several million to about 0.25 billion. This rate of increase, in spite of important cycles of growth and decline, was reinforced during the subsequent 17 and a half centuries. The population tripled to about 0.75 billion on the eve of the Industrial Revolution (an overall rate of growth of 0.6 per 1,000). It was, however, the Industrial Revolution which initiated a period of decisive and sustained growth. During the following two centuries population increased about tenfold, at an annual growth rate of 6 per 1,000 (doubling time 118 years). This process of growth was the result of a rapid accumulation of resources, control of the environment, and mortality decline, and has culminated in the second half of the current century. In the four decades since 1950 population has again doubled and the rate of growth has tripled to 18 per 1,000. In spite of signs that growth may be slowing, the present momentum will certainly carry world population to eight billion by about the year 2020 and ten billion some time during the upcoming century. The acceleration of the growth rate and shortening of the doubling time (which was expressed in thousands of years prior to the Industrial Revolution and is expressed in tens of years at present) give some indication of the speed with which the historical checks to population growth have been relaxed.

Table 1.2 responds to another question which, at first glance, appears to be simply a statistical curiosity. How many people have lived on the earth? The answer requires calculation of the total number of births in each of the periods indicated. Following the courageous hypotheses of Bourgeois-Pichat, [32] we can estimate the total number of births from the origin of the human species to the present day at 82 billion, of which 6.3 billion occurred in the last 50 years, 3 billion less than took place in the hundreds of thousands of years of human existence prior to the Neolithic era. In the year 2000 the 6.2 billion inhabitants of the globe will represent better than 7.6 percent of the total number of human beings ever born. Taking a different approach, and keeping in mind that what we are today represents the accumulated

---

[31]   The estimates in tables 1.2 and 1.3 are taken from J. N. Biraben, "Essai sur l'évolution du nombre des hommes," *Population*, 34 (1979), pp. 13–25. See also J. D. Durand, "Historical Estimates of World Population," *Population and Development Review*, 3 (1977), pp. 253–96; A. J. Coale, "The History of Human Population," *Scientific American*, Sept. 1974.

[32]   J. Bourgeois-Pichat, "Du XXᵉ au XXIᵉ siècle: l'Europe et sa population après l'an 2000," *Population*, 43 (1988), pp. 9–42.

experiences of our progenitors – selected, mediated, modified, and passed on to us – we can observe that 11 percent of these experiences were accumulated prior to the Neolithic era and more than 80 percent before 1750 and the industrial-technological revolution.

If we assign an estimated life expectancy at birth to the individuals in each epoch (these estimates are statistical only for the last period; for the preceding period they are based on fragmentary evidence and before that they are pure conjecture), then we can calculate the total number of years lived by each of these groups. Those born between 1950 and 2000 will have lived (at the end of their lives) about 362 billion years, twice the total number of years lived by all those born prior to the Neolithic era. The 420 billion years that will presumably be lived (during their whole lives) by those alive in 2000 represents a little less than one-fifth of all the years lived since the origin of the human race.

Finally, if we consider energy resources used, we can make one further observation. It is estimated that in 1990 annual world energy consumption amounted to almost 290,000 petajoules[33] and that consumption in the 1980s was about equal to the total energy consumption of humankind in the hundreds of thousands of years leading up to the Neolithic era. These figures are not presented for their shock value, but to demonstrate the extraordinary expansion of resources available to humanity today as compared to earlier agricultural societies.

Population, of course, did not grow continuously, but experienced cycles of growth and decline, the long-term aspects of which are summarized in table 1.3 and figure 1.11. Limiting ourselves to Europe, the tripling of population between the birth of Christ and the eighteenth century did not occur gradually, but was the result of successive waves of expansion and crisis: crisis during the late Roman Empire and the Justinian era as a result of barbarian invasions and disease; expansion in the twelfth and thirteenth centuries; crisis again as a result of recurring and devastating bouts of the plague beginning in the mid-fourteenth century; a strong rallying from the mid-fifteenth to the end of the sixteenth century; and crisis or stagnation until the beginning of the eighteenth century, when the forces of modern expansion came to the fore. Nor do these cycles run parallel in different

---

[33] World Resources Institute, *World Resources 1987* (Basic Books, New York, 1987), p. 300. One petajoule = 34.140 UN standard tons of coal equivalent. The calculation has been made by hypothesizing (with Cipolla) an average daily consumption of 10,000 calories per inhabitant for years lived prior to 1750, according to the calculations of table 1.2.

areas, so that relative demographic weight changes with time: the European share of world population grew from 14.5 to 18.1 percent between 1500 and 1900, only to decline again to 8.2 percent in the year 2000. The entire American continent contained probably less than 2 percent of the world population at the beginning of the seventeenth century, while today the figure is 13.3 percent.

2

Demographic Growth: Between Choice and Constraint

1   Constraint, Choice, Adaptation

We have established a few points of reference: demographic growth takes place with varying degrees of intensity and within a fairly large strategic space, large enough so that rates of growth or decline can lead a population to rapid expansion or extinction. The upper limits of this strategic space are defined by reproductive capacity and survival and so by the biological characteristics of the human species. In the long run, demographic growth moves in tandem with the growth of available resources, the latter imposing an impassable limit on the former. These resources, of course, are not static, but expand in response to incessant human activity. New lands are settled and put to use; knowledge increases and new technology is developed. In a later chapter we shall discuss which is the engine and which the caboose between resources and population – that is, whether the development of the first pulls along the second or vice versa; whether the availability of an additional unit of food and energy allows one more individual to survive or, instead, the fact of there being another pair of hands leads to the production of that extra unit; or, finally, whether they do not both function a little as engine and a little as caboose according to the historical situation.

For the moment, we shall turn our attention to another problem already mentioned in the previous chapter. We have identified three great population cycles: from the first humans to the beginning of the Neolithic era, from the Neolithic to the Industrial Revolution, and from the Industrial Revolution to the present day. The transitional phases between these entailed the breakdown of difficult equilibria between population and resources. However, as we have seen for European populations, demographic growth proceeded irregularly within these cycles as well. Periods of growth alternated with others of stagnation and decline. What were the causes?

In order to provide a theoretical picture, we may conceive of demographic growth as taking place within two great systems of forces, those of constraint and those of choice. The forces of constraint include climate, disease, land, energy, food, space, and settlement patterns. These forces have variable degrees of interdependency, but they do share two characteristics: their importance in relation to demographic change and their own slow rates of change. With regard to demographic change, the mechanisms are intuitive and well-demonstrated. Human settlement patterns (density and mobility) depend on geographic space as does the availability of land. Food, raw materials, and energy resources all come from the land and are important determinants of human survival. Climate in turn determines the fertility of the soil, imposes limits on human settlement, and is linked to patterns of disease. Diseases, in turn, linked to nutrition, affect reproduction and survival directly. And space and settlement patterns are linked to population density and the communicability of diseases. These few comments should already make clear the complexity of the relations which link together the great categories of the forces of constraint as they relate to demographic growth.

The second common characteristic of the forces of constraint is their permanence (space and climate) or slow rate of change (land, energy, food, disease, settlement patterns) in relation to the time frame of demographic analysis (a generation or the average length of a human life). These forces are relatively fixed and can be modified by human intervention only slowly. Obviously, food and energy supplies can be increased as a result of new cultivation and new techniques and technology; improved clothing and housing can blunt the effects of climate; and measures to prevent infection and the spread of diseases can limit their impact. However, the cultivation of previously uncultivated land, the development and spread of new technology, the spread of better styles of housing, and methods of disease control are not developed from one day to the next, but over long periods of time. In the short and medium term (and often in the long as well) populations must adapt to and live with the forces of constraint.

The process of adaptation requires a degree of behavioral flexibility in order that population adjusts its size and rate of growth to the forces of constraint described above. These behavioral changes are partially automatic, partially socially determined, and partially the result of explicit choices. For example, confronted with a shortage of food, body growth (height and weight) slows, producing adults with reduced nutritional needs but equal efficiency. This sort of adaptation to available resources is invoked, for example, to explain the small body size of the *Indios* of Mesoamerica.

Naturally, if this shortage becomes a serious lack then mortality increases, the population declines or disappears, and no adaptation is possible. Another type of adaptation – almost automatic and in any case independent of human action – is the permanent or semipermanent immunity that develops in those infected by certain pathogens, such as smallpox and measles.

Adaptation, however, operates above all by means of those mechanisms which we discussed at length in the previous chapter. The age of access to reproduction (marriage) and the proportion of individuals who enter into this state have for most of human history been the principal means of controlling growth. Prior to the diffusion in the eighteenth century of what has become the primary instrument of control – the voluntary limitation of births – a number of other components had an influence on the fertility of couples and newborn survival: sexual taboos, duration of breast-feeding, and the frequency of abortion and infanticide, whether direct or in the subtler forms of exposure and abandonment. Finally, a form of adaptation to environment and resources that has been practiced by populations in every epoch and climate is migration, whether to escape an existing situation or to find a new one.

The environment, then, imposes checks on growth by means of the forces of constraint. These checks can be relaxed by human action in the long run and their effect softened in the medium and short run. The mechanisms for reestablishing equilibrium are in part automatic, but for the most part are the product of choice (nuptiality, fertility, migration). This is not to say, as is often rashly asserted, that populations are provided with providential regulating mechanisms that maintain size and growth within dimensions compatible with available resources. Many populations have disappeared and others have grown to such a degree that equilibrium could not be restored.

2 From Hunters to Farmers: The Neolithic Demographic Transition

The tenth millennium BC witnessed the beginning of the Neolithic revolution "that transformed human economy [and] gave man control over his own food supply. Man began to plant, cultivate, and improve by selection edible grasses, roots and trees. And he succeeded in taming and firmly attaching to his person certain species of animal in return for the fodder he was able to offer."[1] In short, hunters and gatherers became

---

[1]   V. G. Childe, *Man Makes Himself* (Mentor, New York, 1951), p. 51.

farmers and, with time, switched from a nomadic to a sedentary life-style. This transition, naturally, developed gradually and irregularly, and isolated groups that survive by hunting and gathering still exist today; it occurred independently at times and in places separated by thousands of years and kilometers, in the Near East, China, Mesoamerica.[2] The causes of this transition are complex, and we shall discuss their demographic aspects below. Even given the difficulty of making a quantitative assessment, it is certain that population increased, as revealed by the spread of human population and its increased density.[3] Biraben estimates that prior to the introduction of agriculture the human species numbered about 6 million individuals and these became about 250 million by the beginning of the present era.[4] The corresponding rate of growth is 0.37 per 1,000, less than 1 percent of the rate attained in recent years by many developing countries but many times greater than that hypothesized between the appearance of the first humans and 10,000 BC.[5] One point, however, remains indisputable (though its interpretation is debated): with the spread of agriculture, population increased steadily and by several orders of magnitude and the ceiling imposed by the ecosystem on the hunter-gatherers was raised dramatically.

[2]   J. R. Harlan, "Agricultural Origins: Centres and Noncenters," *Science*, 174 (1971).

[3]   An indirect proof of demographic growth contemporary with the domestication of plants and animals in the Near East, about 8000 BC, is given by the successive waves of migration to the north-east; and these in turn were likely the primary cause of the expansion of agricultural technology. "One consequence of the introduction of agriculture, of course, is an increase in the number of people who can live in a given area. Such an increase in population is often accompanied by a wave of expansion: early farming was in itself a shifting type of agriculture that required frequent movement from old fields to new ones." The average annual amount of expansion was about one kilometer. This is the theory developed by Cavalli Sforza and Ammerman, who have identified the beginning of agriculture in the various zones of Europe by carbon-14 dating the oldest remains of cultivated plants. See L. L. Cavalli Sforza, "The Genetics of Human Populations," *Scientific American*, Sept. 1974, pp. 80–9, from which the above quotation is taken. See also A. J. Ammerman and L. L. Cavalli Sforza, "A Population Model for the Diffusion of Early Farming in Europe," in *The Explanation of Culture Change*, ed. C. Renfrew (Duckworth, London, 1973).

[4]   J.-N. Biraben, "Essai sur l'évolution du nombre des hommes," *Population*, 34 (1979). See also table 1.2.

[5]   The significance of comparisons between growth rates of this sort, based on uncertain data and referring to long periods and vast areas, is purely abstract. Faster growth might also have been the result of a decrease in the frequency of extinction of population groups breaking off and migrating away from earlier groups, as opposed to an increase in the normal growth rate.

In spite of general agreement regarding the quantitative nature of prehistoric population growth, anthropologists and demographers have long debated its causes and mechanisms. One interpretation concentrates more on the way in which the acceleration came about rather than its cause. Clearly there is little sense in talking about a world population or the populations of large geographical areas in the Paleolithic period. We are dealing instead with a collection of small, relatively autonomous, and highly vulnerable groups, each numbering perhaps a few hundred individuals and existing in a precarious balance with its environment. For groups of this sort, a decline in size below a certain level (say 100–200 members), whatever the cause, compromises the reproductivity and survival of the collectivity. Alternatively, a growth in numbers can lead to splitting and the creation of a new group. The aggregate growth or decline of population then is a function of the "births" and "deaths" of these elementary nuclei. In a successful period, the balance between births and deaths is positive and the population grows; in an unsuccessful one, the balance is negative and population declines. Figure 2.1(a) (the x-axis corresponds to the level of success; the y-axis to the number of nuclei) includes 3 possible models: curve A describes a situation in which the successes dominate; C the reverse; and B an equilibrium. The corresponding aggregate growth rates will be positive, negative, and zero. Changes in climate, environment, or disease then will cause the curve to shift either to the left or the right. Figure 2.1(b) shows what may have happened with the transition from the Paleolithic to the Neolithic Age: greater "stability" of the conditions of survival shifted the curve from left to right and so sped up the rate of growth.[6]

In addition to this "technical" hypothesis, there are at least two diametrically opposed theories that attempt to explain the causes behind this acceleration of population growth. The "classic" theory claims that growth accelerated due to improved survival, the consequence of better nutrition made possible by the agricultural system.[7] A more recent theory suggests instead that dependence on crops that varied little lowered the

[6] For a similar discussion, see A. J. Ammerman, "Late Pleistocene Population Dynamics: An Alternative View," *Human Ecology*, 3 (1975). See also E. A. Hammel and N. Howell, "Research in Population and Culture: An Evolutionary Framework," *Current Anthropology*, 28 (1987).

[7] Cohen attributes the theory that I have improperly called "classic" to Childe, *Man Makes Himself*. See M. N. Cohen, "An Introduction to the Symposium," in *Paleopathology and the Origin of Agriculture*, ed. G. J. Armelagos and M. N. Cohen (Academic Press, Orlando, Fla, 1984).

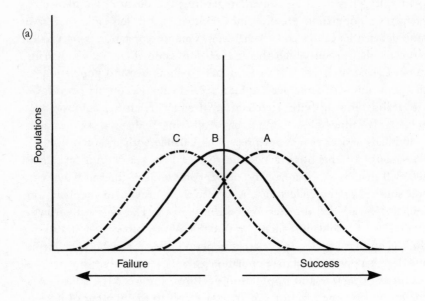

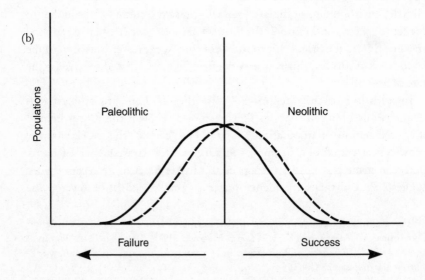

Figure 2.1   Failure and success of individual populations – a model

quality of nutrition, that sedentary habits and higher density increased the risk of transmitting infectious diseases and so also their frequency, while the reduced "cost" of raising children resulted in higher fertility. In other words, the introduction of agriculture brought about an increase in mortality, but also an even greater increase in fertility, with the result that the growth rate sped up.[8] In an extremely synthesized form, these are the postulates on which the two theories are based. It is worthwhile to briefly consider the arguments in favor of each.

The classic theory is based on a simple but convincing argument. Settlement and the beginning of agricultural cultivation and animal domestication permitted a more regular food supply and protected populations that lived off the fruits of the ecosystem from the nutritional stress associated with climatic instability and the changing of the seasons. The cultivation of wheat, barley, millet, corn, or rice – highly nutritional grains that are easily stored – greatly expanded the availability of food and helped to overcome periods of want.[9] Health and survival improved, mortality declined, and the potential for growth increased and stabilized.

In recent decades this theory has been questioned and the problem re-cast in new terms: In sedentary agricultural populations both mortality and fertility increased, but fertility increased more than mortality, and this explains demographic growth.[10] Yet why should mortality have been higher among farmers than among hunters? Two groups of causes are usually cited in response to this question. The first is based upon the as-sertion that nutritional levels, from a qualitative (and some claim also quantitative) point of view, worsened with the agricultural transition. The diet of the hunter-gatherers, which consisted of roots, greens, ber-ries, fruits, and game, was probably more complete than the fare of the sedentary farmers, which, while adequate calorically, was meager and monotonous because of the heavy dependence upon grains.[11] Proof is

---

[8] Statements of this new theory may be found in B. Spooner, ed., *Population Growth: Anthropological Implications* (MIT Press, Cambridge, Mass., 1972). See also Cohen, "An Introduction." For a formulation in demographic terms, see A. J. Coale, "The History of Human Population," *Scientific American*, Sept. 1974, pp. 40–51.

[9] Childe, *Man Makes Himself*, p. 66.

[10] Clearly I am presenting this debate in extremely schematic terms. Transition to agriculture must have been gradual, and during long periods old and new methods coexisted. Pastoral societies, for example, seem to have been characterized by many elements from both phases.

[11] Spooner, *Population Growth*; see pp. xxiv–xxv of his introduction.

found in the study of skeletal remains: body size, height, and bone thickness all seem to have declined when hunters settled and became farmers.[12] Armelagos and his colleagues come to the conclusion that: "The shift in subsistence pattern had a significant impact on the biological adaptation of prehistoric Nubians. The development of agriculture resulted in a reduction in facial dimensions and concomitant changes in cranial morphology. In addition, the intensification of agriculture led to nutritional deprivation. The pattern of bone growth and development, the occurrence of iron-deficiency anemia (as evidenced by porotic hyperostosis), microdefects in dentition, and premature osteoporosis in juveniles and young adult females all suggest that later Nubian populations involved in intensive agriculture were experiencing nutritional deficiencies."[13] I have cited the preceding passage not because the experience of the Nubians is applicable to all other types of transition (assuming that remains from the various epochs were representative, that there was no immigration, and no errors were made in evaluating the remains), but in order to illustrate the sort of evidence offered in support of the nutritional hypothesis.

The second argument in favor of this theory is of a different and perhaps more convincing nature. The stable settlement of population created the conditions necessary for the onset, spread, and survival of parasites and infectious diseases, which were unknown or rare among mobile and low-density populations.[14] Higher demographic concentration acts as a "reservoir" for pathogens, which remain in a latent state awaiting an opportune moment to resurface. The spread of diseases transmitted by physical contact is favored by increased density, and this density in turn increases the contamination of the soil and water, facilitating reinfection.

---

[12] G. J. Armelagos and M. N. Cohen, "Editors' Summation," in *Paleopathology*, ed. Armelagos and Cohen. The interpretation of osteological finds is, however, the subject of open controversy. See J. W. Wood, G. R. Milner, H. C. Harpending, and K. M. Weiss, "The Osteological Paradox," *Current Anthropology*, 33 (1992).

[13] G. J. Armelagos, D. P. van Gerven, D. L. Martin, and R. Huss Hushmore, "Effects of Nutritional Change on the Skeletal Biology of Northeast African (Sudanese Nubian) Populations," in *From Hunters to Farmers*, ed. J. D. Clark and S. A. Brandt (University of California Press, Berkeley, 1984), p. 146.

[14] For a general theory of infectious diseases, see F. Macfarlane Burnet, *Natural History of Infectious Disease* (Cambridge University Press, London, 1962); T. A. Cockburn, *Infectious Diseases: Their Evolution and Eradication* (C. G. Thomas, Springfield, Ill., 1967). On infectious diseases in the prehistoric period: T. A. Cockburn, "Infectious Diseases in Ancient Populations," *Current Anthropology*, 12 (1971). For an excellent summary of theories and data, see M. N. Cohen, *Health and the Rise of Civilization* (Yale University Press, New Haven and London, 1989).

The replacement of the mobile and temporary shelters of nomadic populations with permanent ones encouraged contacts with parasites and other carriers of infectious diseases. In addition, settlement increases the transmissibility of infections brought on by carriers whose life cycle is otherwise interrupted by frequent human movements; this is the case, for example, with fleas whose larvae grow in nests, beds, or dwellings rather than on the bodies of animals or human beings. With settlement, many animals, domesticated and not, come to occupy a stable place in the human ecological niche, raising the possibility of infection from specifically animal pathogens and increasing the incidence of parasitism. Agricultural technology may also have been responsible for the spread of certain diseases like, for example, malaria, which benefited from irrigation and the artificial creation of pools of stagnant water.[15] As confirmation of the lower incidence of acute infectious diseases among preagricultural populations, studies of, for example, Australian Aborigines isolated from contact with the white population are cited.[16] In general, the small dimensions and mobility of present-day hunting and gathering groups seem to provide defense against parasites just as their relative isolation appears to check the spread of epidemics.[17] It should be recalled, however, that many scholars maintain that the biological complexity of the ecosystem (complex in the tropics and simple in desert or arctic areas) is directly related to the variety and incidence of infections affecting populations.[18]

On the whole, then, a more meager and less varied diet and conditions favorable to infectious diseases would seem to justify the hypothesis of higher mortality among farmers relative to their hunting ancestors.[19] But if

---

[15]   Cockburn, "Infectious Diseases," p. 49.

[16]   Ibid., p. 50.

[17]   M. N. Cohen, *Health*, p. 104.

[18]   F. L. Dunn, "Epidemiological Factors: Health and Disease in Hunter-Gatherers," in *Man the Hunter*, ed. R. B. Lee and I. DeVore (Aldine, Chicago, 1968).

[19]   For a recent reassessment of this theory, see M. N. Cohen, *Health*. Cohen's prudent synthesis runs as follows: "Most comparisons between hunter-gatherers and later farmers in the same locale suggest that the farmers usually suffered higher rates of infection and parasitization and poorer nutrition . . . poor as it is, the data also suggest that hunter-gatherers reared a good proportion of their children to adulthood – a proportion commonly equal to or greater than that of later prehistoric populations. The data also suggest that average adult ages at death among prehistoric hunter-gatherers, though low by historic standards, were often higher than those of early farmers" (p. 122). Moreover, we might discern a similar tendency among hunters and gatherers passing from the Paleolithic to the Neolithic periods when the extinction of large prey led to the need for a diet less rich in meat. Ibid., p. 113.

mortality was higher among farmers, then their more rapid population growth can only have been the result of higher fertility. The latter hypothesis finds support in the social modifications attendant upon the transition from hunting to farming. The high mobility of hunter-gatherers, continually moving in a vast hunting ground, made the transport of dependent children both burdensome and dangerous for the mother. For this reason, the birth interval must have been fairly long, so that a new birth came only when the previous child was capable of taking care of itself. In a settled society this necessity became less pressing, the "cost" of children in terms of parental investment declined, and their economic contribution in the form of housework, fieldwork, and animal care increased.[20]

The hypothesis that fertility increases with the transition from hunting to agriculture is something more than conjecture. It has, in fact, been confirmed by several studies of present-day populations. Between 1963 and 1973 a group of scholars led by R. B. Lee studied the !Kung San, a nomadic population that lived by hunting and gathering in northern Botswana (southern Africa) and was at that time beginning a gradual process of settlement.[21] Lee's group observed that about half of the !Kung's edible vegetables were gathered by the women, who in the course of a year traveled several thousand kilometers. During most of their movements these women carried their children under four years of age with them. The age of puberty among the !Kung women was late, between 15 and 17, and a long period of postpuberty sterility followed, so that the first birth came between 18 and 22, followed by birth intervals of three to five years. These intervals[22] are very long for a population not practicing modern birth control and were the result of the continuation of breast-feeding until as late as the third or fourth year. Body growth of the babies was slow, a notable adaptive advantage since it allowed their easier transportation during the long daily movements of the mothers. Consequently, the average number of children per woman was fairly low (4.7). Low fertility of this sort, imposed by the

---

[20]   R. B. Lee, "Lactation, Ovulation, Infanticide and Women's work: A Study of Hunter-Gatherer Population Regulations," in *Biosocial Mechanisms of Population Regulation*, ed. M. N. Cohen, R. S. Malpass, and H. G. Klein (Yale University Press, New Haven, 1980). A very detailed analysis of the !Kung is found in N. Howell, *The Demography of the Dobe !Kung* (Academic Press, New York, 1979). Coale, "History of Human Population."

[21]   The following is based on Lee, "Lactation, Ovulation, Infanticide."

[22]   On birth intervals see chapter 1, section 4.

habits of a hunter-gatherer population, is also characteristic of other groups, like the African Pygmies.[23] Still more interesting is the fact that in the process of settlement !Kung San fertility seems to have increased. In fact, the settled women had birth intervals (36 months) significantly shorter than their hunter-gatherer counterparts (44 months),[24] just as postulated by the supporters of the theory that fertility increases with the transition from hunting and gathering to farming. The comparison between historical and present-day populations gives similar results. Two recent studies reveal differences between the total fertility rates (TFR) of hunter-gatherers (foragers) (5.7 and 5.6) and agriculturalists (6.3 and 6.6).[25]

The postulates of the two theories are summarized in figure 2.2. The evidence in their support is for the most part conjectural, and the gathering of data is slow and often contradictory. Both theories assert that the level of nutrition changed, but in opposite ways. Even if it is true that hunter-gatherers enjoyed a more varied diet (present-day hunter-gatherers seem to be only rarely malnourished), it is hard to imagine that the nutritional level declined with the transition to agriculture. One need only keep in mind the possibility of expanding cultivation, of accumulating reserves, of complementing the products of the earth with those obtained by hunting and fishing, of improving the techniques of food preparation and conservation. It may be, on the other hand, that the level of nutrition had less of an influence on mortality than is suggested by either of these theories, since it is only in cases of extreme want and malnutrition that the risk of contracting and succumbing to certain infectious diseases increases.[26] The hypothesis that the frequency and transmission of infectious diseases increased in higher-density and more permanent

---

[23] L. L. Cavalli Sforza, "The Transition to Agriculture and Some of Its Consequences," in *How Humans Adapt*, ed. D. J. Ortner (Smithsonian Institution Press, Washington, D. C., 1983).

[24] Lee, "Lactation, Ovulation, Infanticide." We should, however, also mention the hypothesis of Rose Frisch, according to which the low fertility of the !Kung women is the result of malnutrition below a critical threshold.

[25] See K. L. Campbell and J. W. Wood, "Fertility in Traditional Societies," in *Natural Human Fertility: Social and Biological Mechanisms*, ed. P. Diggory, S. Teper, and M. Potts (Macmillan, London, 1988); G. R. Bentley, G. Jasienska, and T. Goldberg, "Is the Fertility of Agriculturalists Higher than that of Nonagriculturalists?," *Current Anthropology*, 34 (1993).

[26] This is a position which I advocate in M. Livi-Bacci, *Population and Nutrition* (Cambridge University Press, Cambridge, 1991). It will be dealt with below (chapter 2, section 7).

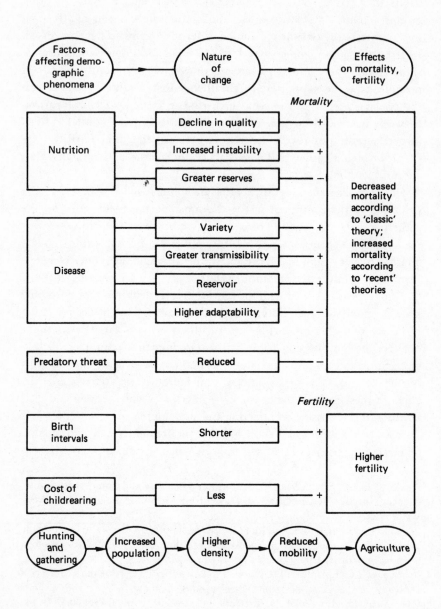

Figure 2.2 Presumed demographic effects accompanying the transition from hunting and gathering to agriculture

populations is better founded, though the matter is too complex to allow simplification.[27]

With regard to fertility, the evidence from present-day preagricultural groups argues convincingly in favor of the possibility that the transition to settled agriculture entailed increased prolificity. Moreover, Childe, an advocate of the classic theory, noted that in an agricultural society "children become economically useful; to hunters children are liable to be a burden."[28]

3 Black Death and Demographic Decline in Europe

Around the year 1000 the population of Europe began a phase of growth which would last three centuries. The data are scarce and fragmentary, but sufficient to reveal the symptoms of solid demographic growth. Settlements multiplied, new cities were founded, abandoned areas were inhabited, and cultivation expanded to progressively less fertile lands. In the course of these centuries European population increased by a factor of two or three, testimony to a growth potential which frequent crises could not suppress. Toward the end of the thirteenth century and in the first decades of the fourteenth there is clear evidence that this cycle of growth was losing steam: crises became more frequent, settlements ceased to expand, and here and there population stagnated. This slowdown was the result of complex causes, probably connected to an agricultural economy made less vigorous

---

[27]   The arguments in favor of caution are many. The density of most prehistoric agricultural populations was very low and urban agglomerations were rare. If, on the one hand, the spread of pathogens was greater among farmers, there is also a process of mutual adaptation between pathogen and host organism which renders the danger less. In a classic and unsurpassed work on the history of infectious diseases and epidemics, Hans Zinsser wrote over 50 years ago: "nothing in the world of living things is permanently fixed . . . on purely biological grounds, therefore, it is entirely logical to suppose that infectious diseases are constantly changing; new ones are in the process of developing and old ones modified or disappearing . . . It would be surprising therefore if new forms of parasitism – that is, infection – did not constantly arise and if, among forms, the modifications in the mutual adjustments of parasites and hosts had not taken place during the centuries of which we have record." H. Zinsser, *Rats, Lice, and History* (Little, Brown, Boston, 1963), pp. 57–9. Finally, we should not forget that the data regarding the pathology of prehistoric populations are few and fragmentary and that many of these hypotheses are entirely conjectural.

[28]   Childe, *Man Makes Himself*, pp. 53–4.

by the depletion of the best land and a halt in technological progress and subject to more frequent shortages due to unfavorable climatic conditions.[29] It might have been a passing phase, a period of adjustment as population sought a more favorable balance with resources, to be followed by another cycle of growth. Instead, toward the middle of the fourteenth century a devastating and long-term catastrophe occurred which caused population to decline, according to the estimates of table 1.3, by almost a third between 1340 and 1400, only to continue to decline during the first half of the following century before beginning to recover. This recovery would not carry population to its precrisis level until the mid-sixteenth century.

The catastrophe was the plague; between its first appearance in Sicily, in 1347, and 1352 when it spread through Russia, it traversed the entire continent. Figure 2.3 shows its expansion: by the end of 1348 it had reached Italy, the Iberian Peninsula, part of France, and southern England; by the end of 1349, Norway, the rest of France, the Rhine valley, Switzerland, Austria, and the Dalmatian coast; between 1350 and 1352, it moved eastward, from Germany to Poland to Russia. In a Europe whose population numbered about 80 million, the number of deaths claimed by the plague represented a significant fraction. Much has been written about the plague, both about its first appearance and its successive waves (of which more is said below).[30] I shall limit discussion here to the essentials of its nature, intensity, and chronology in order to attack the heart of the question, which does not so much concern description as an evaluation of the long-term effects of the plague on growth; the identification, in its most extreme and catastrophic form, of one of the most violent checks to demographic growth; and the individuation of the mechanisms of reaction and compensation activated by the catastrophe.

The bacillus responsible for the plague is called *yersinia pestis* (discovered in 1894 by Yersin in Hong Kong). It is usually transmitted by fleas carried by rats and mice.[31] The bacillus does not kill the flea which bites and so infects its host (the mouse). When the mouse dies, the flea must find a new host

[29] B. H. Slicher van Bath, *The Agrarian History of Western Europe, A.D. 500–1850* (Edward Arnold, London, 1963), appendix; E. Sereni, "Agricoltura e mondo rurale," in *Storia d'Italia* (Einaudi, Torino, 1972), vol. 1.

[30] From this vast literature, I shall limit myself to citing J.-N. Biraben, *Les hommes et la peste en France et dans les pays européens et méditerranéens* (Mouton, Paris, 1974–6), vol. 1: *La peste dans l'histoire*; vol. 2: *Les hommes face à la peste*. See also L. Del Panta, *Le epidemie nella storia demografica italiana (secoli XIV–XIX)* (Loescher, Torino, 1980).

[31] Biraben, *Les hommes et la peste*, vol. 1, pp. 7–31; Del Panta, *Le epidemie*, pp. 34–40.

(another mouse, or a human) and so spreads the infection. Transmitted epidermally, plague has an incubation period of one to six days. The flea bite results in swelling of the lymph glands of the neck, underarms, and groin (buboes). Symptoms of the disease include high fever, coma, cardiac failure, and inflammation of the internal organs. Normally two-thirds to four-fifths of those infected die.[32] The plague was easily transmitted, even over long distances, together with goods carrying infected mice or fleas (clothing, personal objects, foodstuffs).

No one is naturally immune to the plague. Those who contract the disease and survive acquire short-term immunity. Nonetheless, the possibility that successive waves of the plague progressively selected individuals who were for some reason less susceptible to the disease cannot be ruled out, though these processes must evolve over long periods in order to have a perceptible effect.

The plague that appeared in Europe in 1347, while not a new phenomenon, had been absent for six or seven centuries, since the plague of the Justinian period. The latter spread through the eastern Mediterranean in 541–4 and afflicted Italy and, especially Mediterranean, Europe in successive waves from 558–61 until 599–600. It remained in the East until the middle of the eighth century, generating successive epidemics which, though localized, continued to affect Europe.[33]

In September 1347 the unloading of several Genoese galleys in Messina interrupted long centuries of bacteriological peace. These ships came from ports on the Black Sea where the plague, having arrived from the East, raged. In the space of four or five years, as mentioned above, the disease traversed the entire continent; and this was only the first of a series of epidemic waves. In Italy (and progress was little different in the rest of Europe) these waves came in 1360–3, 1371–4, 1381–4, 1388–90, and 1398–1400. In the fifteenth century they were still occurring frequently, but with less synchronicity and severity.[34] Measurement of the mortality of the various epidemic waves is uncertain due to the lack of precise data. Nonetheless, there were for many areas annual series of deaths from which we can discern the levels of mortality in normal and plague years. In Siena, for example, the plague of 1348 caused 11 times more deaths than normal. In the other five epidemics of

---

[32] This description is extremely schematic. In addition to the more common bubonic plague, the so-called "pneumonic" form should also be mentioned. Transmitted directly from one person to another by coughing or sneezing, it was almost 100% lethal.

[33] Biraben, *Les hommes et la peste*, vol. 1, pp. 30ff.

[34] Del Panta, *Le epidemie*, p. 118.

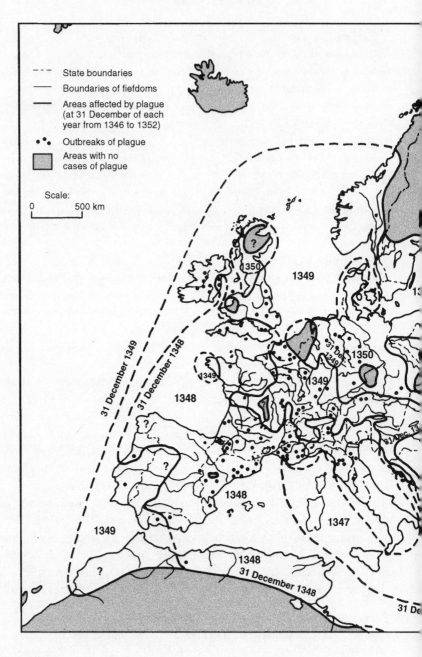

Figure 2.3   The extent of the plague, 1346–52

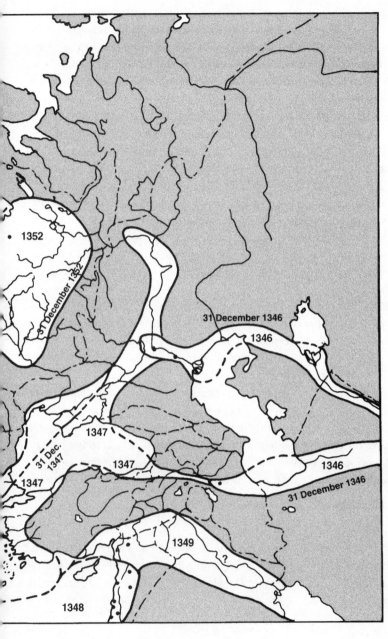

that same century the death total increase varied between five and ten times the norm. Imagining that normal mortality was about 35 per thousand, then an increase of elevenfold would mean about 420 per thousand, or the death of more than four persons in ten. A tenfold increase means, approximately, the elimination of one-third of the population, an increase of fivefold the elimination of one-sixth.

For several parts of Tuscany between 1340 and 1400 I have calculated that on average a serious mortality crisis – defined as an increase in deaths at least three times the normal – occurred every 11 years; the average increase in deaths was at least sevenfold. In the period 1400–50 these crises occurred on average every 13 years and deaths increased fivefold. In the following half century (1450–1500) the average frequency declined to 37 years and the average increase to fourfold.[35] With the passage of time, both the frequency and the intensity of the crises declined, as did the geographic synchronization of their occurrence. Keep in mind that Tuscany is an exceptional case only for the abundance of historical sources to be found there.

The following two centuries were not spared the devastation of the plague, from the cycle of 1522–30 (made worse by the wars that followed the fall of Charles VIII) to that of 1575–77 (especially in the north), 1630–1 (in the center-north), and 1656–7 (especially in the center-south).[36] Although these bouts of plague were terrible (Cipolla calculates that more than a quarter of the center-north population struck by the 1630–1 plague was wiped out),[37] they were no longer the dominating catastrophes they had been in previous centuries. Other crises (typhus, for example) competed with the plague for the prize. With some variations the Italian experience applies to Europe as a whole. After the epidemic of 1663–70 which hit England (the London plague of 1664 described by Defoe), northern France, the Low Countries, and the Rhine Valley, the plague disappeared from Europe as a general geographic event, save for an appearance in Provence in 1720–2 and in a few other limited areas.[38]

Returning to our central concern, in the century that followed the Black Death of 1348 European population declined both as a result of the first and, from a literary point of view, most famous explosion and also the relentless cycles that followed. Only in the sixteenth century would European

[35]   M. Livi-Bacci, *La société italienne devant les crises de mortalité* (Dipartimento statistico, Florence, 1978), p. 41; Del Panta, *Le epidemie*, p. 132.

[36]   Del Panta, *Le epidemie*, p. 118.

[37]   C. M. Cipolla, "Il declino economico in Italia," in *Storia dell'economia italiana*, ed. C. M. Cipolla (Einaudi, Torino, 1959), vol. 1, p. 620.

[38]   Biraben, *Les hommes et la peste*, vol. 1, pp. 125–6.

population once again attain the numerical level of 1340, while the plague would continue to play a role as a check on population growth until its virtual disappearance in the second half of the seventeenth century. There are no precise data on the scale of the decline between the period before 1348 and the population nadir reached during the first half of the fifteenth century, but a loss of 30 to 40 percent is corroborated by local studies in Piedmont and Tuscany,[39] in France, Spain, England, and Germany. Cities emptied within oversized urban boundaries, abandoned villages and deserted countryside rendered concrete testimony, while a labor shortage caused salaries to rise and the abundance of available land lowered the price of food.

The plague constitutes a population check largely exogenous, or external, to the sociodemographic system. It acted independently of modes of social organization, levels of development, density of settlement, and so on. The ability of the plague to infect and kill bore no relation to one's state of health, age, or level of nutrition. It struck urban and rural populations with equal violence and, with the exception of a few isolated areas, density levels presented no obstacle to its spread. The movement of people and goods was sufficient to carry it from one end of the continent to the other. In the long run, of course, societies took measures to defend themselves. The quarantine and isolation of infected or suspect individuals and goods, the shutting up of plague victims' homes, and a few public health measures may partially explain the disappearance of the plague from the European continent.[40] Nonetheless, for over centuries the plague made itself at home there.

Unlike the victims of many other diseases, the few individuals who contracted the plague and survived did not acquire long-term immunity. It is not reasonable, then, to attribute the gradual decline of the plague solely to the existence of a larger immunized portion of the population. The process of *Durchseuchung*, according to which "the accidentally less susceptible survive, and through generations a gradual alteration of the relationship between parasite and host becomes established,"[41] may have had some effect; and

---

[39]   R. Comba, "Vicende demografiche in Piemonte nell'ultimo Medioevo," *Bollettino storico-bibliografico subalpino*, 75 (1977); E. Fiumi, "Fioritura e decadenza dell'economia fiorentina, II: Demografia e movimento urbanistico," *Archivio Storico Italiano*, 116, disp. IV (1958). Other works of Fiumi deal with Prato, and the area of Volterra and San Gimignano. See also for Tuscany D. Herlihy and C. Klapisch-Zuber, *Les Toscans et leurs familles. Une étude du catasto florentin de 1427* (EHESS, Paris, 1978).

[40]   C. M. Cipolla, *Public Health and the Medical Profession* (Cambridge University Press, London, 1976); Livi-Bacci, *La société italienne*, pp. 95–122.

[41]   Zinsser, *Rats, Lice, and History*, pp. 66–7.

"had the disease continued, constantly present, and attacking a large portion of the new generations as they appeared, it might gradually have assumed an endemic, sporadic form, with relatively low mortality."[42]

A disease of such ferocity could have, after repeated attacks, completely eliminated the populations which it infected. This did not happen, and with time the frequency, if not always the intensity, of the crises declined. Neither the specific explanations discussed above (social adjustment, immunity, selection) nor still others (other social or ecological transformations) are sufficient to explain this phenomenon. For reasons not entirely clear the plague underwent a process of mutual adaptation between pathogen (*yersinia*), carrier (flea), and host-victim (human).

As occurs for other sorts of mortality crises, there was also a process of socio-demographic adaptation and response to the plague, both in the short and medium-long term. In the short term a sudden and large increase in mortality has a double effect. The spread of the disease lowers the frequency of conceptions, births (for choice, necessity, and psycho-biological reasons), and marriages. The decline in births accentuates the negative demographic action of the epidemic. Moreover, high mortality ends marriages and breaks up or destroys family units. At the end of the crisis there is a rebound effect which, while not sufficient to compensate for the lost lives and births, nonetheless attenuates their effect. Marriages which had been postponed during the crisis are celebrated and the marriage rate among the widowed increases. In some cases a fertility increase among couples has even been noted. These several factors combine to produce a temporary increase in overall fertility. Mortality too is often below normal after a crisis due to the reduced representation of infant age groups and the selective effects linked to the epidemic. The balance between births and deaths improves and for a few years some of the previous losses are made up. A new crisis can, of course, soon restart the cycle, as in the century after 1348, or it can do so after a longer interval, as in the sixteenth and seventeenth centuries.[43]

In the long term other factors intervene. Depopulation caused by the plague in Europe created abundant available land and a labor shortage. New family units acquired the resources they needed to establish themselves more easily. The checks to marriage generally relaxed and nuptiality increased, stimulating population growth. One may, for example, explain

---

[42] Ibid., p. 89.

[43] Livi-Bacci, *La société italienne*, pp. 8ff and 63ff discusses various aspects of the reaction to mortality crises.

in this way the low age at marriage in early fifteenth-century Tuscany.[44]
Both long- and short-term responses tend to minimize the damage done
to society and population by *yersinia*, flea, and mouse.

4 *The Tragedy of the American* Indios: *Old Microbes and New Populations*

"Thrice happy are those, that inhabiting some yet undiscovered island in
the midst of the ocean, have never been brought into contaminating
contact with the white man."[45] So wrote the young Melville in 1845 on
returning from the Marquesas Islands. The tragic effects of contact
between white Europeans – whether conquerors, colonists, explorers, or
sailors – and the indigenous populations of the New World, the Pacific,
and Oceania were evident from the time of the earliest explorations.
Historical documentation is abundant, and we have only to choose our
examples.

As is well known, Columbus landed in Santo Domingo (christened at
the time La Española) in 1492. The number of inhabitants at the time is of
course unknown, but it seemed densely populated to the first visitors, "like
the countryside of Cordoba."[46] Whether we take the Las Casas estimate of
three or four million or that much smaller one of just under 60,000, the fact
remains that in 1514 the *ripartimientos* of the *Indios* for tax purposes counted
22,000 individuals, and of these only a few tens or hundreds survived 20
years later. The 112,000 *Indios* of 1512 Cuba suffered a similar fate, disappearing in the second half of the century.[47]

---

[44]   In Florence the age at first marriage for women reached a nadir in the first half of
the fifteenth century, after which it gradually increased: 17.6 in 1427, 19.5 in 1458, 20.8
in 1480. In nearby Prato it was 16.3 in 1372, 17.6 in 1427, and 21.1 in 1470. Rural rates must
have followed a similar pattern. See Herlihy and Klapisch-Zuber, *Les Toscans*.

[45]   H. Melville, *Typee* (The New American Library, New York, 1964), p. 29.

[46]   According to the report of Ferdinand Columbus, based on his father's notes. See
S. F. Cook and W. Borah, *Essays in Population History. Mexico and the Caribbean* (University
of California Press, Berkeley, 1971), vol. 1, chap. 6.

[47]   H. Thomas, *La conquista de México* (Barcelona, 1994), pp. 96–8. In striking contrast
to the disappearance of indigenous and imported slave populations, horses, cattle,
swine, and dogs imported from Spain increased dramatically in the wild. Diego
Valasquez, the first governor of Cuba, wrote to the king in 1514 that the small
number of pigs imported four years before had grown to 30,000.

Skipping over the preconquest estimates, based on vague conjecture, those of Cook and Borah for central Mexico – the area of the Aztecs and the most populous of the continent – are relatively well-founded and give a figure of 6.3 million *Indios* in 1548, which subsequently declined to 1.9 million in 1580 and 1 million in 1605.[48] In Incan Peru, the other important demographic concentration of the continent, estimates based on the visit of the Viceroy Toledo in 1572, subsequently updated, report 1.3 million Indios subject to tribute; their number was reduced to 0.6 million by 1620.[49] Farther to the north in Canada, Charbonneau has calculated that there lived no fewer than 300,000 Indians at the beginning of the seventeenth century; that number was reduced to less than a third two centuries later. Thornton claims that in the three centuries after 1500 the Indians of the area that became the United States were reduced from 5 million to 60,000.[50] For all of these groups demographic decline from the moment of contact with Europeans seems to have been the rule. There are also more recent examples: Darwin refers to the disappearance of the inhabitants of Tasmania;[51] the Maoris experienced rapid demographic decline from the time of the voyages of Captain Cook to the end of the following century;[52] and the Australian aborigines presumably suffered a similar fate. The indigenous population of

[48]   Ibid., chap. 2. It should be mentioned that the debate over the pre-Columbian population of the continent is far from resolved. Between the lowest estimates of Kroeber and Rosenblat (9 to 13 million) and the highest of Dobyns (90 to 112 million), the latter supported by the research of Cook and Borah, there is a wide range of intermediate figures. With regard to the Mesoamerican population, the Cook and Borah estimate of 25.2 million for the period just prior to conquest is derived primarily from retrospective extrapolations based on late-sixteenth-century trends and is highly speculative. See the recent criticism of A. Zambardino, "Mexico's Population in the Sixteenth Century: Demographic Anomaly or Mathematical Illusion?," *Journal of Interdisciplinary History*, 11, (1980), pp. 1–27, which, for example, lowers the estimate of 6.3 million for 1548 to 3.6 million. Nonetheless, no one questions the demographic decline, attested to by data from the late sixteenth century and numerous historical reports. See N. Sánchez Albornoz, *La población de América Latina desde los tiempos precolombinos al año 2000* (Alianza Editorial, Madrid, 1994), pp. 53–73.

[49]   Sánchez Albornoz, *La población de América Latina*, p. 65.

[50]   H. Charbonneau, "Trois siècles de dépopulation amérindienne," in *Les populations amérindiennes et Inuit du Canada. Aperçu démographique*, ed. L. Normandeau and V. Piché (Presses Universitaires de Montréal, Montréal, 1984); R. Thornton, *American Indian Holocaust and Survival* (University of Oklahoma Press, Norman, 1987), p. 90.

[51]   C. Darwin, *The Descent of Man* (Random House, New York, n.d.), pp. 543–4.

[52]   D. I. Pool, *The Maori Population of New Zealand, 1769–1971* (Auckland University Press, Auckland, 1977). Pool estimates that the 100,000 to 200,000 inhabitants of 1770 were reduced to little more than 40,000 a century later.

Tierra del Fuego, 7,000–9,000 in 1871, is now almost extinct.[53] In the Amazon basin there are groups which, due to their extreme isolation, have only in this century come into contact with colonists or explorers and have died off before the eyes of contemporary observers.[54]

The above examples should suffice. The demographic collapse of indigenous populations as a result of contact with groups of European origin is a widespread and well-documented phenomenon throughout America and Oceania. The timing, scale, and duration of the decline of course vary according to the historical situation, but the basic mechanism is fairly simple. Indigenous populations were, so to speak, virgin soil for many infectious diseases which they had never before encountered. Once the pathogen had passed – by way of explorer, *conquistador*, or colonist – from the original population (exposed to the disease for many generations) to the virgin population, it spread with a virulence basically ascribable to three factors:

1 Infectious diseases immunize (whether for short or long periods) those individuals who have contracted the illness and recovered. As a result, while the disease continues to wend its way among the population (either because endemic or else continually re-introduced), there is always a larger or smaller immunized portion that resists infection and so limits the damage. On the other hand, all the members of a virgin population are theoretically susceptible, and so the introduction of a new disease produces immense losses.

2 In a nonvirgin population, the disease tends over generations to select the more resistant individuals. In the absence of this factor, the disease attacks the virgin population more ferociously.

3 That process of mutual adaptation over time between pathogen (virus, microbe, parasite) and host – a complex and not entirely understood process which attenuates the virulence of the disease – has not taken place in the case of the virgin population. Syphilis, malaria, measles, and influenza are diseases that seem to grow less harsh with time. It is said that a pathogen is not interested in killing the host upon which it depends for survival, but rather in coexisting with it and not causing too much harm; hence the selection of less lethal strains. In virgin populations, this coexistence has obviously not had time to develop.

[53]   H. F. Dobyns, "Estimating Aboriginal American Population. An Appraisal of Techniques with a New Hemispheric Estimate," *Current Anthropology, 7* (1966), p. 413.
[54]   Ibid., p. 413.

The devastating effects of infectious diseases, even those relatively harmless or benign in their area of origin, is almost always at the root of the quantitative decline (and in the case of smaller or weaker groups even extinction) of virgin populations. The history of Mesoamerica offers a classic example of this process. Table 2.1 records the decline of this population according to the estimates of Cook and Borah. In 1608 the population numbered one-sixth of that estimated for 1548. The decline was more severe along the coast (up to one seventh) than in the highlands (one-fifth). And the population in 1548 must have been a fraction (one-quarter according to these two authors) of what it had been in 1519, the year that Cortés and his soldiers arrived.[55] Although the initial size of the population is unknown, numerous reports point to a demographic decline in that 30-year period. It is difficult to accept the estimate of 25 million: given the restricted area in which the population must have been concentrated, its density would have been about 50 persons per square kilometer, considerably higher than that of the most densely populated country area of Europe at the time (Italy, with about 35 persons per square kilometer). Considering the fairly rudimentary technology of the indigenous population, the harshness of the terrain, and the moderate productivity of their agriculture, one is inclined to subscribe to the opinion of more prudent scholars who place the preconquest population well below 10 million. No one, however, contests that which numerous documents prove beyond a doubt: the population declined rapidly to a low point reached in the first decades of the seventeenth century.[56]

While data are scarce, documentary and literary testimony abound. The

[55]   See, however, the cautions regarding these estimates in note 46.

[56]   Robert McCaa has recently returned to this question and concludes: "It seems to me that close attention to contemporary narratives will lead to consensus on the scale, causes, and consequences of the demographic disaster which struck sixteenth-century Mexico. There is agreement that a demographic catastrophe occurred and that epidemic disease was a dominant factor in initiating a die-off beginning, in Central Mexico, with smallpox in 1520. But the role of disease cannot be understood without taking into account massive harsh treatment (forced migration, enslavement, abusive labor demand and exorbitant tribute payments) and ecological devastation accompanying Spanish colonization. Killing associated with war and conquest was clearly a secondary factor, except in isolated cases . . ." See R. McCaa, "Smallpox and Demographic Catastrophe in Mexico: What can Spanish and Nahuatl Narratives tell us that Numbers cannot?" (unpublished manuscript, 1995). The same author has observed that whatever the estimate of the size of the population of central Mexico before the conquest, nine scholars out of ten estimate the population decline during the sixteenth century (1519–95) somewhere between 55 and 96 percent.

Table 2.1   Population of central Mexico (1532–1608)

Year	Population in thousands			Annual population growth rate[a]		
	Plateau	Coast	Total	Plateau	Coast	Total
1532	11,226	5,645	16,871	–	–	–
1548	4,765	1,535	6,300	−5.4	−8.1	−6.2
1568	2,231	418	2,649	−3.8	−6.5	−4.3
1580	1,631	260	1,891	−2.6	−4.0	−2.8
1595	1,125	247	1,372	−2.5	−0.3	−2.1
1608	852	217	1,069	−2.1	−1.0	−1.9
1532–1608				−3.4	−4.3	−3.6
1548–1608				−2.9	−3.3	−3.0

[a] For the period since the previous date.
Source: S. F. Cook and W. Borah, *Essays in Population History. Mexico and the Caribbean*, 3 vols (University of California Press, Berkeley, 1971), vol. 1, p. 82

first serious epidemic wave was that of smallpox, which arrived with Columbus and decimated the populations of La Española and Puerto Rico before moving on to Mexico. Bernal Diaz del Castillo, a lieutenant of Cortés, wrote: "we shall return now to Narvaez and to a black man whom he brought with him, completely infected with smallpox; a fatal black for New Spain as he was the cause that smallpox took hold and spread throughout the country, causing much death which, according to the *Indios*, has never been equalled. And not knowing better, they washed themselves frequently and because of this died in huge numbers."[57] Smallpox decimated the Aztecs, felled the successor to Montezuma, spread through Guatemala, and then passed from Central America to the Incan Empire, apparently preceding Pizarro and his *conquistadores*.

The second serious epidemic was that of *sarampion* (measles), which between 1529 and 1535 passed from the Caribbean to Mexico to Central America. In the same period, Cabeza de Vaca, who shipwrecked in Florida, managed during his desperate trek to Mexico to infect (possibly with dysentery) the tribe that enslaved him. The tribe was decimated and, ironically, made him a shaman. In 1545 *matlazahuatl* (an Aztec term, perhaps

---

[57]   Bernal Diaz del Castillo, *Historia verdadera de la conquista de la Nueva España* (Espasa Calpe, Madrid, 1968), p. 262; see also the account in F. B. de Sahagún, *Historia general de las cosas de Nueva España* (Editorial Porrua, Mexico City, 1977), vol. 4, p. 58.

typhus) struck and spread throughout the continent. The devastation continued: in 1557 a type of influenza struck, in 1563 smallpox, *matlazahuatl* in 1574–6, and smallpox again in 1588 and 1595. Sánchez Albornoz, from whom I have taken the above information, notes that "during the seventeenth century the continental epidemics occurred at a rate of almost one every ten years . . . The following century they occurred more irregularly and in geographically more limited areas . . . perhaps the *Indios* had developed, after about three quarters of a century, the necessary antibodies and so were better able to resist the attacks of the various diseases. It is even possible that these diseases had become endemic and the local populations attained a certain level of adaptation."[58]

The theory of virgin terrain finds confirmation in the facts. Analogous to the (more lethal) European plague, an adjustment of sorts was achieved a century after the initial contact, evident in the lower intensity, frequency, and synchronicity of the crisis. Demographically the decline was halted and recovery began in the second half of the seventeenth century. Epidemics on virgin terrain constitute the principal explanation for the indigenous population decline, though other factors – genocide as maintained by the Dominican Bartolomé de Las Casas, champion of the *Indios*, or forced labor and the reorganization of production – should not be discounted.[59]

The variety of the lethal diseases that struck the New World populations should also be stressed. In addition to smallpox and probably typhus – scourges in the Old World as well as the New – tuberculosis, measles, influenza, and chicken pox all left their mark. Reports of the awful virulence of smallpox among populations which were strangers to it abound outside of Mesoamerica as well. In the seventeenth century the Huron and Algonquian tribes of Canada were decimated,[60] as were the Cherokee and other tribes of the Great Plains in the following century[61] and the California Indians who settled near the missions established in the late eighteenth century. The effects of measles were similar: "When measles first came to the Fiji Islands in 1875, as a result of the visit of the King of the Fijis and his son to Sydney in New South Wales, it caused the death of 40,000 people in a population of

---

[58] Sánchez Albornoz, *La población de América Latina*, p. 83.
[59] Ibid., pp. 71–80. The influential thesis of Bartolomé de Las Casas appears in the 1542 work, *Breve relación de la distrucción de las Indias occidentales*.
[60] Charbonneau, "Trois siècles de dépopulation amérindienne," pp. 38–9.
[61] A. W. Crosby, "Virgin Soil Epidemics as a Factor in the Aboriginal Depopulation of America," *William and Mary Quarterly*, 3rd series, 33 (1976), pp. 290–1. See also, by the same author, the more general work, *Ecological Imperialism: The Biological Expansion of Europe, 900–1900* (Cambridge University Press, London, 1986).

about 150,000."[62] In the second half of this century measles struck the Indians and Eskimos of the Ungava Bay in northern Québec in 1952, the Brazilian Indians of the remote Xingu reserve in 1954, and the Yanamono tribe of the Orinoco valley on the border between Venezuela and Brazil in 1968. In spite of the aid of modern medicine, mortality in these three cases was close to 10 percent.[63] An analogous but reverse mechanism operated in the case of the Lorrainers, several thousand of whom were sent by the Grand Duchy of Tuscany to colonize the Maremma district along the west coast of Italy in the eighteenth century. Unaccustomed to the climate and, above all, to malaria and other fevers, their numbers were rapidly reduced.[64] For similar reasons, disease-related mortality among European troops stationed in tropical regions was exceedingly high until the middle of the last century. One example will have to suffice: of the 12,000-man English force that laid siege to the Caribbean port of Cartagena for two months, more than two-thirds perished from yellow fever. And even in normal periods, very high losses were a constant source of worry for European armies.[65]

5 The French Canadians: A Demographic Success Story

Having recounted two catastrophic cases of infectious disease-related mortality – the plague and the virtual extermination of the *Indios* – let us turn to a demographic success. A few thousand pioneers arrived in the Canadian province of Québec, centered on the Saint Lawrence basin and five times the size of Italy, in the seventeenth century. Most of the present-day population of 6.5 million trace their ancestry to this original group. Faced with a harsh and inhospitable climate, a few courageous individuals quickly adapted and, thanks to abundant natural resources and available land, rapidly multiplied. In 1776 Adam Smith wrote: "The most decisive mark of the prosperity of any country is the increase of the number of its inhabitants . . . In the British colonies in North America, it has been found

[62] H. Zinsser, *Rats, Lice, and History*, p. 67.

[63] Crosby, "Virgin Soil Epidemics," p. 293; J. Rousseau, "Coupe biogéographique et ethnologique de la pénisule Québec Labrador," in *Le Nouveau Québec*, ed. J. Malaurie and J. Rousseau (Mouton, Paris, 1964), p. 77.

[64] L. Del Panta, "Una fonte per lo studio delle colonie lorenesi in Maremma: i libri parrocchiali di Massa Marittima," *Bollettino della Società Storica Maremmana*, 49, fasc. speciale (1985).

[65] P. D. Curtin, *Death by Migration* (Cambridge University Press, Cambridge, 1989), p. 2.

that they double in twenty or five-and-twenty years. Nor in the present times is this increase principally owing to the continual importation of new inhabitants, but to the great multiplication of the species. Those who live to old age, it is said, frequently see there from fifty to a hundred, and sometimes many more, descendants from their own body."[66] Others, from Benjamin Franklin to Thomas Malthus, made similar observations. We shall see that their claims are essentially correct and explain in large part the demographic increase of a few tens of thousands of colonists in North America who, between the eighteenth century and the end of the nineteenth, became 80 million.

In addition to the vigor of pioneers and colonists, a continual flow of immigration contributed to the demographic success of most of the European populations of North America and Oceania. It has been calculated that in the period 1840–1940 a migratory surplus accounted for almost 40 percent of total growth in Argentina, almost 30 percent in the United States, and a little more than 15 percent in Brazil and Canada,[67] while in French Canada there was consistently net outmigration.[68]

The reasons for choosing French Canada as our example are two. First, from the eighteenth century on immigration had little effect on population growth, and second, the Canadian sources are remarkably rich and have been skillfully exploited, allowing analysis of the demographic reasons for the success of the French in America.

Jacques Cartier explored the Saint Lawrence in 1534, and during the following century a French settlement developed there. Québec was founded in 1608; the Company of 100 *Associés* was formed in 1627 for the purpose of colonization; and in 1663 the royal government took over direction of the colonization process.[69] By 1680 the settlement was well established on the banks of the Saint Lawrence and numbered 10,000 individuals divided among 14 parishes. In the following 100 years the initial nucleus multiplied elevenfold (from 12,000 in 1684 to 132,000 in 1784, with an average annual growth rate of 2.4 percent), almost entirely due to natural increase.[70]

---

[66]   A. Smith, *The Wealth of Nations* (J. M. Dent and Sons, London, 1964), vol. 1, p. 62.

[67]   J.-C. Chesnais, *La transition démographique* (PUF, Paris, 1986), p. 180.

[68]   H. Charbonneau, "Essai sur l'évolution démographique du Québec de 1534 à 2034," *Cahiers québécois de démographie*, 13 (1984), p. 13.

[69]   See H. Charbonneau et al., *Naissance d'une population. Les Français établis au Canada au XVIIe siècle* (Presses de l'Université de Montréal, Montréal, 1987), on which this section is largely based.

[70]   H. Charbonneau, "Essai sur l'évolution démographique," p. 13.

From the foundation of Québec (in 1608) to 1700, total immigration amounted to about 15,000, a tiny fraction of the French population of the day (barely eight emigrants per 1 million inhabitants), while nearby England, with one-third the population, sent 380,000 emigrants to the New World between 1630 and 1700.[71] Careful research has established that barely a third of those who immigrated before 1700 (4,997 individuals) successfully established a family in the colony. The others either returned to France, died before marrying or, but these were few, remained unmarried. Counting only the true biological "pioneers" who began families before 1680 (a few of these married before immigrating while the majority did so after) we have 3,380 individuals (1,425 women), from whom descend, as already mentioned, the vast majority of French Canadians. Analysis of this group of pioneers and their descendants (see also chapter 1, section 3) allows examination of the demographic characteristics of the French Canadians and so the reasons for their success. These are essentially three: (1) high nuptiality, especially due to the young age at marriage; (2) high natural fertility; and (3) relatively low mortality.

Table 2.2 records several demographic measures for both the pioneers and the population remaining in France. The women who came to Nouvelle France wed on average more than two years earlier than their French sisters. In addition, remarriage was much more frequent among the former and, given the high mortality of that period, widowhood at a young age was not

Table 2.2 Comparison of the demographic behavior of French Canadian pioneers and the contemporary French population

Demographic index	*Pioneers*	*French*	*Pioneer/French ratio*
Mean age at first marriage (M)	28.8	25.0	1.15
Mean age at first marriage (F)	20.9	23.0	0.91
% of second marriages (M)[a]	70.0	67.8	1.03
% of second marriages (F)[a]	70.4	48.8	1.44
Completed fertility[b]	6.88	6.39	1.08
Life expectancy at age 20	38.8	34.2	1.13

[a] % of widows and widowers remarried by age 50.

[b] Sum of legitimate fertility rates, from 25 to 50 years of age, for women married prior to age 25.

Source: H. Charbonneau et al., *Naissance d'une population. Les Français établis au Canada au XVII[e] siècle* (Presses de l'Université de Montréal, Montréal, 1987)

---

[71] H. Charbonneau et al., *Naissance d'une population*, p. 21.

uncommon. Within their earlier and more frequent marriages the Canadian women enjoyed higher fertility, due to a shorter interval between pregnancies (25 months versus 29 in France), and more numerous offspring. Finally, pioneer life expectancy, calculated at 20 years of age, was significantly higher (almost five years) than in France.

Although they do not explain the situation completely, selective factors are at the base of these behavioral differences. Those who left on a long and difficult journey to an inhospitable land undoubtedly possessed courage, initiative, and a sound constitution. The long hard weeks of the transatlantic voyage exercised further selection, as mortality on board was high. Many of those who were unable to adapt returned home. This selection, which always accompanies migratory movements, certainly explains the lower mortality and perhaps also the higher fertility of the Canadians. At least during the early phases, low population density must also have contributed to keep down mortality by checking the spread of infection and epidemic. The young age at marriage for women (which was initially as low as 15 or 16)[72] and the frequency of second marriages owes much to the sexual imbalance created by the greater immigration of males. It was again Adam Smith who observed that: "A young widow with four or five young children, who, among the middling or inferior ranks of people in Europe, would have so little chance for a second husband, is there [in North America] frequently courted as a sort of fortune. The value of children is the greatest of all encouragements to marriage."[73]

The advantageous conditions in which the pioneers found themselves allowed each couple to have an average of 6.3 children, of whom 4.2 married, with the result that the population doubled in less than 30 years.[74] The 4 plus children of the pioneers had in turn 28 children, so that each pioneer had on average 34 offspring between children and grandchildren. About a third of the pioneers had more than 50 children and grandchildren, just as Smith wrote in the passage cited earlier.[75]

Subsequent generations continued to enjoy high levels of reproductivity and rapid growth. For while age at marriage for women slowly began to rise as the society became more established,[76] at the same time the fertility of the

---

[72]   H. Charbonneau, *Vie et mort de nos ancêtres* (Presses de l'Université de Montréal, Montréal, 1975), p. 166.
[73]   Smith, *The Wealth of Nations*, p. 63.
[74]   See chapter 1, section 3.
[75]   Charbonneau et al., *Naissance d'une population*, p. 113.
[76]   Charbonneau, *Vie et mort*, p. 165.

daughters of the pioneers, born in Canada and so full participants in the new society, was even higher than that of their mothers (which had in turn been higher than that of the women who remained in France). A few numerical examples: the average number of offspring for women who married between 15 and 19 years of age in northwest France (the area from which most of the pioneers emigrated) was 9.5; for the pioneers it was 10.1, while for the women born in Canada it was 11.4. For women marrying between 20 and 24, the respective figures were 7.6, 8.1, and 9.5; and for those marrying between 25 and 29, 5.6, 5.7, and 6.3.[77] The fertility of the Canadians remained high throughout the eighteenth century and is among the highest ever encountered.[78] With regard to mortality the situation seems to have been better in the seventeenth than in the eighteenth century, perhaps as a result of increasing density and the declining influence of migrational selection. Nonetheless, Canadian mortality seems to have remained a little better than that of northwest France.[79]

An initial selection mechanism, social cohesiveness, and favorable environmental factors were the basis of the demographic success of French migration to Canada. A few thousand pioneers at the beginning of the seventeenth century grew in half a century to 50,000,[80] initiating the demographic growth shown in table 2.3. It is interesting to note that while the French Canadian population grew rapidly, that of France (many times larger) grew slowly or stagnated, and the indigenous Indian population, stricken by disease and geographically displaced by colonial expansion, declined. There is a parallel, not to be interpreted mechanically, between these demographic adjustments and those of animal populations which, emigrating from a saturated area, establish themselves in a new environment at the expense of other species with which they compete. The different fates of the indigenous and colonizing populations – demographic crisis for the indigenous versus success for the colonizers – were a function not only of new diseases, but also of different levels of social and

---

[77]   Charbonneau et al., *Naissance d'une population*, p. 90.

[78]   H. Charbonneau, "Les régimes de fécondité naturelle en Amérique du Nord: bilan et analyse des observations," in *Natural Fertility*, ed. H. Leridon and J. Menken (Ordina, Liège, 1979), p. 450.

[79]   Charbonneau, *Vie et mort*, p. 147

[80]   Charbonneau et al., *Naissance d'une population*, p. 163. In this study the author has attempted to estimate the contribution of the pioneers to the gene pool of the French Canadian population (pp. 107–25). He calculates that the pre-1680 pioneers account for 70% of the gene pool at the end of the eighteenth century, a proportion little changed up to the present day due to the small amount of immigration after that date.

Table 2.3 French Canadian immigration and population (1608–1949)

Period	Immigrants settled	Average population (in thousands)	Immigrants as a % of average population	Contribution of pioneers at end of period (%)[a]
1608–79	3,380	–	–	100
1680–99	1,289	13	10.0	86
1700–29	1,477	24	6.0	80
1730–59	4,000	53	7.5	72
1760–99	4,000	137	3.0	70
1800–99	10,000	925	1.0	69
1900–49	25,000	2450	1.0	68

[a] The data in this column should be understood as an estimate of the contribution of the pioneers to the gene pool of the entire French Canadian population at the end of each period.

Source: H. Charbonneau et al., *Naissance d'une population. Les Français au Canada au XVIIe siècle* (Presses de l'Université de Montréal, Montréal, 1987), p. 1

technological organization. The Europeans controlled energy sources (horse, animal traction, and sail) and technologies (iron and steel tools and weapons, the wheel, explosives) that far outperformed those of the indigenous populations. They were better clothed and housed and were in any case accustomed to cold or temperate climates. In addition, the animals they imported (horses, cattle, sheep, goats) adapted to the new environment with astonishing ease and reproduced rapidly, as did their plants (and weeds).[81]

6 *Ireland and Japan: Two Islands, Two Histories*

In the long run, population and resources develop along more or less parallel lines. However, if we switch from a time frame of several centuries to one of shorter duration, this parallelism is not always so easy to identify. This situation comes about because the human species is extremely adaptable

[81] These comments derive from the very original work of A. W. Crosby, *Ecological Imperialism. The Biological Expansion of Europe* (Cambridge University Press, Cambridge, 1986). The success of cattle in the Argentine Pampas was extraordinary: Crosby (p. 178) takes as a reliable estimate that of the eighteenth-century traveler, Felix de Azara, according to whom there were 48 million head of cattle between the twenty-sixth and forty-first parallels, and these descended from just a few head imported a century before. This figure is comparable to that for the American buffaloes of the Great Plains at the time of their greatest expansion.

and able both to withstand periods of want and also to accumulate large quantities of resources. Nor is it the case that demographic variation always reflects, in a period short enough to render causality obvious, the variations in available resources (which we shall consider here, for the sake of convenience, as independent of human intervention). Furthermore, some of the factors influencing demographic change, above all mortality (see sections 3 and 4 of this chapter), are independent of resource availability. In some cases, however, the interrelationship between resources and demography is clearly evident. If we accept the authoritative interpretations offered, the examples of Ireland and Japan – two islands distant from one another both in culture and space – between the seventeenth and nineteenth centuries represent well this relationship.

Ireland has always been one of the poorest countries of western Europe. Its population, subjugated by the English, deprived of independence and autonomy, and subject to an agricultural tributary economy dominated by absentee landlords, suffered a backward existence. In spite of poverty it grew rapidly – even more rapidly than nearby England, which was by far the most demographically dynamic of the large countries of Europe. Between the end of the seventeenth century and the census of 1841 – a few years before the great famine that would alter Irish demography dramatically – the Irish grew from just over two million to over eight million (table 2.4). Japan, although closing itself off to foreign influence, experienced a significant internal revival from the beginning of the Tokugawa era in the early seventeenth century. Population tripled in 120 years and then entered a long period of stagnation until the second third of the nineteenth century. What were the reasons for rapid growth in both cases and then catastrophe in Ireland and stagnation in Japan?

The case of Ireland was considered by Connell[82] over 40 years ago, and his analysis has withstood the scrutiny of subsequent studies fairly well. Connell's thesis basically is that a natural tendency of the Irish to marry early was inhibited by the difficulty of obtaining land on which to build a house and start a family. This obstacle was removed in the second half of the eighteenth century by a series of complex factors – among them the great success of the potato – which allowed the extension and breaking up of

---

[82] K. H. Connell, *The Population of Ireland (1750–1845)* (Clarendon Press, Oxford, 1950). See also K. H. Connell, "Land and Population in Ireland," in *Population in History*, ed. D. V. Glass and D. E. C. Eversly (Edward Arnold, London, 1965). For a restatement of studies subsequent to Connell, see J. Mokyr and C. O'Gráda, "New Developments in Irish Population History, 1700–1850," *The Economic History Review*, 2d series, 27 (1984).

Table 2.4 Population of Ireland and Japan (17th–19th centuries)

Year	Population (in millions)	Annual growth rate (%)
	Ireland	
1687	2.167	–
1712	2.791	1.01
1754	3.191	0.32
1791	4.753	1.08
1821	6.882	1.19
1831	7.767	1.33
1841	8.175	0.51
1687–1754		0.58
1754–1841		1.08
	Japan	
1600	10–18	–
1720	30	0.92–0.43
1875	35	0.10

Sources: For Ireland, K. H. Connell, *The Population of Ireland (1750–1845)* (Clarendon Press, Oxford, 1950); for the period 1687–1791, estimates; for 1821–41, census data. For Japan, A. Hayami, "Movement de longue durée et structures japonaises de la population à l'époque Tokugawa," *Annales de démographie historique 1971* (Mouton, Paris, 1972).

farmland. As a result nuptiality increased and, together with a high level of natural fertility and a not too high level of mortality, this resulted in a high rate of growth. Finally, this equilibrium became precarious as a result of excessive growth until the Great Famine of 1846–7 permanently upset the previous demographic order.

The data in table 2.4 show rapid Irish demographic growth: in the century prior to 1845 the population grew at an annual rate of 1.3 percent as compared to 1 percent in England. These are the data on which Connell bases his interpretation. They are the product of dependable censuses only for the period 1821–41; the earlier values are an elaboration of the reports made by collectors of "hearth money" (a sort of family tax).

Connell writes: "In the late eighteenth and early nineteenth centuries it is clear that the Irish were insistently urged and tempted to marry early: the wretchedness and hopelessness of their living conditions, their improvident temperament, the unattractiveness of remaining single, perhaps the persuasion of their spiritual leaders, all acted in this direction.'[83] But did the material means exist to permit early marriage? The poor rural population of the island did not share the idea, common to large sectors of European population, of putting off marriage for the purpose of accumulating capital and attaining a better standard of living.[84] The large landowners tended to limit their tenants to a subsistence existence by adjusting rents, and so rendered standard of living improvement difficult. The cost of marriage was small; a new dwelling, usually little more than a shack, could be constructed in a few days with the help of friends and family; and furniture was simple and rudimentary.[85] The true problem in a society of tenant farmers was the availability of a plot on which to establish a new household. As long as this was difficult (for example, dependent on the death of the father), nuptiality was checked. However, toward the end of the eighteenth century conditions changed. The conversion of pasture to cultivated plots and the cultivation of new lands (reclaimed swamps and mountains) – promoted by reforms of the Irish Parliament and by the demand in England, which was at war with France, for food-stuffs – removed this check.[86] Land subdivision increased still more as a result of the introduction and spread of the potato, which quickly became the primary, and often almost sole, food of the Irish.[87] The special role of the potato, perhaps introduced by Sir Walter Raleigh at the end of the sixteenth century and then gradually adopted, was decisive for two reasons. The first was its high productivity. As the population became ever more dependent upon the potato, "land which formerly had been adequate for only one family's subsistence could be parcelled among sons or other sub-tenants,"[88] since "an acre of potatoes sufficed to feed a family of six and the livestock."[89] The second reason was the high nutritional value of the potato,

---

[83] Connell, *Population of Ireland*, pp. 81–2.

[84] Ibid., p. 82; see also R. N. Salaman, *The Influence of the Potato on the Course of Irish History* (Browne and Nolan, Dublin, 1933), p. 23.

[85] Connell, *Population of Ireland*, p. 89.

[86] Ibid., pp. 90ff.

[87] Ibid., p. 133.

[88] Connell, *Population of Ireland*, p. 90.

[89] Salaman, *Influence of the Potato*, p. 23. See also, by the same author, *The History and Social Influence of the Potato* (Cambridge University Press, London, 1949). Much of Salaman's analysis coincides with that of Connell. The latter, however, maintains that the potato became the principal food of the Irish in the second half of the eighteenth century, while Salaman believes that its wide diffusion occurred earlier. Both Connell and Salaman assert the dominant role played by the potato in the socio-demographic history of Ireland. A different point of view is that of L. M. Cullen, "Irish History Without the Potato," *Past and Present*, 40 (1968).

consumed in incredible proportions as part of a diet which also included a considerable amount of milk.[90] Arthur Young, traveling in King's County, observed, "their food is potatoes and milk for ten months and potatoes and salt for the remaining two."[91] A barrel of 280 pounds (127 kilograms) of potatoes fed a family of five for a week at an average daily consumption of 8 pounds (3.6 kilograms) per person, including infants and children. Connell estimates daily consumption at 10 pounds between 1780 and the Great Famine, while Salaman suggests 12 pounds per adult at the end of the eighteenth century, "a quantity exceeded in the next century."[92] It should be added that a diet of 4 kilograms of potatoes and half a liter of milk contains more than sufficient caloric and nutritional value for an adult male.[93] So while one may accuse the potato of having impoverished the Irish peasantry, one cannot accuse it of having exposed them to higher mortality. The availability of new land and the fragmentation of existing plots, made more productive due to potato cultivation, made possible the low age at marriage and high nuptiality of the Irish. These factors, combined with high natural fertility[94] and moderate mortality, produced a high rate of growth in the period leading up to the Great Famine.[95]

Sustained demographic growth (the population doubled between 1781 and 1841) in a rural society for which land, even though made more productive by the introduction of the potato, was the limiting factor of production could not go on indefinitely. Already in the decade before 1841 there is evidence of a gradual rise in the age at marriage and increased emigration. These developments did not, however, avert catastrophe: in 1845 a fungus, *phytophtora infestans*, badly damaged the potato harvest; in

---

[90]   Connell, *Population of Ireland*, p. 149.

[91]   Young's observations are reported in Salaman, *Influence of the Potato*, p. 19.

[92]   Ibid.

[93]   If we consider a daily consumption of ten pounds of potatoes (3,400 calories) and a pint of milk (400 calories), we arrive at 3,800 calories, more than the present-day standard considered adequate for an adult male engaged in intense physical activity. This diet seems also to be adequate for its content of protein, vitamins, and minerals. One might, however, question the advisability of ingesting such an enormous quantity of food.

[94]   Around 1840 the marital fertility rate was about 370 per thousand, 20% higher than that of England and Wales in 1851 (307 per thousand) The standardized index of legitimate fertility, I_g, was 0.82 in Ireland and 0.65 in England and Wales. See Mokyr and O'Gráda, "New Developments," p. 479.

[95]   It is estimated that in the 30 years between Napoleon's defeat at Waterloo and the Great Famine 1.5 million Irish left Ireland for England and North America. See ibid., p. 487.

1846 it destroyed it entirely.[96] The winter of 1846–7 brought famine, poverty, desperate and massive emigration, and epidemics of fevers and typhus. It has been estimated that the Great Famine together with associated epidemics caused between 1.1 and 1.5 million more deaths than normal.[97] Emigration became an exodus, and 200,000 people per year left Ireland between 1847 and 1854.[98]

The Great Famine marked the end of a demographic regime. The potato contributed to rapid demographic growth, but also rendered precarious the diet of a population that depended upon it alone for its nutritional needs. During the following decades a new regime of land use and ownership and a new nuptial order (late marriage and high rates of spinster- and bachelor-hood), supported by the large landowners and the clergy, together with massive emigration resulted in a steady decline in population. The average age at first marriage increased from 23–24 between 1831 and 1841 – apparently a level already above that of previous decades – to 27–28 at the end of the century. The proportion of married childbearing age women declined sharply between 1841 and the end of the century,[99] when about a fifth of the population aged 50 had never married. The island's population declined rapidly from 8.2 million in 1841 to 4.5 million in 1901.

According to the interpretation of one of the most authoritative scholars of Japanese demographic and social history,[100] the case of Japan resembles that of Ireland in the initial phase, though of course the setting is much different. The Tokugawa regime, which stretched over more than two and a half centuries from 1603 to 1867 and the beginning of Meiji

---

[96] On the Great Famine see R. D. Edwards and T. D. Williams, eds, *The Great Famine* (New York University Press, New York, 1957).
[97] J. Mokyr, *Why Ireland Starved: A Quantitative and Analytical History of the Irish Economy, 1800–1850* (Allen and Unwin, London, 1983).
[98] M. R. Davie, *World Immigration* (Macmillan, New York, 1936), p. 63.
[99] The index I_m, a weighted average of married childbearing age women, declined from 0.45 around 1841 to 0.324 in 1901 (−28%). Mokyr and O'Gráda, "New Developments," p. 479; M. S. Teitelbaum, *The British Fertility Decline: Demographic Transition in the Crucible of the Industrial Revolution* (Princeton University Press, Princeton, 1984), p. 103.
[100] A. Hayami, "The Population at the Beginning of the Tokugawa Period. An Introduction to the Historical Demography of Pre-Industrial Japan," *Keio Economic Studies*, 4 (1966–7); A. Hayami, "Mouvements de longue durée et structures japonaises de la population à l'époque Tokugawa," in *Annales de Démographie Historique 1971* (Mouton, Paris, 1972). See also S. B. Hanley and K. Yamamura, eds, *Economic and Demographic Change in Preindustrial Japan 1600–1868* (Princeton University Press, Princeton, 1977).

era modernization, was characterized by domestic peace, closure to both the outside world and Christian penetration, a revival of Confucianism, and political stability. However, during this long period "society prepared itself for modernization, . . . economically motivated behavior gradually modified the lifestyle of the population . . . Initially production, which served to pay off property taxes and meet individual needs, had poverty as its inevitable accompaniment, . . . but when the principal end of production became selling, then suffering became the work by means of which one was able to prosper and improve the qualities of one's life."[101] The amount of cultivated land doubled and agricultural techniques changed from extensive to intensive. Traditional social structures altered: large family groups, including many relatives and servants who were generally not able to marry, were broken up and many independent families established. In the county of Suwa, for example, average family size declined from 7 in the period 1671–1700 to 4.9 in 1751–1800.[102] The servant class of the Genin,[103] only a small fraction of which ever married, was transformed into a class of tenant farmers characterized by normal demographic behavior.

The freeing up of economic resources (new lands, new agricultural technology) was accompanied by sustained demographic growth. Hayami estimates a population of no more than 10 million at the beginning of the seventeenth century, which grew rapidly to 30 million by 1720 (the uncertainty of the sources induces him to adopt a safety margin of plus or minus 5 million), maintaining an average annual rate of growth of between 0.8 and 1 percent for over a century.[104] In the following century and a half this galloping growth slowed to a trot: in 1870, just after the fall of the Tokugawa regime, the population was about 35 million, having grown since 1720 at the reduced annual rate of 0.2 percent. The causes and mechanisms of this stagnation are the subject of considerable debate. There is definite evidence of intentional control of the "production" of children, not so much by delaying marriage but by the practices of abortion and infanticide, and of a "destructive" role played by the cities with regard to the rural population surplus (Edo, today Tokyo, was the largest city in the world at the beginning of the nineteenth century). Detailed studies of several Tokugawa era villages supply ample documentation, as a

---

101 Hayami, "Mouvements," pp. 248–9.
102 Ibid., p. 254.
103 Hayami, "Population of the Tokugawa Period," p. 16.
104 Hayami, "Mouvements," pp. 249–51.

complement to literary and legal reports, attesting to the widespread practice of abortion and infanticide in all social classes.[105] In the village of Yokouchi, for example, women born before 1700 and married at 20 years of age bore on average 5.5 children, while those married at the same age but born between 1750 and 1800 averaged barely 3.2.[106] Beyond infanticide and abortion, another interesting explanation for the slow population growth of the late Tokugawa epoch and the Meiji epoch that followed is the well-documented agricultural transformation that took place and led to an ever greater intensification of farming methods. This transformation improved the general conditions of rural life but also brought with it a notable increase in workloads for men and even more for women. This trend ". . . must have had unfavourable effects on marital fertility, as well as on infant and maternal mortality, and thereby must have counterbalanced some of the favourable demographic effects of long term agrarian development."[107] Whatever the explanation of the demographic stagnation, Japanese society gradually discovered mechanisms to limit demographic growth as the expansion of cultivation encountered natural and insuperable limits.

The Japanese demographic system differed from the Irish in its response to the gradual pressure applied to available resources. In Ireland the system collapsed with the Great Famine and the Great Emigration: this double shock opened the way to changes in the nuptial regime (high ages at marriage and large numbers of unmarried), a less painful adjustment. In Japan the response was gradual and not the result of traumatic events.

---

[105]   T. C. Smith, *Nakahara. Family Forming and Population in a Japanese Village, 1717–1830* (Stanford University Press, Stanford, 1977), p. 11.

[106]   Ibid., p. 13; A. Hayami, "Demographic Aspects of a Village in Tokugawa Japan," in *Population and Economics*, ed. P. Deprez (University of Manitoba Press, Winnipeg, 1968) (Acts of the fifth section of the Fourth Congress of the International Association of Economic History). On low urban fertility see Y. Sasaki, "Urban Migration and Fertility in Tokugawa Japan: The City of Takayama, 1773–1871," in *Family and Population in East Asian History*, ed. S. B. Hanley and A. P. Wolf (Stanford University Press, Stanford, 1985).

[107]   See O. Saito, "Infanticide, Fertility and 'Population Stagnation': the State of Tokugawa Historical Demography," *Japan Forum*, 4 (1992); idem, "Gender, Workload and Agricultural Progress: Japan's Historical Experience in Perspective," Discussion Paper Series A, No. 268 (The Institute of Economic Research, Hitotsubashi University, 1993).

7   On the Threshold of the Contemporary World

During the eighteenth century Europe entered a phase of economic, demographic, and social change of great importance. I shall deal below (see chapter 4) with the developments of this great transformation, which in the following two centuries completed its cycle in both the Old World and, borrowing from Crosby, the neo-Europes overseas before spreading to the rest of the world. It was a transformation that dramatically altered the phenomena determining growth: fertility and mortality, generally high, declined in two centuries to the low levels that we know today, and the forces of constraint were effectively controlled.

In the early phase, however, the forces of constraint were still strong. Birth control was still virtually unknown except in a few isolated cases, like France, and medical and sanitary measures had made little headway against high mortality. Then, between 1750 and 1850 European population growth accelerated. The annual rate of growth, barely 0.15 percent between 1600 and 1750, grew to 0.63 percent between 1750 and 1850. This acceleration involved all the major countries (table 2.5), though it was greater in some (for example, England) than in others (France). However, in spite of the disappearance of the plague and the success in combating smallpox (Jenner discovered a vaccine in 1797), the period between the mid-eighteenth and mid-nineteenth centuries was not free of troubles. The French Revolution and Napoleonic wars devastated Europe for 20 years; the last great subsistence crisis – the 1816–17 famine accompanied by an outbreak of typhus – hit all of Europe;[108] and a previously unknown pestilence, cholera, ravaged the continent. Nonetheless, population grew vigorously and spilled over, with the beginning of large-scale transoceanic migration, to the Americas.

A debate, still open, has developed regarding the causes of demographic acceleration from the mid-eighteenth century, in part because the demographic mechanisms themselves are not entirely understood. In some cases growth was due to increased fertility resulting from increased nuptiality, while in others, the majority, mortality decline was the principal factor.

In the case of England, the country that experienced the greatest demographic growth in the period, recent studies[109] ascribe the demographic acceleration of the second half of the eighteenth century more to fertility

---

[108]   J. Post, *The Last Great Subsistence Crisis in the Western World* (The Johns Hopkins University Press, Baltimore, 1977).

[109]   E. A. Wrigley and R. S. Schofield, *The Population History of England, 1541–1871* (Edward Arnold, London, 1981).

Table 2.5   Growth of selected European populations (1600–1850)

Country	Population (in millions)			Indexed growth			Density (inhabitants/sq. km)	Distribution (%)		
	1600	1750	1850	1750 (1600 = 100)	1850 (1750 = 100)	1850 (1600 = 100)	1750	1600	1750	1850
England	4.1	5.7	16.5	139	289	402	47	7	8	14
Holland	1.5	1.9	3.1	127	163	207	63	3	3	2
Germany	12.0	15.0	27.0	125	180	225	42	22	21	22
France	19.0	25.0	35.8	132	143	188	46	34	34	29
Italy	12.0	15.7	24.8	131	158	207	52	22	22	20
Spain	6.8	8.4	14.5	124	173	213	17	12	12	12
Total	55.4	71.7	121.7	129	170	220		100	100	100

Estimates are for present-day borders. For Spain, only continental territory is considered. For France, Italy, and Spain, the estimates given for the above dates are mine and are based on estimates for nearby dates given in the works cited.

Sources: Data derived or based on the following works: England: E. A. Wrigley and R. Schofield, *The Population History of England 1541–1871* (Edward Arnold, London, 1981, re-issued Cambridge University Press, 1987), pp. 532–4; Holland: B. H. Slicher van Bath, "Historical Demography and the Social and Economic Development of the Netherlands," *Daedalus*, Spring 1968, p. 609; Germany: C. McEvedy and R. Jones, *Atlas of World Population History* (Penguin, London, 1978), pp. 67–70; France: J. Dupâquier, *La population française au XVIIᵉ et XVIIIᵉ siècles* (Presses Universitaires de France, Paris, 1979), pp. 9, 11; Italy: C. M. Cipolla, "Four Centuries of Italian Demographic Development," in *Population in History*, ed. D. V. Glass and D. E. C. Eversly (Edward Arnold, London,1965), p. 579; Spain: J. Nadal, *La población Española* (Ariel, Barcelona, 1984), p. 47.

increase (aided by nuptiality increase) than to mortality decrease. Apparently the Industrial Revolution generated a notable increase in the demand for labor, which in turn stimulated nuptiality and so fertility (the latter was not yet subject to "control" within marriage). However, mortality also declined, and the combined effect resulted in sustained demographic growth and the tripling of population in a century. We shall return to England when analyzing the relationship between demographic and economic systems in chapter 3.

In much of Europe the transition from the eighteenth to the nineteenth century brought with it a decline in mortality. This improvement is evident above all in the lower frequency of mortality crises resulting from epidemic outbreaks and at times famine and want. As an example, in a group of 404 English parishes the frequency of months marked by severe mortality was 1.3 percent in the first half of the eighteenth century, 0.9 percent in the second half, and 0.6 in the first quarter of the nineteenth,[110] a sign of the rapid decline of crisis frequency. In France the incidence of severe crises declined dramatically between the first and second halves of the eighteenth century, so much so that one speaks of the end of *ancien régime* crises, like that, for example, after the harsh winter of 1709 which resulted in a million deaths more than normal or the equally severe crises of 1693–4 and 1739–41.[111] In other parts of Europe – Germany, Italy, Spain – the decline occurs later and less suddenly.

The causes for the attenuation of the great mortality crises are at once biological, economic, and social. The biological effect of mutual adaptation between pathogen and host (see sections 3 and 4 above), furthered by increased population density and mobility, cannot be ruled out as a cause for the reduced virulence of certain diseases. Social causes, instead, include the reduced transmissibility of infection as a result of improved private and public hygiene. Finally, economic causes pertain not only to agricultural progress, but also to the improved system of transportation, and so of the distribution of goods, between areas of abundance and areas of want.

The disappearance of crisis years alone, however, does not explain European mortality decline. Life expectancy at birth, for example, increased in England from 33 to 40 years between 1740–9 and 1840–9; in France the same period witnessed an increase from 25 to 40; in Sweden from 37 to 45 (between 1750–9 and 1840–9); and in Denmark from 35 to 44 (between

---

[110]　Ibid., p. 650.
[111]　Livi-Bacci, *Population and Nutrition*, pp. 50–5.

1780–9 and 1840–9).[112] Clearly mortality decline, whether "crisis" or "normal," was responsible for accelerated demographic growth. One of the theories that has gained favor in recent years is the "nutritional" theory championed by McKeown,[113] according to which eighteenth-century demographic acceleration was due to mortality decline; mortality decline, however, can be explained neither by medical advances (ineffective, except for the small-pox vaccine, until the end of the nineteenth century), nor by changes in public or private hygiene (which in some cases, for example the large cities, probably deteriorated), nor by other causes. The true cause, according to McKeown, was the improvement of the population's nutritional level, which increased organic "resistance" to infection. This improvement came about as a result of the progress made in agricultural productivity thanks to the intro-duction of new, more abundant, crops, from corn to potatoes.

This theory is countered by a number of considerations which make us look to other causes. In the first place, the link between nutrition and resistance to infection holds primarily in cases of severe malnutrition; and while these were frequent during periods of want, in normal years the diet of European populations seems to have been adequate.[114] Second, the latter half of the eighteenth century and the first decades of the nineteenth, the period during which this mortality "transition" began, do not appear to have been such a fortunate epoch. It is true that new crops spread. By the second half of the eighteenth century the potato, its diffusion furthered by the severe famine of 1770–2 in the center-north, had overcome its strongest European doubters and would soon be widespread. A field planted with potatoes could feed twice or thrice the population of a similar field of grain. Versatile buckwheat could be planted late in the season, should the winter crop fail. Corn spread in Spain in the seventeenth century and then passed to southwest France, the Po Valley in northern Italy, and on to the Balkans. As with the potato, its cultivation spread as a result of the subsistence crisis of 1816–17.[115] In many cases, however, the introduction of new crops did not improve per capita consumption. Often, as in Ireland with the potato, the new crops served to feed the additional population but led to the

---

[112]   Ibid., p. 70.

[113]   T. McKeown, *The Modern Rise of Population* (Edward Arnold, London, 1976).

[114]   This position finds an authoritative supporter in Braudel; it is one that I have advocated in Livi-Bacci, *Population and Nutrition*; see especially chapter 5.

[115]   On the spread of new crops and their effects, see F. Braudel, *Civilation materielle, economie et capitalisme, XVe-XVIIIe siècle* (Colin, Paris, 1979), vol. 1: *Les structures du quotidien: le possible et l'impossible*; W. Abel, *Congiuntura agraria e crisi agrarie* (Einaudi, Torino, 1976).

abandonment of more esteemed foods, like grains, and so made for a poorer diet. Cobbett's invective regarding his travels in Ireland is famous in this regard: "It is both my pleasure and my duty to discourage in any way I can the cultivation of this damned root, being convinced that it has done more harm to mankind than the sword and the pestilence united."[116] In England and also in Flanders, there are indications that as potato consumption increased, that of grains declined. In those regions where corn met with greatest success, especially Italy, it became the principal foodstuff and was responsible for the terrible spread of pellagra.[117]

Other, indirect, considerations also cast doubt on the nutritional hypothesis. For one, real wages in general declined throughout Europe during the eighteenth century and into the first decades of the nineteenth.[118] Real-wage decline is an indication of diminished buying power on the part of salaried workers (and perhaps other groups as well), who in this period spent about four-fifths of their wages on food. Another indication is variation in average height, which seems in this same period to have declined in England, in the Hapsburg Empire, and in Sweden. Height is fairly sensitive to changes in nutritional levels, and its decline or stagnation is certainly not a sign of nutritional improvement.[119] Finally, mortality improvement benefited primarily the young (as is always the case when it is due to a decline in infectious disease mortality, a relatively less important cause of death at older ages) and infants. Until weaning, which occurred fairly late, generally between the ages of one and two years, babies were fed mother's milk and so their nutritional level was generally independent of agricultural production and levels of consumption. But infant mortality declined as well – not because of better nutrition, but because of improved childrearing methods and better protection from the surrounding environment.

Mortality decline was certainly due to many causes and perhaps none, taken singly, predominated. However, even given a generous reading, the nutritional hypothesis stands up to scrutiny less well than others. It is nonetheless the case that increased agricultural production accompanied European demographic expansion (population almost doubled in a century), even if nutritional levels did not improve notably. While the possibility of farming new lands – once pasture, swamp, or wild – together with

[116]   "Letters of William Cobbett to Charles Marshall," in *Rural Rides*, ed. G. D. H. and M. Cole (Peter Davis, London, 1930), vol. 3, p. 900.
[117]   Livi-Bacci, *Population and Nutrition*, pp. 95–9.
[118]   Abel, *Congiuntura agraria*.
[119]   Livi-Bacci, *Population and Nutrition*, pp. 107–10.

improved technology and the introduction of new crops may not have been responsible for mortality decline, these elements did allow the agricultural population to expand, forming new centers and increasing nuptiality levels. The growth of the industrial sector, urbanization, and a general increase in demand for nonagricultural labor assisted this process and created an outlet for the rural population.

The demographic growth of the eighteenth century occurred along with the extension of agriculture to previously uncultivated lands. In France during the last 30 years of the *ancien régime*, cultivated land increased from 19 to 24 million hectares.[120] In England the enclosure movement was proceeding at a few hundred acres per year at the beginning of the eighteenth century and 70,000 per year during the latter half of the same century. Swamps and marshes were dried in Prussia and the Italian Maremma, and the draining of bogs and fens helped to satisfy the demand for land in both Ireland and England.[121]

---

[120] Abel, *Congiuntura agraria*, p. 308.

[121] Slicher van Bath, *Agrarian History*. See also D. Grigg, *Population Growth and Agrarian Change: An Historical Perspective* (Cambridge University Press, Cambridge 1980).

3

Land, Labor, and Population

---

1 Diminishing Returns and Demographic Growth

The question of the effect of demographic growth on the economic development of agricultural societies remains open and unresolved. It is a question over which two hardened points of view oppose one another. The first sees demographic growth as an essentially negative force which strains the relationship between fixed or limited resources (land, minerals) and population, leading in the long run to increased poverty. According to the second, demographic growth instead stimulates human ingenuity so as to cancel and reverse the disadvantages imposed by limited resources.

The first position finds immediate and short-term empirical verification: increased population density creates competition for the use of fixed resources which must satisfy a larger number of people. Historical observation, however, presents a valid objection to this position, as economic progress is generally accompanied by demographic growth. A large population allows for better organization and specialization of tasks; it can more easily find ways to substitute fixed resources, creating systems which a small or sparse population could not maintain. The reconciliation of short- and long-term observations has not proved to be easy.

The second, opposing, theory has to resolve another and perhaps more serious contradiction. Even if we admit that demographic growth stimulates the human spirit of innovation and inventiveness (what economists call "technical progress"), it is hard to imagine how this spirit can expand those fixed resources (land, space, and other essential natural elements) necessary to human survival and well-being.

Consider an agricultural population isolated in a deep valley. The difference between births and deaths results in slow growth, so that the population doubles every two centuries. Initially the more fertile, easily irrigated, and accessible lands are cultivated – those in the plain along the river. As population grows, and so the need for food, all the best land will be used, until it becomes necessary to cultivate more distant plots on the slopes of the valley, difficult to irrigate and less fertile than the others. Continued growth will require the planting of still less productive lands, higher up the sides of the valley and more exposed to erosion. When all the land has been used up, further increase of production can still be obtained by more intensive cultivation, but these gains too are limited, as the point will eventually be reached when additional inputs of labor will no longer effectively increase production. In this way demographic growth in a fixed environment (and, it must be added, given a fixed level of technology) leads to the cultivation of progressively less fertile lands with ever greater inputs of labor, while returns per unit of land or labor eventually diminish.

The concept of diminishing returns is fundamental to the thought of both Malthus and Ricardo[1] and can be applied to nonagricultural situations as well. It is easy to imagine that while the contribution of each additional worker to a fixed stock of capital (the workers operating a single machine) may increase overall production, nonetheless the contribution to that increase made by each additional worker will progressively decline.

The law of diminishing returns, then, would seem to dictate a per capita decline of production given the combination of population increase and a fixed supply of land or capital. Worker productivity, however, is not constant, and throughout human history innovations and inventions have continuously caused it to increase. In agriculture, metal tools replaced those of wood, the hoe gave way to the plough, and animal power was added to human power. Analogous progress has characterized the technical innovations of production: crop rotation, the selection of seed strains, and improvements in fertilization. In short, the introduction of a technological innovation, whether it increases production per unit of land or of labor, entails an increase in available resources. The positive effects of this increase, however, may be only temporary, since continued demographic growth will

---

[1]   Malthus introduced the concept of diminishing returns at the beginning of his *Essay*: "When acre has been added to acre till all the fertile land is occupied, the yearly increase of food must depend upon the melioration of the land already in possession. This is a fund which, from the nature of all soils, instead of increasing, must be gradually diminishing." T. R. Malthus, *Essay on the Principle of Population*, 7th ed. (Dent, London, 1967), p. 8. Ricardo expressed the concept this way: "Although, then, it is probable that, under the most favourable circumstances, the power of production is still greater than that of population, it will not long continue so; for the land being limited in quantity, and differing in quality, with every increased portion of capital employed on it there will be a decreased rate of production, whilst the power of population continues always the same." D. Ricardo, *The Principles of Political Economy and Taxation* (Dent, London, 1964), p. 56.

neutralize the gains achieved. It should also be added that no degree of progress can indefinitely increase the productivity of a fixed resource like land.

In 1798, Malthus described the above relationship in the first edition of his famous *Essay*, asserting the incompatibility of the growth potential of population, "which increases in a geometrical ratio," and that of the resources necessary for survival, especially food, which "increases only in an arithmetical ratio." Because laws of nature require that humans have food, "this natural inequality of the two powers of population and of production in the earth and that great law of our nature which must constantly keep their effects equal form the great difficulty that to me appears insurmountable."[2] Demographic increase strains the relation between resources and population until a check to further growth intervenes. Malthus calls these "positive" checks; famine, disease, or war reduce population size (as happened with the medieval cycles of the plague or the Thirty Years War) and reestablish a more suitable balance with resources. Reachieved equilibrium, however, will only last until another negative cycle begins, unless population can find some other way to limit its reproductive capacity. This "preventive" and virtuous check exists in the form of celibacy or at least the delay of marriage, practices that reduce the reproductivity of populations wise enough to choose this alternative. The fate of population depends upon the battle between positive and preventive checks, between careless and responsible behavior, between being a victim of constraint and necessity or making an active choice.

The Malthusian model, though repeatedly revised and updated over the years, is still basically contained in its initial formulation, and may be summarized as follows:

1   The primary resource is food. Its scarcity causes mortality to increase, slowing (or reversing) population growth and reestablishing equilibrium.
2   The law of diminishing returns is unavoidable. Cultivation of new land and intensification of labor in response to demographic growth adds progressively smaller increments to production for each additional unit of land or labor.
3   Production or productivity increases resulting from invention or innovation provide only temporary relief, since any gains achieved are inevitably canceled by demographic growth.

[2]   T. R. Malthus, *An Essay on the Principle of Population* (1798) (Norton, New York, 1976), p. 20.

4   Awareness of the vicious cycle of population growth and positive checks may lead a population instead to check its prolificity (and so demographic increase) by means of nuptial restraint.

Figure 3.1 depicts the relationship between population and resources according to which equilibrium is reestablished after a period of growth or decline. In both cases the figure shows two paths, according to whether or not the preventive check is operating. As population grows so does the demand for food, and prices consequently rise. At the same time labor is less well paid as its supply increases. The combination of increased prices and decreased wages results in a still greater decrease in real wages, which is to say a worsening of the population's standard of living. This worsening cannot continue indefinitely and must eventually lead to a new equilibrium imposed either by the wise choice of the preventive check (path 1), the consequences of its refusal, namely increased mortality (path 2), or a combination of the two. Whichever path is followed, a worsening standard of living leads to a reduction of population (or at least slower growth) as a result of increased mortality or reduced nuptiality and fertility and so the reestablishment of equilibrium between population and resources.

Innovations and discoveries only delay operation of the restabilizing mechanism by introducing a discontinuity, without, however, altering its basic functioning. The above model applies particularly to agricultural economies, the growth of which is limited by the availability of land, and to poor populations, which spend a good part of their income acquiring food. Until the time of Malthus and the Industrial Revolution, almost all the countries of the world fit into these categories; many poor countries still do today.

The application of the Malthusian model to industrial societies (which has recently been done with considerable public, if not scientific, success by the Club of Rome) presents no logical problems. However, the forceful logic of Malthus becomes less compelling when dealing with industrial processes, subject to continual technological innovation and employing resources which are for the most part renewable or replaceable.

2   Historical Confirmations

According to the Malthusian scheme, population must suffer periodic mortality increases in the absence of the virtuous preventive check because of the declining standard of living. However, if the preventive check is operating, then population growth can be controlled and both the accumulation

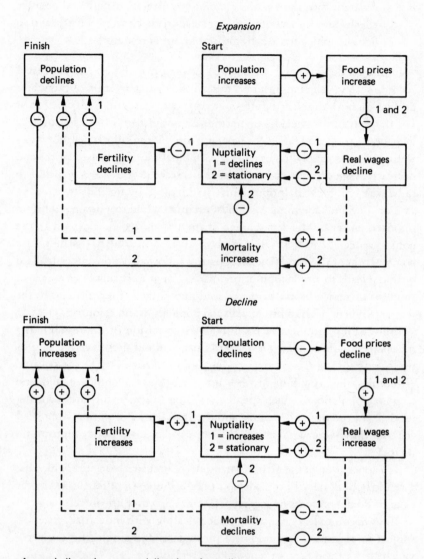

Figure 3.1 The Malthusian system of positive and preventive checks during phases of demographic expansion and decline

of wealth and a general improvement of living standards becomes possible.[3] According to Malthus the preventive check was stronger in his day than it had been in ancient Europe, an implicit proof of human progress. Preventive checks, however, act slowly and only in highly civilized societies. Unfortunately, the positive check seems to have been historically more prevalent, as demonstrated by the frequency and intensity of catastrophes and mortality crises. Mortality crises, it is true, were often caused by epidemic cycles largely independent of living standards (see chapter 2, section 3 on the plague), but in modern times subsistence crises have been frequently accompanied by mortality increase. Increases in the price of grain – which made up two-thirds of the population's caloric intake – by factors of two, three, four, and more above that of normal years were followed after several months by violent mortality increases. One or more bad harvests, generally caused by weather conditions, caused jumps in the price of grain, a situation possibly made worse by a lack of reserves, the impossibility of substitution with other foods, obstacles to trade, and the basic poverty of the populations affected. The periodic elimination of excess population in crisis years is one of the more frequent arguments cited in support of the Malthusian model. Figure 3.2 charts the price of wheat in Siena and deaths in the same city (together with several other localities in Tuscany) for a number of periods, centered on years of large price increases coinciding with peaks in mortality between the middle of the sixteenth century and the beginning of the eighteenth.[4] Similarly, years of want are often years of nuptiality decline, since marriages are postponed until conditions improve, a situation that leads also to temporary fertility decline.

The situation for the various European countries is not much different from that of Siena. The sixteenth, seventeenth, and early eighteenth centuries are characterized by subsistence crises, with the attendant adverse demographic consequences, at a rate of two, three, four, or more per century.[5]

---

[3] T. R. Malthus, *A Summary View of the Principle of Population* (1830) (Penguin, Harmondsworth, 1970), pp. 251–2.

[4] M. Livi-Bacci, *Population and Nutrition. Essay on the Demographic History of Europe* (Cambridge University Press, Cambridge, 1991), pp. 51–4.

[5] For England, see A. B. Appleby, "Grain Prices and Subsistence Crises in England and France 1590–1740," *The Journal of Economic History*, 39 (1979), pp. 865–87. For France, see F. Lebrun, "Les crises démographiques en France au XVIIème et XVIIIème siècles," *Annales ESC*, 35 (1980). For Italy, see L. Del Panta, *Le epidemie nella storia demografica italiana (secoli XIV-XIX)* (Loescher, Torino, 1980). For Spain, see V. Perez Moreda, *Las crisis de mortalidad en la España interior, siglos XVI-XIX* (Siglo Veintiuno, Madrid, 1980). For Germany, see W. Abel, *Massenarmut und Hungerkrisen in vorindustriellen Europa* (Paul Parey, Hamburg, 1974).

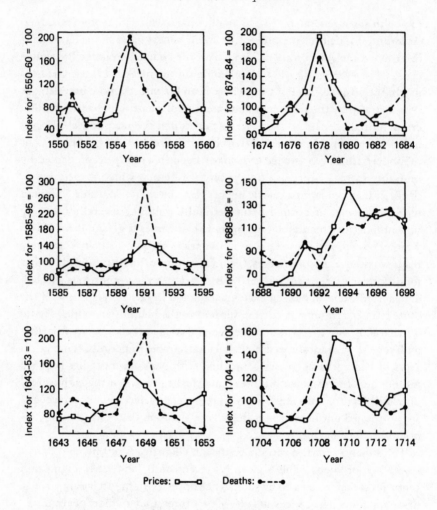

Figure 3.2 Sienese death and grain-price indices (sixteenth and
seventeenth centuries)

Sources: For prices, G. Parenti, *Prezzi e mercato a Siena (1546–1765)* (Cya, Florence, 1942),
pp. 27–8. For deaths, an unpublished study by the Department of Statistics of the
University of Florence.

The great crises of 1693–4 and 1709–10 doubled the number of deaths in
France relative to normal years in the period and left a lasting mark on both
the demographic structure and historical memory of the populations
affected.[6]

---

[6]   Livi-Bacci, *Population and Nutrition*, p. 55.

The negative effects of a decline in living standards should be more persistent and the operation of the Malthusian model more clearly in evidence in the long run than in the short. In fact, if we ignore the effects of epidemic crises not attributable to food shortages (plague and smallpox, for example), then it turns out that the demographic impact of subsistence crises does not adequately explain the cyclical succession of growth and decline. These cycles are better explained by the less-transitory action of the positive and preventive checks – that is, by the long-term modification of mortality and nuptiality in reaction to periods of improving or worsening living standards. Wage and price series provide a clue to the relationship between population and the economy, since by these measures the latter two quantities progress in keeping with the Malthusian model over the long run (see figure 3.3). During the negative phase of a demographic cycle – as, for example, in the century after the Black Death or during the seventeenth century – the decline or stagnation of population, and so demand, contributes to a reduction of prices and at the same time to an increase in the demand for labor, and so wages. Between the early fourteenth and the late fifteenth centuries, for example, wheat prices were more than halved, only to rise again afterward in both France and England. As Slicher van Bath writes: "Then came the recession of the fourteenth and fifteenth centuries. The population had been reduced by epidemics, and because the area of cultivation was now larger than necessary for the people's sustenance, cereal prices fell. Through the decline in population, labour became scarce, so that money wages and real wages rose considerably."[7] Strong demographic recovery in the sixteenth century reversed the situation: increasing demand forced up the price of grain and other foods while real wages declined,[8] a trend which reached a critical point at the beginning of the seventeenth century.[9] The demographic slowdown of the seventeenth century and the catastrophic decline of the German population as a result of the Thirty Years War are among the causes of a new inversion of the cycle (accompanied by declining demand and prices and increasing wages) that continued until the mid-eighteenth century, when demographic growth reversed the situation once again.

The English case – from the sixteenth to the eighteenth century – seems to conform well to the Malthusian model. Changing population size and an

---

[7]   B. H. Slicher van Bath, *The Agrarian History of Western Europe, A.D. 500–1850* (Edward Arnold, London, 1963), p. 106.

[8]   Ibid., p. 107.

[9]   Ibid., pp. 108–9.

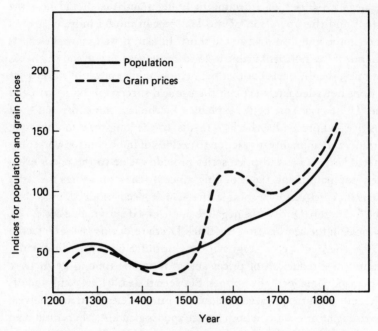

Figure 3.3   Population and grain prices in Europe (1200–1800;
1721–45 = 100)
Source: B. H. Slicher van Bath, *The Agrarian History of Western Europe, A.D. 500–1850*
(Edward Arnold, London, 1963), p. 103.

index of real wages are shown in figure 3.4.[10] Statistics reveal an apparently
direct link between population and prices – in keeping with the idea that
demographic growth or decline leads to an increase or decrease in prices –
particularly at the two points of inversion occurring in the middle of the
seventeenth and eighteenth centuries. The figure highlights the inverse
relationship between demographic and wage movement, though there is a
discrepancy regarding the timing of the turning points. Finally, figure 3.5
clearly reveals that of the two factors in demographic change – mortality,
expressed by estimates of life expectancy at birth, e_0, and fertility, expressed
by total fertility rate (*TFR*) – the first varies independently of the standard of
living (expressed by real wages) while the second (reacting to changing
nuptiality) seems to follow, after a delay, its variations.

   The English example would appear to conform to path 1 (figure 3.1) of the

[10]   E. A. Wrigley and R. S. Schofield, *The Population History of England, 1541–1871*
(Edward Arnold, London, 1981), chap. 10.

Malthusian model, according to which the balance between population and resources is restored by means of changing nuptiality and fertility rather than the dreary check of mortality.

Other studies covering long chronological periods, while not so rich in data, nonetheless provide similar interpretations. The social life of the area of Languedoc in southern France is characterized by marked economic-demographic cycles.[11] A first cycle was completed prior to the plague of 1348. As in much of Europe, population expanded and marginal land – rugged and not very productive – was progressively settled. Signs of frequent famine and demographic slowdown are evident at the end of the thirteenth and in the first half of the fourteenth centuries, followed by plague and population decline. This decline had several sociodemographic effects – for example, the recombination of family nuclei into extended families and land redistribution, both suited to an agricultural system suddenly rich in land and poor in labor. The most significant economic effect for our purposes, however, was the reduction of prices and the increase of wages until demographic recovery gained momentum and

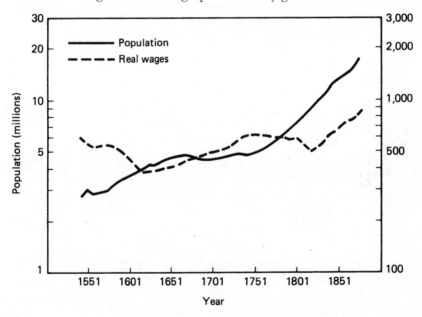

Figure 3.4 Population and real wages in England (1551–1851)
Source: E. A. Wrigley and R. S. Schofield, *The Population History of England, 1541–1871* (Edward Arnold, London, 1981), p. 408.

[11] E. Le Roy Ladurie, *Les paysans de Languedoc* (SEVPEN, Paris, 1969).

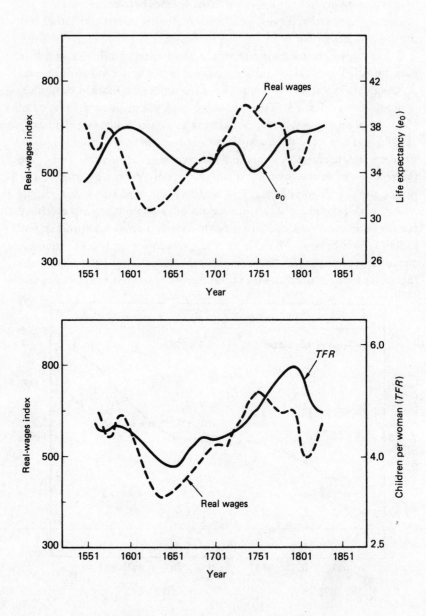

Figure 3.5 Real wages, fertility (*TFR*), and life expectancy (*e₀*) in England (1551–1801)

Source: Adapted from E. A. Wrigley and R. Schofield, *The Population History of England, 1541–1871* (Edward Arnold, London, 1981).

accelerated in the sixteenth century. Once again land became scarce; new and progressively less productive land was tilled; real wages declined; the society became poorer; and, in the period spanning the seventeenth and eighteenth centuries, population declined. Le Roy Ladurie interprets these alternating cycles of growth and decline in Malthusian terms. Population grows more rapidly than resources, and in the long run, in the absence of technological improvements, positive checks intervene. The case of Languedoc differs from that of England in that it follows path 2 of figure 3.1, according to which mortality is the regulating mechanism.

Similar interpretations exist for other regions of both southern and northern Europe.[12] Common to all of these is the observation that demographic growth and the process of diminishing returns lead to a decline in per capita production and so increased poverty and that this spiral, or "trap," can be avoided or at least attenuated by innovation or by the control of demographic growth.

3   Demographic Pressure and Economic Development

The logic of diminishing returns implies a continual contest between the growth of resources and population, unless the latter is controlled by reproductive restraint and so permits the accumulation of wealth and increased well-being. Demographic growth, in any case, acts as a check to economic development.

The opposing theory to that of Malthus, according to which population increase stimulates development, has a still longer history. Economists of the seventeenth and much of the eighteenth centuries, worried by the negative economic effects associated with the depopulation of a number of countries (especially Spain and Germany) and convinced that the poverty of many others rich in resources was connected with population scarcity, viewed

---

[12]   For Catalonia, see J. Nadal, "La població," in *Història de Catalunya*, ed. J. Nadal, I. Farreras, and P. Wolff (Oikos-Tau, Barcelona, 1982); J. Nadal and E. Giralt, *La population catalane de 1552 à 1717* (SEVPEN, Paris, 1960). For Provence, see R. Baehrel, *Une croissance: La Basse Provence rurale* (SEVPEN, Paris, 1961). For Italy, see A. Bellettini, "La popolazione italiana dall'inizio dell'era volgare ai nostri giorni. Valutazioni e tendenze," in *Storia d'Italia* (Einaudi, Torino, 1973), vol. 5, a multicentury study following the Malthusian model; see also M. A. Romani, *Nella spirale di una crisi* (Giuffrè, Milano, 1975). For the Low Countries, see B. H. Slicher van Bath, "Historical Demography and the Social and Economic Development of the Netherlands," *Daedalus* (Spring 1968).

demographic growth favorably: "With rare exceptions they were enthusiastic about 'populousness' and rapid increase in numbers. In fact, until the middle of the eighteenth century, they were as nearly unanimous in this 'population- ist' attitude as they have ever been in anything. A numerous and increasing population was the most important *symptom* of wealth; it was the chief *cause* of wealth; it *was* wealth itself – the greatest asset for any nation to have."[13] In the context of the limited development and low-density population of the period, demographic growth meant a multiplication of resources and there- fore the increase of individual income.[14] This opinion was, as I have said, fairly widespread, and only at the end of the eighteenth century did the negative effects associated with the first phase of the Industrial Revolution induce Malthus, and many others with him, to take the opposite point of view.

Can demographic growth generate economic development? If "fixed" resources are abundant or can be substituted, then there is no reason why not, an observation that social and economic history confirms. It is easy to see how, within certain limits, development may be checked or absent for small populations, characterized by low density, limited trade, minimal possibilities for division or specialization of labor, and inability to make sub- stantial investments. Historically, areas depopulated or in the process of los- ing population have almost always been characterized by backward economies. Many European governments in the seventeenth and eighteenth centuries took action (often unsuccessfully) to populate sparsely inhabited areas or areas where demographic decline had lowered the standard of living.[15]

It is important to understand the logic of the link between development and demographic growth. How can increasing population pressure and the consequent straining of available resources possibly constitute the prerequisite for development? A recent theory proposed by Ester Boserup explains this relationship with reference to agricultural economies.[16]

The variable population density of rural areas is naturally associated with the fertility of the land: high density in areas of rich, easily irrigated soil; decreasing density in areas less well suited to cultivation. This interpretation can, however, be reversed so that demographic growth is seen to create the

[13]   J. A. Schumpeter, *History of Economic Analysis* (Oxford University Press, Oxford, 1954), p. 251.

[14]   Ibid., pp. 251–2.

[15]   For example, the eighteenth-century attempt to colonize Andalusia under Charles III and that in the Italian Maremma during Lorraine rule.

[16]   E. Boserup, *The Conditions of Agricultural Growth* (Allen and Unwin, London, 1965).

conditions necessary for the adaptation of progressively more intensive methods of cultivation. Population pressure is then the cause and not the consequence of agricultural innovation.

The various systems of land cultivation spread across a continuum that stretches from forest-fallow systems (slash and burn preparation of the terrain followed by one or two years of cultivation and then a long fallow period of 20 to 25 years during which the forest reestablishes itself and the fertility of the soil is restored) at one end to multiannual cropping on the same piece of land at the other. Between the two extremes brush-fallow cultivation is identical in method to forest-fallow, but shorter, as a covering of shrubs reestablishes itself after six to eight years. In a short-fallow system (one or two years) there is only time for a grassy covering to grow back, while annual cropping allows but a few months for the soil to rest. Demographic growth determines the transition to progressively more intensive and shorter fallow cultivation systems which permit the feeding of a progressively larger population in a fixed area. This intensification process, however, is accompanied by an ever greater labor requirement and often also by declining worker productivity. For example, land preparation and the sowing of seed is extremely rudimentary in a slash and burn system: hatchet and fire clear the terrain of forest, ash fertilizes the soil, a pointed stick is all that is needed to sow the soft earth, and productivity per hour of work is high. Shorter fallow periods require more laborious soil preparation, and the simple action of fire must be replaced by work with hoe or plough; fertilization, weeding, and irrigation all become necessary. In a forest-fallow system, "fire does most of the work and there is no need for the removal of roots, which is such a time-consuming task when land has to be cleared for the preparation of permanent fields. The time used for superficial clearing under the system of forest fallow therefore seems to be only a fraction – perhaps ten or twenty per cent – of the time needed for complete clearing."[17] Tools, too, change at the various stages: while a pointed stick suffices for the sowing of seed in a slash and burn system, a hoe is needed to clear the soil of shrub when fallow is shorter and a plough to eradicate weeds when it is shorter still. When animal power is introduced for ploughing, the livestock produce fertilizer, but at the same time must be fed and cared for, tasks requiring additional labor. In order to obtain the same product, each farmer must work longer; in other words, his productivity per hour worked (in the absence of technological innovations) tends to decline. When population becomes too large in relation to available

[17]   Ibid., p. 30.

land, farmers are forced to use new techniques which, by virtue of increased inputs of labor, allow for greater production per unit of land. In many cases, so goes the argument, certain populations do not adopt more intensive techniques not because they are unaware of these alternatives but because land availability renders them disadvantageous. In fact, intensification would mean lower production per unit of labor.

This process of agricultural innovation differs from that according to which innovations or discoveries are "immediately" adopted because they are labor saving. In the first case, innovation is a consequence of demographic growth and the fact that a certain threshold of population density has been attained. In the second, innovation is independent of demographic factors.

The link between agricultural systems and population density is also supported by the fact that the above process of agricultural innovation seems to have been reversed in periods of population decline (several of which are discussed in chapter 2): lower density favors a return to less intensive systems. "Many of the permanent fields which were abandoned after wars or epidemics . . . remained uncultivated for centuries after. The use of labour-intensive methods of fertilization, such as marling, were abandoned for several centuries in France and then reappeared in the same region, when population again became dense."[18] More recent examples of this "technological" regression may be found in developing countries, for example in Latin America, "when migrants from more densely populated regions with much higher technical levels become settlers in . . . sparsely populated regions."[19] The slash and burn agriculture practiced in equatorial forests by new colonists, for example in the Amazon, is an unfortunate contemporary example of this phenomenon.

Boserup's model (synthesized schematically in figure 3.6) refers generally to the slow transformation of historical societies under the pressure of gradual population increase, the latter seen as an independent variable, external to the model.[20] It loses much, although not all, as we shall see below, of its explanatory force when applied to mixed economies or to developing countries experiencing modern demographic acceleration. This model does not rule out the operation of other factors, but posits

---

[18]   Ibid., p. 62.
[19]   Ibid.
[20]   Elements of Boserup's model are found in a number of modern authors. See, for example, C. Clark and M. Haswell, *The Economics of Subsistence Agriculture* (Macmillan, London, 1964), chapters 1 and 2.

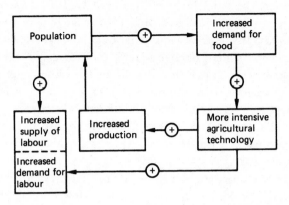

Figure 3.6 Population and agricultural intensification

demographic growth as one of the driving forces of economic transformation. It overturns the Malthusian model as population becomes not a variable dependent upon development but one which itself determines that development.

4   More on Demographic Pressure and Development: Examples from the Stone Age to the Present Day

The positive theory of demographic pressure has been applied with intriguing results to the "rapid" transition from hunting and gathering to agriculture which I discussed earlier. This transition allowed the human race – which for hundreds of thousands of years had depended on those animal and vegetable products supplied spontaneously by the ecosystem – to develop, in just a few thousand more, a system for the man-made production of resources.

According to the traditional theory, this transition is explained by the development and diffusion of innovations and inventions. The invention of new techniques of animal domestication, planting, and harvesting led to increased and more stable production and so provoked demographic acceleration.[21] In other words, people modified the environment and so established the conditions for population growth. Mark Cohen, like Boserup, turns the process around.[22] When, 11,000 to 12,000 years ago,

[21]   V. G. Childe, *Man Makes Himself* (Mentor, New York, 1951).
[22]   M. N. Cohen, *The Food Crisis in Prehistory. Overpopulation and the Origin of Agriculture* (Yale University Press, New Haven, 1977).

hunter-gatherer societies had settled all the land then available, demo-graphic growth forced them to enlarge their range of gathering to include inferior foods, less nutritional and lacking in flavor. Then, beginning 9,000 years ago, hunter-gatherers were forced to enlarge still further this range of food, cultivating not tastier foods but those easily reproduced, and so the transition to agriculture began. This argument is based on two primary arguments and a series of corollaries.

According to the first argument, agriculture consists of a series of prac-tices and techniques which were known to hunter-gatherers but not adopted because unnecessary: "Any human group dependent in some degree on plant materials, possessing the rudiments of human intelligence, and having any sort of home-base camp structure . . . will be almost bound to observe the basic process by which a seed or shoot becomes a plant . . . Agriculture is . . . a combination of behaviors . . . including such things as the creation of clearings in which certain plants thrive; the enrichment of certain soils; the planting of seeds; the irrigation of plants; the removal of competing species; the practice of conservation measures; the transporting of species beyond their original ecological boundaries; or the selection of preferred types. None of these behaviors alone constitutes agriculture; taken together they *are* agriculture."[23]

The second argument involves the level of nutrition and the work required to obtain this level with the transition to agriculture. In the first place, this transition entailed a deterioration of both the quality and variety of diet, as the food acquired by fishing, hunting, and gathering is much richer in nutrition and flavor than that of sedentary agriculture, dominated by a monotony of grain. Consequently, this transition would not have been expedient in the absence of the demographic growth that made it necessary. In addition, the work of a sedentary farmer was considerably more onerous than that of a hunter-gatherer who often con-sidered the search for food not so much a form of labor as a natural way of life.

This theory is based primarily on observation of groups of hunter-gatherers that have survived to the present day. The hypothesis regarding the light workload entailed by this survival model is confirmed by the Bushmen of the Kalahari, among whom the adult males devote on average two or three hours a day to obtaining food, by the Arnhem Land Aborigines, who average three to five hours, and by the tribes of Tanzania, at barely two.[24]

---

[23] Ibid., pp. 22–3.
[24] Ibid., pp. 30–1.

Similar observations were made in the nineteenth century by Grey.[25] Comparisons between primitive farmers and their hunter-gatherer predecessors presumably also confirm the lesser effort exerted by the hunter-gatherers for acquiring adequate food. In conclusion, "agriculture permits denser food growth supporting denser populations and larger social units, but at the cost of reduced dietary quality, reduced reliability of harvest, and equal or probably greater labor per unit food."[26] Agriculture spreads, then, when demographic growth requires greater production per unit area. Keeping in mind the fact that there existed a reequilibration mechanism (migration) which distributed excess population among areas, reducing demographic pressure, one can understand why the transition to agriculture (driven by demographic growth) took place in a relatively short period of time as compared to the duration of human history.

Cohen's approach has provoked intense debate and many attempts at confirmation. In particular, attention has been focused on the hypothesis that the period leading up to agricultural transition was characterized by a decline in living standards and nutritional levels. Confirmation, however, remains elusive, and both archaeological finds and paleopathological studies are inconclusive on this point.[27]

The theory according to which the first known demographic revolution led to the invention of agriculture shares with that of Boserup the belief that population acts as a stimulus to development. Later demographic developments – the period of growth in medieval Europe prior to the plague, for example – also provoked changes in the organization of production in keeping with the above model. "The new system, which spread in the period between the ninth and fourteenth centuries, was a three-course rotation of all the fields in a village, in which two cereal crops were followed by one year of fallow. The stubble and fallow were utilized for supervised grazing by domestic animals belonging to all the villagers. Stubble-grazing animals fertilized the fields with their droppings, helping to compensate for loss of soil fertility by shorter fallowing, and for loss of natural pastures due to expansion of the cultivated area. Even so, it is possible that crop yields were lower than

---

[25] Cited in M. Sahlins, *Stone Age Economics* (Aldine, Chicago, 1974). Moreover, Sahlins provides detailed examples of the limited workload of contemporary hunter-gatherer populations.

[26] Cohen, *Food Crisis in Prehistory*, p. 39; see also Clark and Haswell, *Economics of Subsistence Agriculture*, pp. 33, 46.

[27] M. N. Cohen and G. J. Armelogos, eds, *Paleopathology and the Origins of Agriculture* (Academic Press, Orlando, 1984); see the final chapter authored by the two editors.

they had been under the long-fallow system, and it is likely that there was some shift of diet from animal to vegetable food as population continued to increase. When the Black Death later reduced population densities, an opposite shift to less vegetable food took place, as arable fields, made superfluous by the decline of population, returned to pasture."[28]

Evidence from present-day agricultural societies using traditional technique also confirms the theory of the propulsive role of demographic growth. A recent study employs a series of cases taken from Latin America, Africa, and Asia during the last half century.[29] In these, the level of population pressure has been much greater than in the past due to higher rates of growth. The cases analyzed illustrate the response of agricultural societies to growth rates of 2 to 3 percent per year; in almost all cases urban growth has absorbed a fraction of rural demographic excess (or excess rural population), and in some the nonagricultural sector has actually come to dominate.

Given approximately equal technological levels, the work required for the cultivation of a given crop on a given unit of land increases with increasingly intensive cultivation systems. For example, comparing forest-fallow cultivation – employing the slash and burn technique and long fallow periods – to annual cultivation, the yearly total of hours worked per hectare jumps from 770 to 3,300 in Cameroon.[30] The increased labor requirement is the result of both the greater amount of work needed for each phase of cultivation (preparation of the soil, weeding and so forth) and the larger number of phases (irrigation and fertilization, for example). Three operations are sufficient for slash and burn agriculture: preparation of the soil by burning, which requires 300 to 400 hours per hectare in Liberia or the Ivory Coast; planting with a stick or hoe in the fire-softened terrain; and harvesting. Virtually no work is performed in the period between sowing and harvesting, since neither fertilization nor weeding nor irrigation are required. As cultivation intensifies, the latter operations become indispensable and progressively more laborious. Considering all 52 of the cases studied by Pingali and Binswagen, and

[28]   E. Boserup, *Population and Technological Change* (University of Chicago Press, Chicago, 1981), pp. 95–6.

[29]   P. L. Pingali and H. R. Binswagen, "Population Density and Agricultural Intensification: A Study of the Evolution of Technologies in Tropical Agriculture," in *Population Growth and Economic Development*, ed. D. G. Johnson and R. D. Lee (The University of Wisconsin Press, Madison, 1987).

[30]   Ibid., p. 38.

calculating indices of cultivation and labor intensity,[31] one notes a positive correlation between the two variables: a 10 percent increase in cultivation intensity corresponds on average to a 4.6 percent increase in hours worked per hectare. The same analysis reveals that the 10 percent increase in cultivation intensity corresponds to a 3.9 percent increase in production per hectare. Productivity per hour worked, then, declines slightly, but if we also take into account the work hours not strictly employed in cultivation (such as the raising and care of livestock, maintenance of irrigation systems and of tools) the decline in productivity per hour worked is greater. This productivity decline (calculated in the absence of innovations) can, of course, be compensated for by sufficient investment and by new technology.

The experience of developing countries confirms many aspects of the theory. Agricultural intensification implies more work per unit of cultivated terrain and, given a constant level of technology, more work per unit of production. This trend has been effectively countered in recent history by technological innovation, but it is conceivable that in earlier epochs, when the pace of such innovation was either slow or static, the adoption of new methods of cultivation came about as a result of necessity and at the price of greater workloads.

5   Space, Land, and Development

For much of human history, the well-being of a population has depended upon the availability of space and land, and on the constraints imposed by their lack or limited supply. The ways in which populations have succeeded in overcoming or sidestepping these constraints by means of innovation and adaptation have been the leading determinants of survival and growth. The models described above, whether Malthusian or Boserupian, depend on space; in the first case primarily as a determining factor of demographic change and, in the second, as a dimension which responds to and is altered by population growth or decline. In the course of the history of population, these models have alternated, overlapped, and intersected; nor is it easy to

---

[31]   The index of cultivation intensity is the number of annual harvests per unit of land (a plot subject to forest-fallow cultivation with 24 years of fallow and 1 of cultivation represents a minimum index of 0.04; a plot harvested twice a year would have an index of 2). The index of labor intensity represents an estimate of the annual hours of work per unit of land.

make out their separate influences. In order to study long-term demographic growth, we must take "space" into account and all that it implies, in particular land, the products of the land (food, manufactured goods, energy), and those characteristics which determine settlement patterns. Demography has for too long ignored or at best paid scant attention to these themes and so deprived itself of valuable interpretative tools. Indeed the relevance of space for the understanding of demographic trends should be both directly and indirectly evident throughout this book, whether in relation to the Neolithic revolution, the settlement of new territories, or the events in Ireland and Japan.

Let us take Europe as an example, a continent – or perhaps more appropriately the western extension of the large Eurasian continent – for which we have access to abundant information for studying the relationships between space and demography. It is a continent marked by at least three fundamental characteristics. The first is its relatively easy access; it is almost entirely surrounded by seas, is penetrated by numerous waterways, and includes important orographic features that regulate but do not prevent communications. The second is its favorable climate, for the most part temperate and supportive of a wide range of crops. The third is the great variability of its environmental conditions which require adaptation on the part of the populations but at the same time favor specialization.

The area of Europe (taken to extend to the Urals, the Caspian Sea, and the Caucasus) measures 9.6 million square kilometers of which about half belongs to Russia. It would be superficial in this context to examine the complex relations between space and population in such a vast and varied area, though there are many interesting points to be made. According to Cavalli Sforza and Ammerman, it was because of the availability of space that agriculturalists progressively migrated northwest from Asia Minor to Europe bringing new settlement and cultivation techniques and either causing or at least encouraging the Neolithic revolution there. Similarly, the increasing pressure exerted by nomadic peoples against the eastern borders of the Roman Empire must be ascribed to the conquest of space and resources.

In order to understand better the relationship between space and demographic change at least three lines of analysis need to be investigated. The first concerns the occupation of uninhabited or sparsely populated regions within a settled area; the second the transformation of existing space by means of deforestation, land reclamation, and swamp draining; and the third the expansion outside of settled areas through emigration and the colonization of new territories. These three processes are intimately linked and can conceptually be put in chronological order (though in fact they can all happen at the same time) according to the growing economic, social, and human costs they require.

The occupation of uninhabited or sparsely populated regions

This sort of expansion accompanied the Medieval demographic growth of the eleventh to thirteenth centuries, a period during which European population multiplied by a factor of two or three. According to Grigg, "In AD 900 much of Europe was covered by forest, but the following centuries saw the removal of woodland to allow cultivation. Between AD 1000 and 1300 much of the lowland forest was removed in central and western Europe, and cultivation also extended into mountain areas, notably in the Vosges, Alps and Pyrenees."[32] It was a widespread process, as already-settled territories were expanded by means of the cultivation of new land, often accompanied by the consolidation of population in towns, castles, and new cities.[33] The expansion of cultivated land came about in varied ways, though in the majority of cases it was the individual peasant who put to the plow open space bordering already cultivated fields or else cleared woodland. In other cases new settlements were organized by landlords.[34] This process is a well-documented one, in Italy, Spain, France, Germany, and elsewhere. Obviously, the increasing demands for resources made by an expanding population were also satisfied to some extent by land reclamation, settlement at higher elevations, and costly land transformations (within the limits of available technology and usually by means of that intensification of agriculture we have already discussed). Still, it is hard to imagine that Medieval expansion would have been as dynamic as it was without an abundance of easily acquired land.

Transformation and land reclamation

At considerably higher costs, land reclamation helped to sustain Medieval population growth. Dams were built to control stream waters and to protect

---

[32] D. Grigg, *The Transformation of Agriculture in the West* (Basil Blackwell, Oxford, 1992), p. 13.

[33] H. Dubois, "L'essor médiéval," in *Histoire de la population française*, vol. 1, *Des origines à la Renaissance*, ed. J. Dupaquier (PUF, Paris, 1988).

[34] G. Pinto, "Dalla tarda antichità alla metà del XVI secolo," in *La popolazione italiana dal Medioevo a oggi*, ed. L. Del Panta, M. Livi Bacci, G. Pinto, and E. Sonnino (Laterza, Rome-Bari, 1996).

lowlands from flooding by both rivers and the sea: "Coastal areas saw much reclamation, and embankments were built to protect low-lying land both from the sea and from estuarine flooding in Lincolnshire and Norfolk, on the Elbe, the Loire, the coast of Flanders, and most notably in the Zuiderzee."[35] Similar hydraulic work was carried out in the Po Valley including projects financed by cities in Lombardy, Emilia, Romagna, and in the Venetian plain.[36]

Land reclamation took on larger proportions during the demographic recovery that followed the crisis of the fourteenth and fifteenth centuries. In England wet and swampy areas, both internal (in Lancashire and in Fenland) and along the coasts of Sussex, Norfolk, and Essex, were drained.[37] Similar work was carried out in France, along the northern coast with the help of Dutch workers and also in the south along the malarial and swampy coasts of Provence and Languedoc.[38] And in Italy reclamation activity took off again as well: "all of the lower Po Valley was affected by the great reclamation movement in the sixteenth century. To the west the first rice paddies were created in the eastern part of Piedmont between Novara and Vercelli, but the greatest activity was in the east; massive and surprising transformations took place on either side of the Po: in the Venetian *terra firma*, in the Duchies of Parma, Reggio, Mantua, and Ferrara, and in Emilia."[39] Yet it was in the Netherlands in response to population growth and the increase in grain prices between the late fifteenth and mid-seventeenth centuries that the reclamation of land from sea and marsh by means of dikes, canals, and pump-works took on formidable dimensions. "Between 1540 and 1565, 125,000 hectares of polders were diked; one-half of this was in Zeeland and North Brabant, one-third in Holland, the remaining sixth in Friesland and Groningen."[40] There were also reclaimed lands in the interior of the country: "The area brought into cultivation was remarkable: between 1550 and 1650 the population of the Netherlands increased by some 600,000 but the area reclaimed was some 162,000 hectares".[41] If we assume that one hectare

[35]   D. Grigg, *Transformation*, p. 13.
[36]   G. Pinto, "Dalla tarda antichità."
[37]   D. Grigg, *Population Growth and Agrarian Change: an Historical Perspective* (Cambridge University Press, Cambridge, 1980), pp. 90–1.
[38]   Ibid., p. 106.
[39]   M. Aymard, "La fragilità di un'economia avanzata: L'Italia e la trasformazione dell'economia europea," in *Storia dell'economia italiana*, vol. II, *L'età moderna verso la crisi* (Einaudi, Turin, 1991), p. 26.
[40]   D. Grigg, *Population*, p. 150.
[41]   Ibid., p. 151.

can sustain on average two or three people then the added land would have fed between one-half and three-quarters of the added population. In the Netherlands land reclamation followed demographic growth apace. Elsewhere the demographic awakening of the second half of the eighteenth century was accompanied by the revival of reclamation projects as well: in England and Ireland, Poitou and Provence, Schleswig-Holstein and Prussia, and Catalonia and the Italian Maremma.

External expansion

The third element in the complex relationship between space and population is the existence of accessible space outside of already-settled areas. Europe has been both a receiver and a supplier of population in this regard. Prior to the Middle Ages, population flowed in from the steppes to the east and the Mediterranean to the south. In the period since the Middle Ages, it would be difficult to understand the development of European demography and society without taking into account the availability of inhabitable spaces to the west and east and so the phenomena of emigration and colonization. The accessibility of these spaces and the force of attraction they exert is one of the two major factors behind the great migrations; the other is the existence of forces of expulsion tied to economic difficulties in the sending regions. We shall discuss at greater length below the great nineteenth-century transoceanic migrations, which took place in a period of rapid economic and industrial change, but for the moment let us restrict our attention to Europe between the Middle Ages and the Industrial Revolution and focus on three great movements. The first is the German colonization of the territory east of the Elbe River between the eleventh and the fourteenth centuries. The second includes the Iberian migration to Central and South America and the British migration to North America as well as the relatively minor movements of the Dutch and the French to their respective colonies in the period from the sixteenth to the eighteenth centuries; these movements constitute the prelude to the great migrations of the nineteenth century. The third is the expansion of the Russian frontier to the east and to the south.

The drive to the east – *Drang nach Osten* – was a phenomenon of great proportions as it determined the peopling of large areas east of the Elbe and then successively of Poland, the Sudetenland, and Transylvania. It was a colonization process begun in the twelfth century by Dutch and Flemish pioneers – in part organized, in part spontaneous – who moved into open areas sparsely inhabited by Slavs. It is estimated that this migration involved 200,000 people who in the course of the twelfth century occupied the region between the Elbe and the Oder and that the wave of the thirteenth century that helped populate Silesia and Pomerania was of a similar size. It was a relatively modest migratory flow but one of considerable importance in the long run: at the end of the nineteenth century the Germanic population east of the Elbe–Saale line was about 30 million.[42] In the eighteenth century, by calling on several tens of thousands of German colonists, Catherine the Great of Russia produced a new wave of migration into the valley of the Volga in an attempt to push the border southward. Between 1764 and 1768, 104 colonies were founded on the banks of the Volga for 27,000 immigrants. Other settlements in the Crimea, North Caucasus, Kazakhstan, and Siberia followed.[43] From a demographic point of view, the interest of these migrations lies not so much in their size, which was modest in both absolute and relative terms, but in their makeup: the migrants were for the most part young workers, many without families; they represented a significant portion of the reproductive age population and so an outlet for demographic increase. Their progeny was considerable: as with the French Canadian pioneers (see chapter 2, section 5), their reproductivity was high, because of both the selective effects of migration and the abundance of available resources better exploited by large families. A few hundred thousand Germanic colonists then became a few centuries later tens of millions, and the few tens of thousands who migrated to Russia founded colonies which grew into large settlements by the end of the nineteenth century.

The second great migratory outlet was the American continent and, to a lesser extent, other overseas settlements. At the end of the eighteenth century, as the colonial system was collapsing, the American continent was home to modest but significant European settlements: about 4 million in Latin America and 4.5 in North America.[44] These settlements, fed by migrations from Spain and the British Isles and to a lesser degree Portugal, were small in comparison to the physical dimensions of the continent but nonetheless constituted a third of its population. As compared to the population of Europe (excluding Russia) they amounted to only about a fifteenth.

On the basis of indirect estimates derived from maritime traffic, the Spanish contribution is thought to be 3,000–5,000 emigrants per year for

---

[42]   C. Higounet, *Les Allemands en Europe centrale et orientale au Moyen Age* (Aubier, Paris, 1989).

[43]   R. Caratini, *Dictionnaire des nationalités et des minorités en URSS* (Larousse, Paris, 1990).

[44]   C. McEvedy and R. Jones, *Atlas of World Population History* (Penguin, Harmondsworth, 1978), p. 279.

the 150 years ending in the mid-seventeenth century. They came almost exclusively from Castile and constituted a loss (according to the highest estimate) of one per thousand per year, a significant figure given their young age structure and the weak demographic growth of the period. After 1630, and in conjunction with the general (including demographic) crisis, emigration declined and reached a minimum between 1700 and 1720.[45] The drain on England was greater, amounting to a net figure of 7,000 emigrants a year during the seventeenth century from a population that numbered little more than 4 million at its beginning.[46] The emigration from Holland was comparable to that from England; it is estimated that 230,000 net emigrants went to Asian locations between the beginning of the seventeenth century and the end of the eighteenth, to which were added 15,000 to Latin America and the Caribbean and 10,000 to the United States.[47] France, the most populous country in Europe (see chapter 2, section 5), contributed relatively little to these migrations. Transoceanic migration between the beginning of the sixteenth century and the end of the eighteenth was numerically significant and constituted the demographic and political base for the great migrations of the nineteenth century; it made possible then an enormous expansion of European space beyond the Atlantic barrier that had enormous long-term demographic consequences.

The third movement consisted of the shift of the Russian border to the south and east. The peopling of Siberia in the nineteenth century – which takes us beyond the chronological limits here imposed – resembled that of the American continent though the numbers were smaller. As McNeill writes: "By 1796, therefore, when the Empress Catherine II died, the Russian flood had engulfed the once-formidable Tartar society . . . All the vast steppe region north of the Crimea and west of the Don had been occupied by landlords and settlers, and their political and social institutions had been effectively assimilated to those prevailing in the Russian empire as a whole . . . Yet new towns had arisen (Kherson, 1778; Nikolaev, 1788; Odessa, 1794) and throve as administrative centers and grain ports; and with urban life the manifestations of higher culture – flavored by a distinctly cosmopolitan tincture owing to admixture of Greeks, Bulgars, Poles, Jews,

---

[45] J. Nadal, *La población española (siglos XVI a XX)* (Ariel, Barcelona, 1984), pp. 73–6.
[46] E. A. Wrigley and R. Schofield, *The Population History of England, 1541–1871* (Arnold, London, 1981), p. 219.
[47] J. Lucassen, *Dutch Migrations*, paper presented at the XVII International Congress of Historical Sciences (Madrid, 1990).

and a few western Europeans – soon appeared".[48]

These notes on an enormously complex and little-known story should give some idea of the intimate relation between demographic change and the availability of space, whether internal or external, to the relevant populations. It is an argument with ties naturally to the migrations which have traversed the continent in various directions. It helps us in turn to understand how in the space of a millennium the availability of new spaces not strictly defined by political boundaries played a great and varied role in shaping demographic change. Space, then, has made possible the expansion of the European economy into a wider world.

6   Population Size and Prosperity

In the preceding pages I have discussed several possible dynamic relations between population and economic development. It is also worth taking a moment to consider the effect of the simple "number" of inhabitants on societal well-being. I have already touched this argument in passing; it merits, however, something more than the observation that the level of complexity of social organization is also a function of numerical size. Many scholars have grappled with the question of whether there exists an "optimum" population size,[49] but this academic exercise is not particularly helpful for understanding the historical reasons for demographic develop-ment. The concept of an optimum population, which may be defined as that theoretical population size at which individual well-being is maximized (and above or below which well-being declines), is an essentially static concept and applies poorly to dynamic populations.

Population size acts by means of two mechanisms well known to classical economists. The first is linked to the principle of division of labor and so to the more efficient use of individual abilities. The second derives from the observation that the complexity of societal organization is also a function of demographic dimensions, both absolutely and relative to a given unit of territory (density).

The benefits of division of labor were masterfully demonstrated by Adam

Smith, and before him by William Petty. Referring to the advantages of large cities, Petty wrote: "In the making of a Watch, If one Man shall make the Wheels, another the Spring, another shall Engrave the Dial-plate, and another shall make the Cases, then the Watch will be better and cheaper, than if the whole Work be put upon any one Man."[50] Smith's examples of the black-smith making nails and of the advantages to be gained from dividing up the work required for the production of pins are classic: "One man draws out the wire, another straights it, a third cuts it, a fourth points it, a fifth grinds it at the top for receiving the head, to make the head requires two or three distinct operations, to put it on is a peculiar business, to whiten the pins is another; it is even a trade by itself to put them into paper; and the important business of making a pin is, in this manner, divided into about eighteen distinct operations, which in some manufactories, are all performed by distinct hands,"[51] and while a single worker might turn out at most 20 pins a day, a factory employing a team of 10 workers manages to produce 12 pounds a day, or 48,000 pins, 4,800 per worker. Division of labor, however, is a function of the size of the market. If the market is small, division is moderate, as are the advantages to be gained. Smith observed that in the Highlands of his native Scotland, where families were widely scattered, each performed the tasks of butcher, baker, and brewer for itself. Smiths, carpenters, and masons were few, and those families 8 or 10 miles from town did much of this work themselves.[52]

Where it has been impossible to adequately divide labor, this situation has contributed in some measure to the backwardness of scattered groups; to the development difficulties encountered by small, isolated communities, the dimensions of which do not allow specialization; to the failure of colonization undertaken by small nuclei; and to the instability of small island populations even when the environment is favorable. The maximum of inefficiency according to this formula is that population consisting only of Robinson Crusoe.

The second advantage to be gained from population size or density is the

[50] W. Petty, *The Economic Writings*, ed. C. H. Hull (A. M. Kelley, New York, 1963), p. 473. For the quotation from Petty I am indebted to J. L. Simon, *Theory of Population and Economic Growth* (Blackwell, London, 1986). Simon is the most explicit supporter of the positive causal link between demographic growth and increasing levels of innovation/invention. The first four chapters of the above work are dedicated to this argument.
[51] A. Smith, *The Wealth of Nations*, Everyman's Library (J. M. Dent and Sons, London, 1964), vol. 1, p. 5.
[52] Ibid., p. 15.

economies of scale acquired at increasing population levels. Better systems of resource utilization and production are only feasible when population attains a certain density in relation to the territory inhabited. We have already considered an example according to which the processes of agricultural intensification respond to the incitement of demographic growth. In our own time, a country like Canada is considered, by representatives of both the government and the citizenry at large, too "empty" to maintain that development which its extension and natural wealth would seem to ensure. Other classic examples include the development of irrigation systems, the establishment of cities, the improvement of communications, and, in general, those investments in infrastructure which require a critical mass of resources and a critical mass of demand – neither of which are obtainable from small groups and limited markets.

The development of irrigation systems in Mesopotamia allowed the few hunter-gatherers living in the Zagros Mountains in 8000 BC to evolve into a large population of plain-dwellers in the following millennia. "This dense population used intensive systems of agriculture based upon flow irrigation; multicropping was also introduced. Fields were prepared by plows with mulboards and iron shares, drawn by oxen. The irrigation system used water-wheels for lifting water to fields located above the major river, which provided the water. Thus over a period of some eight thousand years, Mesopotamia became densely populated . . . Gradually, the population changed from primitive food gatherers to people who applied the most sophisticated systems of food production existing in the ancient world."[53] The transformation of the Italian Maremma into swampland that accompanied the medieval population decline was a result of the reverse process which saw the deterioration of water control systems.

Considerations of this sort have also been applied to the development of road networks, which is strongly correlated to population density.[54] Clearly the advantage and usefulness of a road is a function of how heavily it is traveled. Once built, it exerts multiple effects on development, speeding up communication, helping trade, and allowing the creation of a larger market. The differences in prices for basic goods in primitive societies are largely

---

[53]   Boserup, *Population and Technological Change*, p. 51.

[54]   Clark and Haswell, *Economics of Subsistence Agriculture*. Chapter 9 studies the role of transportation and communication in primitive economies. J. L. Simon, *The Economics of Population Growth* (Princeton University Press, Princeton, 1977). According to Simon there exists a very strong relation between population density and the density of road networks. This is one of the principal benefits of scale made possible by demographic growth (pp. 262–77).

explained by difficulties of transportation and uncertain communications.

City growth too has obvious links to demography. I take for granted that the creation of cities allows for greater specialization and more efficient organization of the economy. While these advantages may well be compromised in the present day by the ever more evident "diseconomies" of scale created in the great urban centers, for the primarily rural economies that we are discussing the situation was altogether different. Clearly the maintenance of an important centralized population, not directly involved in food production, implies the creation of an agricultural surplus by the rural population; and the wealthier the latter, the greater the available resources. The early growth of cities in Mesopotamia, northern India, and China is certainly a function of the large populations allowed by the fertility of the land and agricultural abundance. It is once again Ester Boserup who provides an original explanation for this situation, proposing a causal chain: Demographic growth drives agricultural intensification, but it is not so much the level of per capita production – which increases with increasingly intensive cultivation – as it is increasing population density (and so the multiplicative factor of per capita surplus) that allows for the creation of the surplus resources requisite for the birth of cities. "Even the best technologies available to the ancient world, when used on the best land, did not allow one agricultural family to supply many nonagricultural families . . . The size of the population available to supply an urban center was far more important than how much food could be delivered or sold per agricultural worker."[55]

The links between division of labor, economies of scale, and demographic dimensions are easily grasped and demonstrated by numerous historical examples. Less easily demonstrated is another thesis, upheld by a number of scholars, which employs the following logical sequence: When resources are available, development is a function of what Kuznets calls "tested knowledge."[56] Employing a restrictive hypothesis, the "creators" of "new knowledge" (investors, innovators) exist in proportion to population size. The creation of "new knowledge," however, is probably helped by factors of scale (the existence of schools, universities, and academies that multiply both the efficiency of already acquired knowledge and also the opportunities for the creation of new knowledge) and so enjoys increasing returns as

---

[55]   Boserup, *Population and Technological Change*, p. 65.

[56]   S. Kuznets, "Population Change and Aggregate Output," in *Demographic and Economic Change in Developed Countries*, Report of the NBER (Princeton University Press, Princeton, 1960), pp. 328–30.

population grows. In this way, all things being equal, population increase leads to increased per capita production.

As Kuznets himself confesses, this is a hazardous argument,[57] though he is not its sole advocate. Indeed, it was Petty who remarked: "And it is more likely that one Ingenious Curious Man may rather be found out amongst 4 Millions than 400 Persons."[58]

7 Increasing or Decreasing Returns?

During the last 10,000 years the human race has managed to multiply by a factor of 1,000 and at the same time increase the per capita availability of resources. Those who argue for the inevitability of decreasing returns maintain that this has come about because the limits of fixed resources have never been reached, either because these limits have been repeatedly pushed back as new land is cultivated and sparsely populated continents inhabited or because resources have been used more productively thanks to innovations and discoveries. Nonetheless, for long historical periods the bite of diminishing returns has severely tested the ability of population to react. Moreover, certain resources would seem to be not only limited but non-substitutable, and so in the long run neither innovation nor invention can avert the onset of diminishing returns and impoverishment.

According to the opposing view, there is no reason to believe that the onset of diminishing returns is inevitable. Kuznets expresses this position well in historical terms, asking: "Why, if it is man who was the architect of economic and social growth in the past and responsible for the vast contributions to knowledge and technological and social power, a larger number of human beings need result in a lower rate of increase in per capita product? More population means more creators and producers, both of goods along established production patterns and of new knowledge and inventions. Why shouldn't the larger numbers achieve what the smaller numbers accomplished in the modern past – raise total output to provide not only for the current population increase but also for a rapidly rising supply per capita?"[59] In other words, diminishing returns from fixed resources are more than compensated for by the increasing returns of human ingenuity and by the ever more favorable conditions created by demographic growth.

---

[57] Ibid., p. 329.
[58] Petty, *Economic Writings*, p. 474.
[59] S. Kuznets, *Population, Capital and Growth* (Norton, New York, 1973), p. 3.

This dilemma is unresolvable only if we insist on finding hard and fast rules to explain complex phenomena. Time is a factor of primary importance. The bite of diminishing returns can create insurmountable obstacles in the short and medium run, lasting a few decades or a few generations. The costs generated by these obstacles are not easily evaluated. Nor are they necessarily reflected by mortality fluctuations, as population is characterized by a high level of resistance to hardships and historically the infectious and epidemic disease component has been largely independent of the human condition. They are, however, reflected in a general increase of poverty that in the long run can only be checked or reversed by innovation. The price paid in terms of human suffering can be high, though historically one is more impressed by the ability of societies to reverse a negative trend. If we transfer this dilemma to the present day, it takes on dramatic proportions. Rapid demographic growth may in the long run be accompanied by unexpected development, but meanwhile the medium-term problems are serious. Should we judge historically in terms of centuries or millennia, or with greater attention to problems foreseeable in our own lifetime?

4

Toward Order and Efficiency: The Recent Demography of Europe and the Developed World

1 From Waste to Economy

In 1769 James Watt built a steam engine with a separate condenser. Compared to the earlier Newcomen engine used to pump water out of mines, Watt's design increased efficiency enormously: in order to produce the same power, Watt's engine consumed one-fourth the fuel of its predecessor, saving the energy wasted to reheat the cylinder after each piston stroke. This saving was decisive in determining the important role the steam engine would play in all sectors of the economy.[1]

During the past two centuries, Western populations have undergone a similar process. Previously, slow growth was accompanied by considerable demographic waste. Women had to bear a half dozen children simply in order to achieve replacement in the following generation. Between a third and a half of those born perished before reaching reproductive age and procreating. From a demographic point of view, old regime societies were inefficient: in order to maintain a low level of growth, a great deal of fuel (births) was needed and a huge amount of energy was wasted (deaths). The old demographic regime was characterized not only by inefficiency but also by disorder. The probability that the natural chronological hierarchy would be inverted – that a child would die before its parent or

[1] D. S. Landes, "Technological Change and Development in Western Europe 1750–1914," in *Cambridge Economic History*, 2nd ed, ed. H. J. Habakkuk and M. Postan (Cambridge University Press, Cambridge, 1965), vol. 6, pt 1, pp. 274–661.

grandparent – was considerable. High levels of mortality and frequent catastrophes rendered precarious any long-terms plans based on individual survival.

The modern demographic cycle in the West has passed through all phases of its trajectory during the past two centuries: European population has multiplied fourfold; life expectancy has increased from the range of 25–35 to 75–80; the average number of children per woman has declined from five to less than two; birth and death rates have both declined from values generally between 30 and 40 per thousand to about 10. This profound transformation, an integral part of the social transformation of the previous century, is generally referred to as the "demographic transition," a term that has entered into common usage much as has "Industrial Revolution." It is a complex process of passage from disorder to order and from waste to economy. In the developing countries, with which we shall deal in the following chapter, this transition is in process; in the more backward countries it has just begun, while in others it is near completion. Keeping in mind the necessary historical adjustments, the European experience – and that of the West in general – can serve as a useful guide to that which is occurring in the rest of the world. It is this experience which we shall now consider in its general outline, attempting to identify common points rather than manifestations peculiar to specific societies and cultures. The latter limitation ignores a rich area of research, but one which it is impossible to include in a synthetic treatment of the type I have proposed.

The strategic space discussed above (see chapter 1, section 5, figures 1.8a–c) is reproduced in figure 4.1. Recall that the space is traversed by "isogrowth" curves, each of which represents the locus of points that combine life expectancy (e_0) and number of children per woman (TFR) to give the same rate of growth. Historically, populations have occupied an area between the 0 and 0.5 percent curves, with low life expectancy and a large number of children. We have also seen that this space has expanded greatly in present-day developing countries as rapid mortality decline is often not accompanied by similar declines in fertility, with the result that many of these countries occupy the space between the 2 and 4 percent curves.

For the European countries, instead, the transition of the last two hundred years has taken place without growth rate "explosions," but rather by means of a gradual and in part parallel modification of mortality and fertility, so that the various populations have occupied a more limited area, generally bounded by the 0 and 1.5 percent curves. Figure 4.1

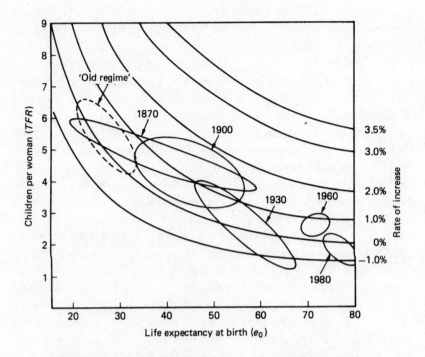

Figure 4.1 The strategic space of growth for 17 European countries
(nineteenth through twentieth centuries)
Source: A. J. Coale, "The Decline of Fertility in Europe since the Eighteenth
Century," in A. J. Coale and S. C. Watkins, *Human Demographic History* (Princeton
University Press, Princeton, 1986), p. 27.

displays fairly well the area of strategic space occupied by 17 European
countries at various times during the past two centuries. For each date an
ellipse represents the area occupied by these countries. Within a fairly
narrow strip, the ellipses move gradually from the upper left (high
fertility and mortality) to the lower right (low fertility and mortality).
Much of the 1870 and 1900 ellipses occupy an area between 1 and 2
percent, revealing that period of the demographic transition when the
distance between fertility and mortality was greatest. By contrast, most of
the 1930 and 1980 ellipses are below the 0 percent curve, periods when
fertility was below replacement.

As I have already mentioned, the demographic transition had several
phases. In order to better describe the movement simplified in figure 4.1,
it will be useful to consider several aspects: the beginning of both
mortality and fertility decline, the end and duration of the phase of

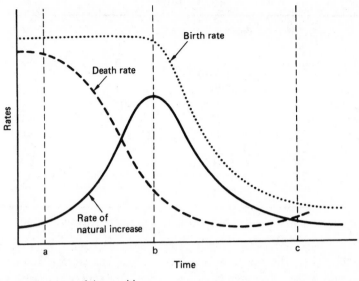

a = beginning of the transition
b = greatest difference between birth and death rates
c = end of the transition

Figure 4.2 Demographic transition model

decline, and the maximum and minimum distances between the two variables.

Figure 4.2 presents an abstract model of transition. The beginning of mortality decline generally precedes that of fertility, and during this phase the separation between the two components (the natural rate of increase) reaches a maximum; as fertility decline accelerates and that of mortality slows down, the two curves approach one another again and the natural rate of increase returns to a low level (similar to that at which it began the transition). Implicit in this model is the hypothesis that once fertility and mortality decline have begun the process will continue until low rates are reached, an hypothesis upheld for the most part by European experience.

The duration of the transition, the steepness of the two curves, and the distance between them varied considerably from country to country. Population increase during the transitional phase, a phase characterized by accelerated growth, is a function of these parameters. The ratio between population size at the beginning and the end of the transition

Table 4.1 Beginning, end, duration, and "multiplier" of the demographic
transition for several countries

Country	Beginning and end of the transition	Duration in years	Multiplier
Sweden	1810–1960	150	3.83
Germany	1876–1965	90	2.11
Italy	1876–1965	90	2.26
USSR	1896–1965	70	2.05
France	1785–1970	185	1.62
China	1930–2000	70	2.46
Taiwan	1920–1990	70	4.35
Mexico	1920–2000	80	7.02

Source: J.-C. Chesnais, *La transition démographique* (PUF, Paris, 1986), pp. 294, 301

may be called the transition "multiplier."[2] In France, for example, the
transition began at the end of the eighteenth century and lasted more
than a century and a half; mortality and fertility declined in similar,
almost parallel, fashion, not diverging greatly from one another in time,
and the multiplier was barely 1.6. In Sweden, on the other hand, mortality
decline proceeded ahead of fertility decline and the transition was shorter; the multiplier was more than double that of France (3.8). Should we
want to compare European experience to that of present-day developing
countries, we might choose Mexico and imagine that the transition will
be complete by the year 2000, having lasted 80 years. Mortality decline
came much before fertility decline; natural increase has reached very high
levels; and the multiplier would be about 7. Table 4.1, borrowed from
Chesnais, lists the duration of transition and value of multiplier for a
number of European and (by extrapolation) developing countries. The
multiplier tends to be considerably higher for developing countries than
for the European ones, with the exception of China, whose population is
controlled by a Draconian demographic policy.

I have intentionally focused on the mechanical aspects of the transition, leaving until now discussion of the causes. The mortality decline

---

[2]   The data in table 4.1, the concept of multiplier, and the above description of the
transition model are taken from J.-C. Chesnais, *La transition démographique* (PUF,
Paris, 1986), p. 33; idem, "Demographic Transition Patterns and Their Impact on
Age Structure," *Population and Development Review*, 16 (1990).

which began in the second half of the eighteenth century is generally ascribed partly to exogenous factors, including the reduced frequency of epidemic cycles and the disappearance of the plague; partly to the reduction of famine due to better economic organization; and to socio-cultural practices which helped to reduce the spread of infectious diseases and improve survival, especially of infants. Mortality decline spurred demographic growth and so increased pressure on available resources, which in turn led to lower fertility by means of both reduced nuptiality and the spread of deliberate attempts to limit births. Equilibrium was only reestablished at the end of the process of fertility decline, the timing of which depended upon the level of progress of the various populations. The above is an adaptation of the Malthusian model that implies an adjustment of population to available resources by means of a check on reproduction – reproduction being less and less conditioned by biological factors and more and more dependent on individual fertility control, a possibility which Malthus did not foresee.

Widely varying opinion seems to agree that the social transformation associated with the Industrial Revolution induced a change in the fertility choices of couples. In particular, the growth of urban industrial society increased the "cost" of childrearing: Children became autonomous wage earners and producers at a much later age than in agricultural societies and required greater "investments," both material and in terms of health care and education, which deprived the mother, especially, of employment opportunities. The increased cost of children appears to have been the spur behind fertility control; its progress was made easier by gradual relaxation of societal control exercised by tradition, institutions, and religion, proceeding in tandem with the economic and social development of European society. Improved communication aided the spread of these practices from city to country, from the upper to the lower classes, and from the more central to the peripheral regions.

In the following sections we shall consider mortality and fertility decline in more detail. Here we can conclude that, as with Watt's steam engine, the energy wasted by the traditional European demographic regime had, by the second half of the twentieth century, been enormously reduced. In the contemporary "economic" regime, a small number of births are sufficient to compensate for a small number of deaths; and yet, as we approach the end of this century, these societies seem no longer inclined to produce even those few births that would maintain demographic equilibrium.

2   From Disorder to Order: The Lengthening of Life

In the second half of the eighteenth century mortality began to show signs of decline: life lengthened and the hierarchical sequence of death, dictated by age, became firmly rooted. Out of the disorder of earlier times, due to random and unpredictable mortality, the processes of life became orderly. Two connected factors essentially explain the earlier capricious nature of death. The first was the frequent and irregular occurrence of mortality crises which, stemming from a variety of causes, slashed away sectors of all ages and classes, seriously upsetting the life of a society. Leaving aside the catastrophes brought about by the plague (the 1630 plague wiped out almost half of the population of Milan; that of 1656 half that of Genoa and Naples[3]), a doubling of the already high number of annual deaths (a frequent enough occurrence) was a traumatic experience for the social body. The second factor was the risk that the natural age-linked and chronological succession of death would be over-turned. Ignoring infant mortality – so frequent as to be considered almost normal – the probability that young or adolescent children would die before their parents was high. If we take, for example, French mortality of the mid-eighteenth century (e_0 between 25 and 28 in the period 1740–90), then we can estimate that the probability that a 40-year-old mother would outlive her 10-year-old son over the course of the following 20 years was 1 in 4. With today's low mortality, this same probability is almost insignificant.[4]

If I have emphasized the importance of the introduction of order and

[3]   L. Del Panta, *Le epidemie nella storia demografica italiana (secoli XIV–XIX)* (Loescher, Torino, 1980), pp. 160, 168.
[4]   According to the model life tables of Coale and Demeny (A. J. Coale and P. Demeny, *Regional Model Life Tables and Stable Populations* (Princeton University Press, Princeton, 1966)), for example, taking life expectancies of 27.5 years for women and 25.3 for men (model West), we obtain the following results. The probability that a 40-year-old woman lives to 60 is 0.536 and the probability that a 10-year-old boy lives to 30 is 0.764. During a 20-year period, a mother and son aged 40 and 10 present four possiblities: (1) that both survive, the probability for which is $0.536 \times 0.764 = 0.410$; (2) that the mother outlives the son, with a probability of $0.536 \times (1 - 0.764) = 0.126$; (3) that the son outlives the mother, with a probability of $0.764 \times (1 - 0.536) = 0.354$; (4) that both die, with a probability of $(1 - 0.536) \times (1 - 0.764) = 0.110$. The sum of the four probabilities of course equals 1. Should the mother survive (probability 0.536), she outlives her son in one case out of four ($0.126: 0.536 = 0.235$). Given present-day mortality, the probability of this happening is about 1 in 60.

regularity – I shall discuss the lengthening of life below – it is because these are essential prerequisites for development: "Perhaps only a society freed from the fear as well as from the material and spiritual consequences of sudden death was able to achieve that high rate of intellectual and technical progress without which population growth could not have been sustained."[5]

The decline in the intensity and frequency of mortality crises, of those sudden and short-term – from a few weeks to a couple of years in the case of a serious epidemic – increases of the normal death rate, constitutes the first aspect of the mortality transition. A wide range of events come under the general heading of "crisis": the destruction of war, famine, and recurring bouts of epidemic diseases. Figure 4.3 provides an example of the attenuation of crises. The solid line traces the progress of the Swedish crude death rate for the period 1735–1920; the dashed lines connect (somewhat arbitrarily) the maximum and minimum values. One can easily make out the progressive narrowing of the band of oscillation and also secular decline. Table 4.2 lists maximum and minimum values, and the differences between the two, of French and Swedish crude death rates for 25-year periods between the mid-eighteenth century and 1975. The progressive contraction of the range of variation is clear: normally between 10 and 20 until the end of the last century, it shrinks by a factor of 10, to 1 or 2, in the last period. The declining incidence of mortality crises in Western Europe during the eighteenth and

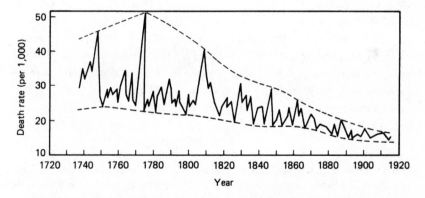

Figure 4.3 Attenuation of mortality swings in Sweden (1735–1920)

5   K. F. Helleiner, "The Population of Europe from the Black Death to the Eve of the Vital Revolution," in *The Cambridge Economic History of Europe* (Cambridge University Press, Cambridge, 1967), vol. 4: *The Economy of Expanding Europe in the Sixteenth and Seventeenth Centuries*, ed. E. E. Rich and C. Wilson.

Table 4.2 Maximum and minimum death rates (per 1000) in France and
Sweden (18th–20th centuries)

| | Sweden | | | France | | |
Period	Maximum	Minimum	Difference	Maximum	Minimum	Difference
1736–49	43.7	25.3	18.4	48.8	32.3	16.5
1750–74	52.5	22.4	30.1	40.6	29.5	11.1
1775–99	33.1	21.7	11.4	45.2	27.1	18.1
1800–24	40.0	20.8	19.2	34.4	24.0	10.4
1825–49	29.0	18.6	10.4	27.7	21.1	6.6
1850–74	27.6	16.3	11.3	27.4	21.4	6.0
1875–99	19.6	15.1	4.5	23.0	19.4	3.6
1900–24	18.0	11.4	6.6	22.3	16.7	5.6
1925–49	12.7	9.8	2.9	18.0	15.0	3.0
1950–74	10.5	9.5	1.3	12.9	10.5	2.4

early nineteenth centuries is well documented.[6] During the nineteenth century, improvements in social and economic organization were seconded by
progress in the control of infectious diseases, including the smallpox vaccine
(Jenner's discovery was made public in 1798 and spread rapidly in the first
half of the nineteenth century) and the identification of the pathogens
responsible for the most devastating epidemics.[7] Progress, however, was difficult. In the nineteenth century, epidemic disease (old ones like smallpox,
but also diseases new to Europe, like cholera) still took a heavy toll, as would
the influenza pandemic that followed the First World War; not to mention the
still more serious destruction of life caused by two world wars, civil wars in
the USSR and Spain, mass deportations, and the Holocaust.

Nonetheless, mortality declined, and not only because of the reduced
frequency and severity of crises but also because of a decline in the

---

[6] The literature on this subject is vast. I shall limit myself to the following citations:
for Italy, L. Del Panta, *Le epidemie*; for England, E. A. Wrigley and R. S. Schofield, *The
Population History of England, 1541–1871* (Edward Arnold, London, 1981); for Spain, V.
Perez Moreda, *Las crisis de mortalidad en España interior, siglos XVI–XIX* (Siglo
Veintiuno, Madrid, 1980); for France, G. Cabourdin, J.-N. Biraben, and A. Blum,
"Les crises démographiques," in *Histoire de la population française*, ed. J. Dupaquier
(PUF, Paris, 1988), vol. 2: *De la Renaissance à 1789*.
[7] On the great microbiological discoveries of the nineteenth century, see G. Penso,
La conquista del mondo invisibile (Feltrinelli, Milan, 1973).

Table 4.3 Life expectancy in several Western countries (1750–1985)

Country	1750–9	1800–9[a]	1850–9[b]	1880[c]	1900[d]	1930[e]	1950	1993[f]
England	36.9	37.3	40.0	43.3	48.2	60.8	69.2	76.2
France	27.9	33.9	39.8	42.1	47.4	56.7	66.5	77.4
Sweden	37.3	36.5	43.3	48.5	54.0	63.3	71.3	78.1
Germany	–	–	–	37.9	44.4	61.3	66.6	76.2
Italy	–	–	–	35.4	42.8	54.9	65.5	77.7
The Netherlands	–	32.2	36.8	41.7	49.9	64.6	71.8	77.0
USSR	–	–	–	27.7	32.4	42.9	64.0	65.4
United States (white population)	–	–	41.7	47.2	50.8	61.7	69.4	75.7
Australia	–	–	–	49.0	55.0	65.3	69.6	77.9
Japan	–	–	–	35.1	37.7	45.9	59.1	79.4

[a] For the Netherlands, 1816–25.
[b] For the Netherlands, the average of 1841–50 and 1851–60; for the US, 1850.
[c] For Sweden, Germany, and the Netherlands, the average of 1871–80 and 1881–90; for England, 1876–80; for Japan, 1891.
[d] For England, Sweden, Germany, the Netherlands, and Australia, the average of 1891–1900 and 1900–1; for Russia, 1897.
[e] For Sweden, the average of 1926–30 and 1931–5; for Germany, 1932–4, for the USSR, 1926–7; for the Netherlands, the average of 1921–30 and 1931–40.
[f] For England and Wales, 1991; for the US, 1992; for the USSR: Russian Federation.
Source: L. I. Dublin, A. J. Lotka, and M. Spiegelman, *Length of Life* (Ronald Press, New York, 1949), pp. 61, 346–51; for the United States see also A. J. Coale and M. Zelnick, *New Estimates of Fertility and Population in the United States* (Princeton University Press, Princeton, 1963), pp. 8–9, 56–7; for Japan, Z. Nanjo and K. Kobayashi, *Cohort Life Tables*, NUPRI Research Paper no. 20 (Tokyo, 1985). For 1993; C. de Guibert-Lantoine and A. Monnier, "La Conjoncture démographique," *Population*, 4–5, July–October 1995.

probability of death at the various ages during normal periods. Table 4.3 reports the progress of life expectancy (e_0) for some of the major developed countries between the mid-eighteenth century and the present day. Initial values, which for some countries are below 30, gradually increase to about 75 in the 1980s. Some countries show noticeable improvement from the mid-eighteenth century; almost all make considerable progress before the impact of medical discoveries could be felt.[8]

For our purposes, two aspects of mortality decline are particularly significant: first, the effect that the reduced probability of death at various ages had on life expectancy; the greatest reductions came in the first years

[8] T. McKeown, *The Modern Rise of Population* (Edward Arnold, London, 1976).

of life due to improved infant care and measures taken to block the spread of infectious diseases. The second, related, aspect was the decline in deaths due to various causes, primarily infectious diseases.

This picture of mortality decline has been confirmed by Caselli. Table 4.4 provides a breakdown by cause of the lengthening of life expectancy in England and Wales between 1871 and 1951 (from 40.8 to 68.4) and in Italy between 1881 and 1951 (from 33.7 to 66.5).[9] The results for these two countries, in spite of their different social histories, are similar. In both cases about two-thirds of the gains in life expectancy are due to the control of infectious diseases (especially among infants: measles, scarlet fever, diphtheria), respiratory diseases (bronchitis, pneumonia, influenza), and intestinal diseases (diarrhoea, enteritis). From the point of view of age, about two-thirds of the lengthening of life expectancy (a bit less for

Table 4.4 Life expectancy gains in England (1871–1951) and Italy (1881–1951) broken down by contributing causes of death

	England		Italy	
	Gains in e_0		*Gains in e_0*	
Causes of death	*(years)*	*(%)*	*(years)*	*(%)*
Infectious diseases	11.8	42.9	12.7	40.1
Bronchitis, pneumonia, influenza	3.6	13.1	4.7	14.8
Diseases of the circulatory system	0.6	2.2	0.8	2.5
Diarrhoea and enteritis	2.0	7.3	3.4	10.5
Diseases of infancy	1.8	6.5	2.3	7.3
Accidents	0.7	2.5	0.5	1.6
Tumors	−0.8	−2.9	−0.4	−1.3
Other diseases	7.8	28.4	7.7	24.3
Total	27.5	100.0	31.7	100.0

Life expectancy was 40.8 years in England in 1871 and 68.4 in 1951; in Italy it was 33.8 in 1881 and 65.5 in 1951.

Source: G. Caselli, "Transition sanitaire et structure par cause de mortalité" (paper presented at the IUSSP conference, "Medicine and the Decline of Mortality," Annecy, France, 1988).

[9] G. Caselli, "Transition sanitaire et structure par cause de mortalité" (paper presented to the IUSSP conference, "Medicine and the Decline of Mortality," Annecy, France, 1988).

England, a bit more for Italy) derive from mortality decline in the first 15 years of life. Improvements in the older ages, over 40, account for only a sixth or seventh of the total increase.

Mortality transition in the developed countries has been relatively slow. For example, the date at which female life expectancy reached 50 (at which level a cohort's losses due to mortality between birth and the onset of reproductive age is still considerable, between 20 and 25 percent, and the "waste" of reproductive potential is about 30 percent) varies between 1861 for Norway and the 1930s for Bulgaria, Portugal, and the Soviet Union. The median date for European countries is 1903.[10]

Gains in life expectancy accelerated until the middle of the present century. Between 1750 and 1850 England, France, and Sweden gained less than a month of life expectancy for each calendar year. These three countries, together with the Netherlands and the United States, gained about two months per year between 1850–9 and 1880. In the following four periods the average annual gains for the ten countries listed in table 4.3 were 3.3 months (1800–1900), 4.6 (1900–30), 5.8 (1930–50), and 2.6 (1950–87). The transition is not yet finished, though its pace has slowed after a period of maximum progress (1930–50) during which the disasters of the Second World War did not succeed in blocking the pharmacological successes (sulpha drugs and penicillin) of the 1930s and 1940s.

The mortality decline of the last century and a half has proceeded in tandem with economic and social progress (a vague expression which includes the expansion of those material, technical, and cultural resources which improve survival). It is the task of social and demographic historians to sort out the when and where of the dominant factors of this decline, which probably include social and cultural factors (methods of childrearing, personal hygiene, improved organization of markets, and so forth) in the first phase of the transition; economic factors (improvements in the material quality of life, improvements in infrastructure) in the second; and medical, scientific, and behavioral factors in the last and ongoing phase. Though, of course, in every period a combination of factors acted together.

---

[10] Values of e_0 equal to 50 are obtained by linear interpolation (and in some cases extrapolation) of series for the various countries found in L. I. Dublin, A. J. Lotka, and M. Spiegelman, *Length of Life* (Ronald Press, New York, 1949). For Sweden, Denmark, Belgium, the Netherlands, Switzerland, Australia, and the United States the date at which female life expectancy reached 50 falls between 1880 and 1900; for England, France, and Germany it is between 1900 and 1910; for Finland, Austria, and Italy between 1910 and 1920; for Greece, Hungary, and the USSR after 1920.

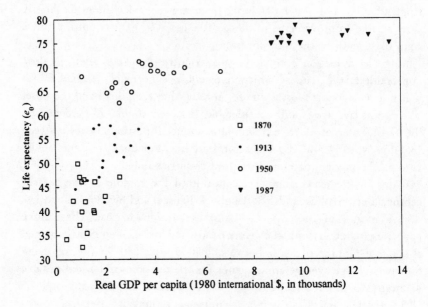

Figure 4.4   Relation between real GDP per capita and life expectancy (e_0)
for 16 industrialized countries (1870, 1913, 1950, 1987)

Figure 4.4 offers a simplified picture of the relation between the
increase in life expectancy in 16 Western countries (see table 4.8) and a
rough indicator of material well-being, namely estimates of the value of
goods and services produced (real gross domestic product, or GDP) per
capita, expressed in 1980 international dollars. These values have recently
been recalculated retrospectively using a uniform method.[11] The graph
compares the value of e_0 with that of the per capita GDP for 1870, 1913,
1950, and 1987 for each country and includes 64 points (4 for each country)
which describe the long-term relationship between life expectancy and
material well-being. I shall pass over discussion of the apparent simplifications upon which the graph is based[12] and concentrate on the results.
These are surprisingly clear: in the first phase of the transition increased

[11]   A. Maddison, *The World Economy in the Twentieth Century* (OECD Development Center, Paris, 1989). Other sources used below do employ GNP (Gross National Product)
which includes foreign-earned income.
[12]   The most significant of these is that the two variables are not independent from
one another: while it is true that mortality depends in part on well-being, it is also the
case that there would not have been material progress without mortality decline.

production corresponds to considerable improvement in life expectancy, improvements which become progressively more modest until, in the final phase, even large increases in wealth are accompanied by small gains in e_0. The fact that in the final phase of the transition countries with differing levels of per capita production have nearly identical levels of e_0 reveals that, beyond a certain limit, the availability of goods has virtually no influence on survival. In 1987 the United States had a per capita GDP 50 percent higher than that of Italy, but US life expectancy (74.9) was slightly below Italian (75.9). This is not to say, of course, that greater well-being will not result in increased life expectancy, but these increases will probably be linked to "immaterial" progress – changes in individual behavior or scientific advances opening previously unimagined horizons. The simple increase of production as measured by GDP has ceased to play a role, at least in this historical phase. In the first phase of the transition increased production translated into greatly improved survival, for obvious reasons: more food, better clothing, better houses, and more medical care have a notable effect on those who are malnourished, scantily clothed, poorly housed, and forced to trust fate in case of sickness. On the other hand, when increased production benefits already prosperous populations the effects are minimal or nonexistent, if not negative, as may be the case with overeating and environmental deterioration.

3   From High to Low Fertility

Fertility decline, like that of mortality, was a gradual and geographically varied process. I have already discussed the combination of factors, both biological (which determine birth intervals) and social (which determine the portion of the reproductive period devoted to childbearing: age at marriage, proportion marrying), which regulate the "production" of children (see chapter 1, section 4).[13] As we have seen, these factors were able to significantly influence fertility, so that prior to the transition European levels ranged from a low of about 30 per thousand to a high above 45.

---

[13]   There exists, of course, fertility outside of marriage, generally (and mistakenly) called illegitimate. Historically, levels of illegitimate fertility in the West have been insignificant as (at least until the last few decades) the vast majority of reproduction has taken place within the context of marriage.

Nonetheless, voluntary fertility control[14] was the decisive factor in fertility decline – certainly a more efficient method than extended breast-feeding, late marriage, or remaining single.

Figure 4.5 records the effectiveness of the marital check in Europe during the period leading up to the fertility decline. Low nuptiality female populations occupy the upper left portion of the graph: they are characterized by a high age at first marriage (over 27 in Switzerland, Belgium, Sweden, and Norway) and a low proportion of women who have married before the end of the reproductive period (a little over 80 percent). In the lower right of the graph are high nuptiality populations (Romania, Bulgaria), with low age at first marriage (around 20) and a high percentage married (over 95 percent). In the premodern age there existed a fairly strong (and inverse) relationship between the two components of nuptiality, as revealed by the graph.

Figure 4.5 gives an idea of the variability of pre-transition nuptiality and, indirectly, the degree to which it controlled the production of births. And while the level of control was considerable, it was not sufficient to regulate fertility during the rapid social transformation of the previous century; more efficient control was provided by voluntary fertility limitation. Birth control, for a time virtually unknown except to select groups (nobility, the urban bourgeoisie),[15] appeared in France and a few restricted areas toward the end of the eighteenth century[16] and spread rapidly throughout Europe during

[14] It is a conceptually subtle distinction that separates voluntary from nonvoluntary fertility control. Demographers call fertility which is not voluntarily controlled "natural fertility." Its level can vary considerably as a function of the behavior of couples or mothers (sexual taboos, frequency of intercourse, length of breast-feeding, and so on – see chapter 1, section 4). Nonetheless, these types of behavior are presumably "structural" and do not reflect the desire of couples to achieve a particular family size; procreational behavior does not vary as a function of the number of children already born. Voluntary fertility control by means of contraception or coitus interruptus, on the other hand, has as its aim the production of certain number of children. Control is practiced above all by couples who have reached the desired number, so that reproductive behavior tends to change as a function of children born. A decline in the average age of the mother at last birth or in fertility at the youngest ages is a sign of fertility control in a population; both situations lead to a change in the "shape" of the fertility curve by age.

[15] M. Livi-Bacci, "Social-Group Forerunners of Fertility Control in Europe," in *The Decline of Fertility in Europe*, ed. A. J. Coale and S. C. Watkins (Princeton University Press, Princeton, 1986).

[16] Urban fertility was generally lower than rural, though this was due in part to the particular makeup of urban population and its high mobility. However, contrary to the model of slower rural decline, fertility began to drop in some areas of Hungary from the late eighteenth century. See R. Andorka, "La prévention des naissances en Hongrie dans la région Ormansag depuis la fin du XVIIIe siècle," *Population*, 26 (1971), pp. 63–78.

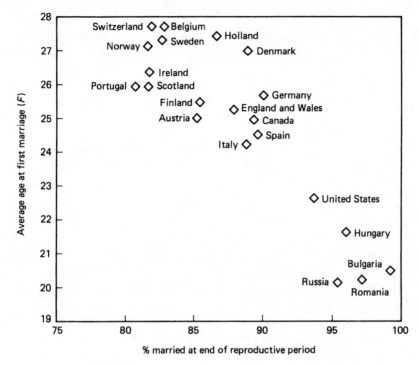

Figure 4.5 Relation between average age at marriage and proportion of women married at the end of the reproductive period for several countries; generations born toward the end of the nineteenth century

Source: P. Festy, *La fécondité des pays occidentaux de 1870 à 1970*, PUF, Paris, 1979, p. 29.

the second half of the nineteenth – though some rural and peripheral areas seem only to have adopted these practices in the middle part of this century.

The European fertility transition from 1870 to 1960 is depicted in the graphs of figures 4.6a–e, which are based upon a recent international study of European fertility decline.[17] We have used graphs of this type previously (figures 1.8 and 4.1). Here, however, the axes are changed, and the curves are of "isofertility": Each curve represents the locus of those points that combine

---

[17] The general aims, characteristics, and results of this study, directed by Ansley Coale and coordinated by the Office of Population Research at Princeton, are summarized in Coale and Watkins, *Decline of Fertility*. The figure 4.6 graphs (a–e) include points for the following countries: Belgium, Denmark, England and Wales, Finland, France, Germany, Hungary, Ireland, Italy, the Netherlands, Norway, Portugal, Scotland, Spain, Sweden, and Switzerland.

legitimate fertility (the abscissa) and nuptiality (the ordinate) to give the same "general fertility" (an index of the rate of production of children, strongly correlated with the average number of children per woman, *TFR*). The indices of legitimate fertility (I_g) and nuptiality (I_m), explained in a note,[18] tell us the following:

1   The index of legitimate fertility measures the intensity of child-bearing within marriage as it relates to the maximum value ever encountered in a normally constituted population (value equal to one). Prior to the spread of voluntary fertility control, I_g values generally fall between 0.6 and 1 as a function of those factors (the length of breast-feeding and others discussed in chapter 1, section 5) which determine the birth interval. The spread of birth control usually reveals itself by a "continuous" decline of legitimate fertility. In the above study a 10 percent decline relative to an initial stable level is considered an unequivocal sign of control. Values of 0.5 and less are definitely those of countries practicing fertility limitation.

2   The nuptiality index is simply a measure of the proportion of child-bearing age women who are married (weighted for potential fertility

---

[18]   The indices I_m, I_f, I_g (indices of the proportion of childbearing age women who are married, general fertility, and legitimate fertility) and I_h (a similar index of illegitimate fertility not discussed here) are calculated in the following manner. f_i, g_i, and h_i represent, respectively, total births, legitimate births, and illegitimate births per woman of age interval *i*. Similarly, w_i, m_i, and u_i represent total women, married women, and unmarried women in the same age interval. F_i is the fertility coefficient for the model population, namely Hutterite women married in the period 1921–30, a group notable for having the highest fertility ever recorded in a regularly constituted population. Given the above information, the following indices can be calculated:

General fertility	$I_f = \Sigma f_i w_i / \Sigma F_i w_i$	(1)
Legitimate fertility	$I_g = \Sigma g_i m_i / \Sigma F_i m_i$	(2)
Illegitimate fertility	$I_h = \Sigma h_i u_i / \Sigma F_i u_i$	(3)
Proportion of women married	$I_m = \Sigma F_i m_i / \Sigma F_i w_i$	(4)

The numerators of 1, 2, and 3 are, respectively, the total births, legitimate births, and illegitimate births of the population studied. The values of F_i are: ages 15–19 = 0.300, 20–24 = 0.550, 25–29 = 0.502, 30–34 = 0.447, 35–39 = 0.406, 40–44 = 0.222, 45–49 = 0.061. The four indices are related by the following equation: $I_f = I_g \times I_m + I_h \times (1 - I_m)$. When I_h is very low, say below 0.05 (or 5 percent), as has traditionally been the case for all Western populations, then the index of general fertility closely approximates $I_g \times I_m$. All the indices have values below 1. In the case of I_g the value of the index represents the ratio between the legitimate fertility of the population studied and the theoretical maximum of the Hutterites. Values below 0.6 generally indicate a degree of voluntary fertility control.

at the various ages). It is then a synthesis of the effects of age at marriage and proportions marrying (as well as of widowhood, declining in the period considered due to reduced mortality) presented in figure 4.5.

The graphs of figures 4.6a-e illustrate the progressive decline of general fertility in European countries as a function of the indices described above. In 1870, fertility levels varied considerably: from below 0.3 for France (where fertility control was already well established) to about 0.5 in Eastern European countries (not shown in graph) characterized by high nuptiality and high legitimate fertility. Excepting France, the range of positions occupied by the different countries at this date is due more to nuptiality variation than to that of legitimate fertility; the area enclosing these points is stretched vertically. The decline of general fertility at successive dates, on the other hand, is due primarily to a drop in legitimate fertility as a result of the spread of birth control; the area acquires a progressively more horizontal orientation, and in 1960 general fertility levels are about 0.2. In more than one case the decline of legitimate fertility is accompanied by an increase in nuptiality. The latter phenomenon can be interpreted as a reaction to the availability of an efficient means of fertility control (contraception), which rendered the nuptial check superfluous and relaxed inhibitions to marriage.

The point at which fertility registered a 10 percent drop relative to a previous stable level (and without subsequent increases) signified the onset of irreversible decline. This date is an important moment in the demographic transition and signals the substitution of the traditional system of fertility regulation (marriage) with a new one (contraception). It occurred first in France, in 1827, and latest in European Russia and Ireland, in 1922 – almost a century apart. For Belgium, Denmark, Great Britain, Germany, the Netherlands, and Switzerland the date falls between 1880 and 1900; for Sweden, Norway, Austria, and Hungary between 1900 and 1910; and for Italy, Greece, Finland, Portugal, and Spain between 1910 and 1920. The date of 10 percent decline has also been calculated for approximately seven hundred European provinces or districts; their distribution by decade is reported in figure 4.7. There are essentially two distributions: that on the left represents French departments which clearly preceded the rest of Europe, beginning fertility decline in the period between 1780 and 1850; that on the right represents the rest of Europe. In 60 percent of all cases the date of decline falls between 1890 and 1920; the most crowded decade is 1900–10. The last areas only began decisive decline in the 1940s.

A complete geography of the transition of legitimate fertility, like that of

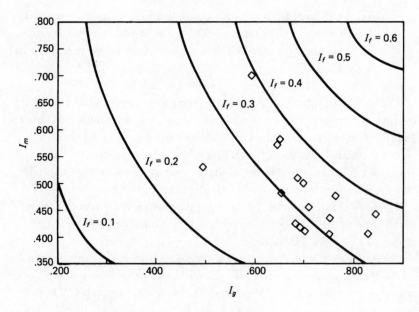

Figure 4.6a   1870

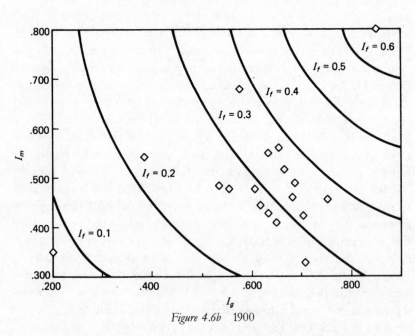

Figure 4.6b   1900

Figure 4.6   Relation between general fertility (I_f), legitimate fertility (I_g), and proportion married (I_m) in 16 European countries (1870–1960)

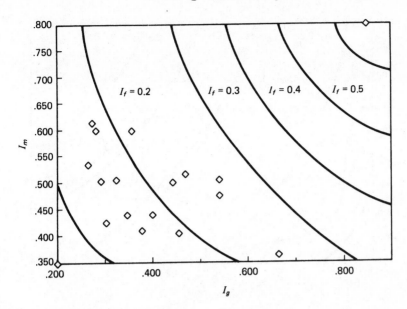

Figure 4.6c 1930

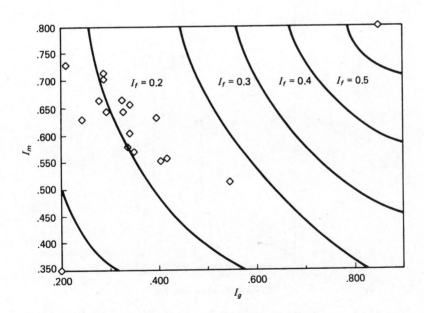

Figure 4.6d 1960

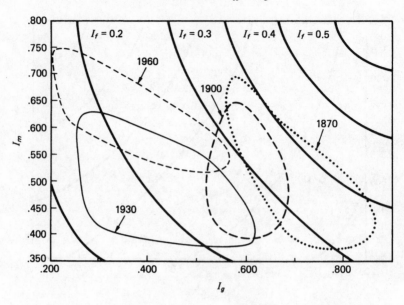

Figure 4.6e   Fertility areas for 16 countries (1870, 1900, 1930, 1960)

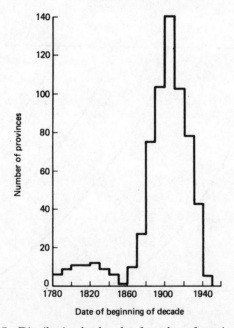

Figure 4.7   Distribution by decade of number of provinces of Europe
experiencing 10 percent decline in legitimate fertility (I_g)

Source: A. J. Coale and S. C. Watkins, eds, *The Decline of Fertility in Europe* (Princeton
University Press, Princeton, 1986), p. 38.

the detailed Princeton study, reveals a process of decline which began in France and spread to the more developed regions of Europe, including Catalonia, Piedmont, Liguria, and Tuscany in the south and England, Belgium, Germany, and Scandinavia in the center-north; subsequently it reached more generally the regions of southern and Eastern Europe. The most peripheral regions (some areas of Mediterranean Europe, the Balkans, Ireland) and areas geographically central but culturally traditional (certain areas of the Alps) were the last strongholds of high fertility, gradually conquered in the middle of this century.[19]

We may now turn from this general, long-range view of the fertility transition to consideration of the indices of the production of births and their evolution in time. The most suitable index is the TFR (average number or children per woman), which for some countries has been calculated for generations of women born at 25-year intervals (table 4.5). Levels range from a high near or above five children per woman for generations born around 1850 or before in England and Wales, Germany, and the Netherlands, to a low of about two children for the generations born around 1950 (who have already completed their reproductive cycle). It is also certain that the generations born in the years after 1950 will have a level of completed fertility well below two and so significantly below replacement.[20] Current fertility levels have become a cause of concern. Do they mark the beginning of a prolonged period of very low fertility that might jeopardize the development of European society or simply the low point of a cycle, soon to be followed by increase?

It will be interesting to compare, as we did for life expectancy, TFR[21] and per capita GDP for the 16 industrialized countries at the usual four dates: 1870, 1913, 1950, and 1987 (figure 4.8). The relationship is just the reverse of that

---

[19] Among the results of the Princeton study are maps of fertility and nuptiality trends from the second half of the previous century to 1960. See Coale and Watkins, *Decline of Fertility.* For more detailed "geography," see the national monographs, all published by the Princeton University Press, for the following countries: France (E. van de Walle), Great Britain (M. Teitelbaum), Germany (M. Knodel), USSR (B. Anderson, A. J. Coale, E. Harm), Italy (M. Livi-Bacci), Belgium (R. Lesthaeghe), Portugal (M. Livi-Bacci).

[20] It is estimated that women born around 1960 in Western Europe will have on average 1.7 to 1.8 children, a figure well below the hypothetical level of generational replacement, which is about 2.1.

[21] The values of TFR used here are "period" rates as opposed to the "cohort" rates used in table 4.6. Period rates are calculated by combining fertility levels for women of different ages at the same date (and so born on different dates and having different fertility histories) and so emphasize the temporary influence of economic factors.

Table 4.5 Average number of children per woman (*TFR*) for several generations in Western countries (1750–1950)[a]

Country	1750	1775	1800	1825	1850	1875	1900	1925	1950
Sweden	4.21	4.34	4.68	4.40	4.28	3.51	1.90	2.05	1.98
England and Wales	5.28	5.87	5.54	5.05	4.56	3.35	1.96	2.15	2.00
Germany[b]	–	–	–	–	5.17	3.98	2.08	2.06	1.65
France	–	–	–	3.42	3.27	2.60	2.14	2.59	2.13
The Netherlands	–	–	–	–	4.98	3.98	2.86	2.76	1.85
Spain	–	–	–	–	–	4.64	3.38	2.51	2.18
Italy[c]	–	–	–	–	4.67	4.50	3.14	2.27	1.90
United States	–	–	–	–	4.48	3.53	2.48	2.94	1.90
Australia	–	–	–	–	–	3.22	2.44	2.98	2.00

[a] Periods are centered on the indicated dates. For the Netherlands, 1841–50 for 1850; for Australia, 1876–85 for 1875.
[b] For Germany, 1925 and 1950 values refer only to West Germany.
[c] Italian values for 1850 and 1875 are based on a 1931 fertility study.
Sources: P. Festy, *La fecondité des pays occidentaux de 1870 à 1970* (PUF, Paris 1979). J.-P Sardon, "Le remplacement des générations en Europe depuis le début du siècle," *Population*, 45 (1990). For England: E. A. Wrigley and R. Schofield, *The Population History of England, 1541–1871* (Edward Arnold, London, 1981). Data for the 1950 generations are estimates, see EUROSTAT, *Demographic Statistics 1994* (Luxembourg, 1994).

between per capita production and e_0: the growth of per capita GDP is initially accompanied by sustained fertility decline; subsequently, GDP increases combine with ever smaller reductions in fertility until the current state of economic maturity is reached and fertility is essentially unchanging. We should not accept as "law" a relationship observed during an historical period in which increased well-being seems to have favored the spread of voluntary fertility control. The present-day lack of correlation between fertility and income levels suggests that other complex motivations, only slightly connected with the availability of material goods, govern the fertility decisions of couples.

During the past two centuries social and economic transformation has been an important factor in fertility decline, confirmed by its generally slower progress in peripheral and backward areas. There have of course been important exceptions which, as often happens in the social sciences, have frustrated those scholars looking for simple solutions to complex problems. The following are a few examples from the many which the literature offers: (1) In rural France, fertility decline began much before it did in England, a richer and more advanced country in the midst of the Industrial Revolution. (2) In many

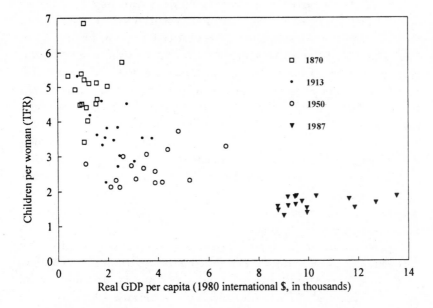

Figure 4.8   Relation between real GDP per capita and children per woman (*TFR*) in 16 industrialized countries (1870, 1913, 1950, 1987)

countries the rate of fertility decline is only minimally explained by social and economic indices, such as levels of education, rurality, industrialization, or urbanization. (3) It is often the case that cultural factors – membership in a linguistic or ethnic group, religious or political affiliation – seem to be more significant to fertility decline than economic factors.

But if we look at the entire process, we see that no population has maintained high levels of fertility for long in the face of increasing well-being and declining mortality. The demographic transition has clearly been an integral part of the transformation of European society.

4   *European Emigration: A Unique Phenomenon*

The synthesis of the transition I am presenting here would not be complete without reference to the great currents of migration that populated two continents while at the same time lowering European demographic pressure. I have already discussed the importance of the availability of space (and so of land) in shaping European demographic growth prior to the Industrial

Revolution. At the end of the eighteenth century, more than 8 million people of European extraction, about equally divided, inhabited the two halves of the American continent. Over three centuries Europe had by means of Iberian and British imperialism established the political, economic, and demographic foundations for the coming mass migration. The causes of that migration were both economic and demographic: economic because the Industrial Revolution and technological progress increased productivity and so rendered masses of workers superfluous, especially in rural areas; and demographic because the transition entailed a large demographic "multiplier," which is to say it sped up population growth, and so worsened the problems created by economic changes. The availability of land and space in North and South America and to a lesser degree in Oceania combined with the demand for labor in these new societies created the conditions for massive migration.

The following are estimates for European transoceanic migration between 1846 and 1932 from the major countries of departure: 18 million from Great Britain and Ireland, 11.1 million from Italy, 6.5 million from Spain and Portugal, 5.2 million from Austria-Hungary, 4.9 million from Germany, 2.9 million from Poland and Russia, and 2.1 million from Sweden and Norway. This flood of emigration, which was of course balanced to some degree by a countercurrent of return migration, went primarily to the United States (34.2 million), Argentina and Uruguay (7.1 million), Canada (5.2 million), Brazil (4.4 million), Australia and New Zealand (3.5 million), and Cuba (0.9 million). In the first 15 years of this century the annual rate of European emigration exceeded 3 per thousand, equal to about one-third of natural increase.[22]

Between 1861 and 1961, net Italian population loss due to emigration was 8 million. Imagining that this population had grown at the same rate as that of the Italian population in Italy (a fairly restrictive hypothesis), it would in 1981 have numbered 14 million, about 25 percent of the national population at that time.[23]

---

[22] Chesnais, *La transition démographique*, p. 164.

[23] By combining US immigration statistics with census results (which asked for the nationality of those censused), I have been able to calculate that between 1880 and 1950, 50.2 percent of Italian immigrants returned to Italy after stays of varying lengths. M. Livi-Bacci, *L'immigrazione e l'assimilazione degli italiani negli Stati Uniti* (Giuffrè, Milano, 1961), pp. 34–5. In order to calculate the present-day population descended from net Italian migration in the period 1861–1961, I applied the Italian growth rate for each decade to the net migration for the same period, supposing that it was maintained (by both the first migrants and their descendants) up until 1981.

These brief notes should give an idea of the importance of emigration for the European demographic system. All in all, from the viewpoint of aggregate economic growth, this emigration was certainly beneficial. It made possible rapid economic growth in the areas of emigration, utilization of labor where it could be most productive, and a general increase of resources both in Europe and overseas.

Figure 4.9, taken from Chesnais, compares demographic increase in continental Europe with the intensity of emigration about 25 years later, a period which corresponds more or less to the average age of the emigrants. There is a striking relationship between growth rate increases and decreases and emigration trends a quarter century later. Emigration serves to lower demographic pressure caused by the influx of larger cohorts of workers into the labor market.[24] A strong overseas demand for workers is of course the complement to this process for the export of excess population. From the point of view of the demographic development of Europe, the implications

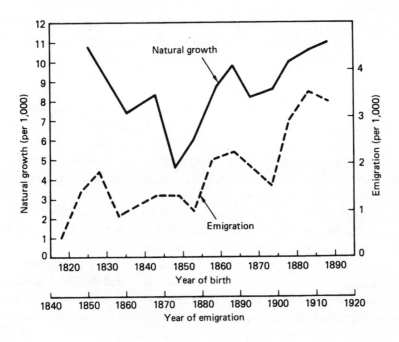

Figure 4.9 Emigration and natural growth for continental Europe

[24] Chesnais, *La transition démographique*, pp. 169–72.

are several, and not only quantitative. These implications, however, relate primarily to the nature of the emigrant selection process and would take us beyond the scope of the present study.

A word on the causes of European migration is, however, in order. We have already referred to these in general terms: the creation of surplus population which the economic system could not absorb (figure 4.9), the availability of land and capital combined with a strong demand for labor in America, and the "shrinking" of the world due to easier and more rapid transportation. But this analysis needs to be pursued further in order better to understand the reasons behind the gigantic transfer of population. In particular, three complex phenomena and their interrelationships need to be identified: first, rural population growth, the availability of land both in Europe and outside of it, and agricultural productivity; second, the rural population dynamic; and third, the contemporary growth of nonagricultural activities.

With regard to the first point, in the latter half of the eighteenth century about three-quarters of the population of all European countries except England, which was rapidly industrializing, were employed in agriculture. This proportion dropped rapidly though not uniformly during the following century: in 1850 it was about one-half and by the beginning of the twentieth century about a third. Nonetheless, the size of the agricultural population grew during the first part of the century because of rapid European demographic growth (a doubling during the course of the century) and stabilized in the latter part.[25] Demographic expansion increased demand for food, and this demand was for the most part met thanks to the increase in cultivated land. New land was available in northern Europe and also east of the Elbe; elsewhere the usual fallow periods were gradually eliminated. Productivity, however, remained low: in the mid-nineteenth century the wheat yield for one hectare of land was about a ton; by the beginning of the twentieth century this figure had increased by a modest 20 percent.[26] The scarcity of land – which multiplied the number of peasants who had none – combined with its slowly-increasing productivity would have imposed new "Malthusian" limits on population had it not been for the vast expansion of land cultivated outside of Europe. Grigg has calculated that arable land in Europe grew from 140 to 147 million hectares between 1860 and 1910; in that same period the land cultivated in Russia grew from 49 million to 114 million

[25]   P. Bairoch, *International Historical Statistics*, vol. 1: *The Working Population and its Structure* (New York, 1969).

[26]   D. Grigg, *The Transformation of Agriculture in the West* (Basil Blackwell, Oxford, 1992), table 4.2, p. 35.

hectares, in the United States from 66 to 140 million, and in Canada and Argentina from insignificant levels to 33 million.[27] The low production costs in the new areas of European settlement and the lowering of shipping costs were in fact the basis of a fall in agricultural prices that plunged the European countryside into crisis beginning in the 1870s. Finally, while the productivity of land grew sluggishly, the injection of capital into the countryside and mechanization combined to increase the productivity of labor. And masses of peasants characterized by limited proprietorship and increased productivity of labor translates into a rapid increase in surplus labor, and so workers frequently found themselves torn away from traditional activities and lifestyles and facing crisis situations. The pool of potential emigrants as a result grew.[28]

The second point refers to the population dynamic of rural areas where birth control spread with a notable lag as compared to the cities, fostering higher rates of natural population increase during the period of the transition. In some cases – analogous to the situation in many developing countries – the first phases of the transition and the attendant improvements in sanitary conditions led to an increase rather than a decrease in fertility.[29]

The third point refers to the rapidity with which new nonagricultural activities sprang into existence in Europe and so provided an alternative outlet for rural population excess. This phenomenon is not of course independent of the stage of evolution of agriculture; indeed the two are intimately connected: tools, machines, and fertilizers which had previously been produced by agricultural concerns came gradually to be more efficiently created by the industrial system. But it was the growth of this latter system and of predominantly urban service activities that created new opportunities for surplus rural labor. In those areas where this process occurred relatively early, emigration was low or in any case short-lived; by contrast, in those areas where it took place relatively late, emigration tended to be massive.

---

[27] Ibid., table 2.2, p. 19.

[28] See D. Massey, *Economic Development and International Migration in Comparative Perspective* (Commission for the Study of International Migration and Cooperative Economic Development, Washington, D.C., 1990).

[29] A typical case is that of Venetia which, in the 1920s, was the last region of north-central Italy to initiate fertility control. Legitimate fertility (I_g) increased considerably in the period just prior to the onset of decline (almost 20 percent between 1881 and 1911). Factors of increase included improved living conditions and the elimination of pellagra, a vitamin deficiency-related disease resulting from excessive dependence on corn (maize). See M. Livi-Bacci, "Fertility, Nutrition and Pellagra: Italy during the Vital Revolution", *Journal of Interdisciplinary History*, 16 (winter 1986).

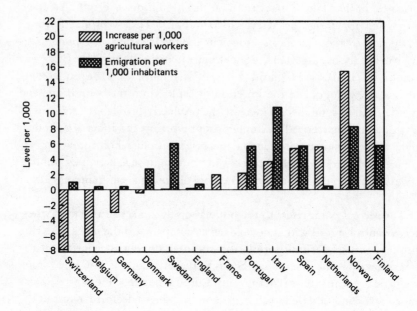

Figure 4.10   Increase of agricultural employment (1870–1910) and
emigration (1900–10)

Figure 4.10 compares emigration levels (particularly high at the beginning of this century) with the rate of growth of agricultural employment
in 13 European countries during the last 30 years of the nineteenth
century. The two variables correlate directly: transoceanic emigration
was low from those countries where agricultural employment declined
or remained stationary (Switzerland, Belgium, Germany, Denmark, and
England), while there was much emigration from those countries where
rural employment grew (Finland, Norway, Italy, and Spain). Figures 4.11a–
b consider the same problem from another point of view: the great wave
of emigration, propeled by rural population surplus, ebbed when the
latter became less significant. The ratio between those employed in
manufacturing industries and those employed in agriculture serves as an
index of the changing situation. When this ratio is greater than one (that
is, when those employed in manufacturing exceed those in agriculture),
then the pressure to emigrate becomes weaker and eventually disappears
as the modern sector of the economy – which initially consisted of the
manufacturing industries but then grew to include transportation,
services, building, and so on – becomes sufficiently important to absorb

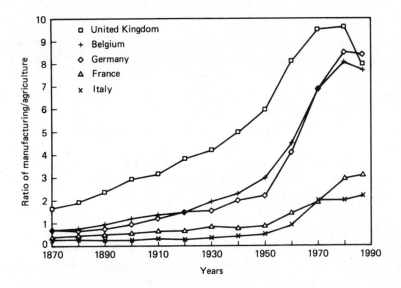

Figure 4.11a United Kingdom, Belgium, Germany, France, Italy

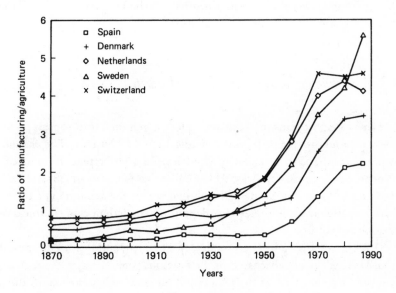

Figure 4.11b Spain, Denmark, the Netherlands, Sweden, Switzerland

Figure 4.11 Ratio of those employed in manufacturing industries to those engaged in agriculture (1870–1987)

the remaining agricultural surplus population. Great Britain, from which mass emigration had long ceased, well exceeded a one-to-one ratio during the late nineteenth century. Prior to World War I, this ratio was surpassed by those countries undergoing a rapid process of industrialization: Belgium, where mass emigration had never taken hold, and Germany and Switzerland, where it had ceased. Mediterranean countries like Italy and Spain, where industrialization came late, only exceeded this ratio in the 1960s and 1970s, at which time large-scale emigration came to an end. In other countries where manufacturing industries came to dominate the national economy in the period between the wars (Denmark, Sweden, the Netherlands), emigration had been halted first by receiving country restrictions and then by the economic crisis.

The experience of Europe – throughout the nineteenth century and for much of the twentieth the main source of population for the "neo-Europes" overseas – cannot simply be applied to the present day. The current situation of demographic pressure which fuels migration from the poorer to the richer countries differs fundamentally in that "empty" areas open to immigration no longer exist and national policies severely limit the possibilities for human movement. We can hypothesize, however, that the incentive to emigrate from these countries should rapidly diminish as the modern sectors of the economy come to dominate the agricultural.

5   A Summing Up: The Results of the Transition

The demographic transition and associated migration left European population profoundly changed, both dynamically and structurally. The changes associated with the achievement of a high level of demographic efficiency can be expressed by several indices. Table 4.6 lists these for Italy in 1881 and 1981, approximately the beginning and ending dates for the demographic transition in that country. With certain adaptations the Italian case is typical of Europe as a whole.

Table 4.6 requires a brief commentary. The birth and death rates repeat what we have already discussed in the previous pages, namely the reduced intensity, by about two-thirds, of both phenomena; at the same time, life expectancy more than doubled as survivorship increased immensely. In 1981, 98 percent of each generation arrived at reproductive age (15 years) and 48 percent achieved the respectable age of 80. At the earlier date these figures were 58 and 6 percent. Clearly these dramatic changes effect important

Table 4.6 The results of the transition: demographic indices for Italy (1881 and 1981)

Demographic index	ca. 1881	ca. 1981
Births (per 1,000 population)	36.5	11.0
Deaths (per 1,000)	28.7	9.6
Natural increase (per 1,000)	7.8	1.4
Life expectancy (e_0, M and F)	35.4	74.4
Survivorship at age 15 (per 1,000)	584	982
Survivorship at age 50 (per 1,000)	414	936
Survivorship at age 80 (per 1,000)	65.0	422
Age at first marriage (F)	24.1	24.0
Average age at childbirth	(30.0)	27.6
Average age at birth of last child	(39.0)	30.0
Unmarried (F) at age 50 (%)	12.1	10.2
Children per woman (*TFR*)	4.98	1.58
Net reproduction rate	1.26	0.76
Intrinsic rate of natural increase (%)	0.77	−0.99
Population 0–14 (%)	32.2	21.4
Population 15–64 (%)	62.7	65.3
Population 65 and over (%)	5.1	13.3
Children per married woman	5.6	1.7
Average family size	4.5	3.0

changes on a society.[30]

The measures of nuptiality and family structure provide a less clear picture, revealing both stability and change at the same time. Age at marriage and the proportion of women remaining single at the end of the reproductive period were stable, confirmation that in the West the nuptial check

---

[30] It is, however, generally considered obvious that the increased survivorship of the last century is responsible for the demographic aging of the population – that is, the increased proportion of old people. That aging has in fact been due exclusively to the progressive decline of fertility as a result of which the younger levels of the age structure have not been sufficiently replenished. Moreover, one can show that improved survivorship was proportionately more significant for younger age groups than for older and so created a greater increase, all things being equal, among the young than the old; the age structure actually became younger. The situation today and in the near future, however, is different. Improvements in survivorship will almost exclusively benefit the old (there being virtually no room left for improvement at the younger ages). As a result further mortality decline will contribute to population aging. Historically, however, this has not been the case.

played a minimal role in the dramatic changes which took place. While fertility declined, utilization of the reproductive space decreased considerably, as revealed by the decrease in average ages at birth and at last birth – the latter lower by almost ten years. As a result, in the modern demographic regime the last child reaches maturity when the mother (or father) is relatively young (about 50) and still has a large portion of her life to live. By contrast, in the old regime maturity for the last-born occurred when the parents were about 60 and so fairly old given the lower life expectancy of the period. Finally, fertility decline is largely responsible for reduced family size (3 persons per family in 1981 as opposed to 4.5 a hundred years before).[31]

The last group of indices, relating to age structure, is especially revealing. Fertility decline has reduced the relative size of the younger age groups (the percentage of the population under 15 has declined from 32.2 to 21.4) and increased that of the older (from 5.1 to 13.3 percent over 60), advancing the process of "demographic aging." Still more intriguing is the "projection" in time of the mortality and fertility behavior of 1881 and 1981 so that they remain constant until the population achieves "stability."[32] In 1881 the difference between the stable state and the real state of the population was minimal. In 1981, however, the implications are disconcerting: should fertility (0.76 daughters per woman) and mortality remain at 1981 levels, the growth rate will become about – 1 percent per year, implying a halving time of 71 years, and population will suffer further and severe aging.

These comments round out the picture of the demographic transition in the developed world, a transition which followed a basic plan common to many countries. It entailed general demographic expansion which, by means of emigration, extended to other continents. This largely positive development, however, did not come without a price: while populations today are far more "economical" and efficient than they were a hundred or two hundred years ago, they have acquired new weaknesses. In the case of mortality, increased demographic order has not entirely eliminated the risks of disorder (the loss of an only child or of parents at an early age), and these,

---

[31] Obviously fertility alone does not determine the change in family size. Survivorship, age at which the children leave home, widowhood and second marriages, the frequency of extended families (composed of more than one biological nucleus), and cohabitation of nonrelated persons are also factors determining family size.

[32] A population with fixed fertility and mortality behavior ultimately achieves a fixed age structure (determined by this behavior) as well as fixed crude birth, death, and growth rates. A theoretical population of this sort is called a "stable" population. In table 4.6, the parameters reported refer to the stable populations which would be produced by Italian mortality and fertility behavior in 1881 and 1981.

precisely because of their rarity, are more devastating to their victims. Family structures are reduced and so are more fragile in the face of risk. And population aging, beyond certain limits, constitutes a heavy burden on the social system.

6 Theoretical Considerations on the Relationship between Demographic and Economic Growth

The advent of the Industrial Revolution, the introduction of machinery, the exploitation of new sources of energy, and increased trade all combined to rapidly alter the terms of the population/land/labor equation. Population growth no longer led, by means of increased demand, to a rise in prices and a decline in wages. Beginning in the nineteenth century, European population, in spite of considerable growing pains, nonetheless grew in a climate of declining prices and increasing wages. The difficult balance between population and land was broken as economic and demographic growth became not competing but complementary forces. This, however, is only a general picture; clearly the attempt to describe more specifically the nature of the relationship between population and economy is a difficult undertaking. One is inclined to adopt Schumpeter's point of view, according to which population plays a secondary or background role in economic development: "The fundamental impulse that sets and keeps the capitalist engine in motion comes from the new consumers' goods, the new methods of production or transportation, the new markets, the new forms of industrial organization that capitalist enterprise creates."[33] My task, however, will not be to discuss whether or not demographic variation determines economic development, but rather to consider how and to what degree the one conditions the other.

Once again we may consider the problem in terms of the returns from the factors of production, labor included, and whether these tend to increase or decrease. It is certainly the case that dependence on the availability of land decreases as an economy expands beyond agriculture, but the dependence on other resources, like coal, iron, or other minerals derived from the earth, increases. Due to market integration, the opening of new continents, the substitution of raw materials, and unceasing human innovation

---

[33] J. A. Schumpeter, *Capitalism, Socialism, and Democracy,* 2nd ed (Harper and Brothers, New York, 1947), p. 83.

and technological progress, the limits of these resources have not yet been reached. The secular decline of the relative prices of raw materials, food, and industrial products attests to this fact.

Land scarcity and diminishing returns have not been avoided simply because of the opening of the North American continent to European agriculture, but above all because of the dramatic increase in agricultural productivity, especially over the last half century during which the cultivation of new lands has ceased.[34] Over a century ago, the economist Jevons feared that coal supplies would be used up,[35] and about 20 years ago the Club of Rome made similar predictions regarding other raw materials,[36] while the specter of declining petroleum reserves haunted the 1970s. None of these fears has been realized, though it is reasonable to believe that resource scarcity might in the future present an obstacle to development. Those resources used to produce energy (petroleum, coal, wood) clearly have become neither more rare nor more costly, as demonstrated by their reduced incidence over time in relation to a constant product. In the United States, the energy required in 1850 to produce $1,000 of goods or services (GDP, expressed in constant prices) amounted to 4.6 tonnes of petroleum equivalent; by 1900 this figure had dropped to 2.4, by 1950 to 1.8, and by 1978, at the peak of the oil crisis, to 1.5. In other words, a unit of energy (whatever source used) in 1978 produced triple the value (in constant prices) that it did in 1850.

In 1910, Alfred Marshall wrote: "There have been stages in social history in which the special features of the income yielded by the ownership of land have dominated human relations . . . But in the present age, the opening out of new countries, aided by low transport charges on land and sea, has almost suspended the tendency to diminishing return, in that sense in which the term was used by Malthus and Ricardo, when the English laborer's weekly wages were often less than the price of half a bushel of good wheat."[37]

Returning to consideration of the long-term relationship between demographic growth and economic development, between 1820 and 1987 the population of the four leading Western nations (Great Britain, France, Germany, and the United States) grew by a factor of 5.5, while their combined

---

[34]   Y. Hayami and V. W. Ruttan, *Population Growth and Agricultural Productivity* (Johns Hopkins University Press, Baltimore, 1985).

[35]   W. S. Jevons, *The Coal Question* (Macmillan, London, 1865).

[36]   Club of Rome, *The Limits to Growth* (Universe Books, New York, 1972).

[37]   A. Marshall, *Principles of Economics* (Macmillan, London, 1920), pp. xv–xvi. A bushel is equivalent to 35.2 liters.

GDP (in constant prices) multiplied by 93. Per capita production, then, increased seventeenfold. Given that per capita production (a rough indicator of individual well-being) doubled every four decades during the past 170 years, it would appear that demographic growth, by whatever means it may have acted, was at best a modest check to economic development; in fact, at first glance it might seem more reasonable to adopt the opposite opinion, namely that population increase reinforced economic growth.

Abandoning any attempt to determine a causal relationship between population and economy, we may nonetheless discuss several factors linked to demographic growth that may have sped up, rather than slowed down, development or, in other words, brought increasing returns for each additional individual. These factors may be grouped into three categories: (1) purely demographic factors; (2) factors of scale and dimensional factors in general; and (3) the stock of knowledge and technological progress.

Purely demographic factors

These are changes associated with the demographic transition discussed earlier in this chapter. Their influence is considered positive for a number of reasons. First, mortality decline and the reduced frequency of disease increased not only the length of life but also the efficiency of the population. Second, the fact that mortality began to follow a more hierarchical and chronological order largely eliminated the risk of premature death and allowed for longer-term planning, certainly an aid to development. Third, the decline of fertility – previously accompanied by high infant mortality – reduced the amount of energy and resources devoted to the raising of children and so allowed these resources (particularly in the form of female employment) to be devoted to more directly productive activities. And finally, up until at least the middle of this century, age structure was shifting to favor the more productive ages, improving the ratio between the productive and dependent sectors of the population.[38]

These factors probably acted to increase the average efficiency of the population over the time period considered. As we shall see below, however, it will not be possible to repeat this sort of progress in the future. From the point of view of purely demographic variables, the low fertility of the last decades, the aging of the population, and the fact that the beneficial aspects of mortality gain have all been realized lead to the conclusion that a turning

---

[38] These arguments are developed in S. Kuznets, *Modern Economic Growth* (Yale University Press, New Haven, 1966), p. 57.

point has been reached and Western populations are entering a phase of decreasing efficiency.

Factors of scale and dimensional factors in general

We have already discussed these factors at some length (chapter 3, section 5). It is likely that economies of scale were realized in the West during the past two centuries as a result of the fivefold demographic increase which greatly expanded markets. Many studies have confirmed the existence of net gains in efficiency and productivity for individual industrial sectors as a result of market expansion.[39] More generally, Denison has estimated that factors of scale contributed about 10 percent to the post-World War II growth of Europe and the United States.[40] Clearly economies of scale do not derive merely from demographic growth, but also from the expansion of the economy and market integration. However, even given these limitations, the demographic component of economies of scale must be considerable.

The example of the manufacturing industries can probably be extended to other sectors of the economy, but not all – perhaps to service industries, much less to public administration. While economies of scale derived from demographic expansion are fairly evident for small populations, they are less so for large ones. Moreover, the elimination of international barriers to trade can be a strong substitute for demographic growth with regard to market expansion. We may, in this regard, cite the opinion of E. A. G. Robinson: "There are no penalties for being bigger than the minimum size . . . there are no possibilities of diseconomies of scale arising from the excessive size of the market."[41]

Finally, demographic growth appears to have a positive effect not only by virtue of the economies of scale it makes possible but also because of the possibility of market expansion. When population grows entrepreneurs are encouraged to embark upon new undertakings and strengthen those already begun, a process which generates investment and growth. The opposite, of course, occurs in periods of demographic decline or

[39] J. J. Spengler, *Facing Zero Population Growth* (Duke University Press, Durham, 1978), pp. 136–9.
[40] E. F. Denison, *Accounting for the United States' Economic Growth* (Brookings Institution, Washington, D.C., 1974), pp. 71–5; and by the same author: *Why Growth Rates Differ* (Brookings Institution, Washington, D.C., 1967), pp. 232–3.
[41] E. A. G. Robinson, ed., *Economic Consequences of the Size of Nations* (Macmillan, London, 1960), p. xxii of Robinson's introduction.

stagnation. Keynes used an argument of this sort to explain the economic stagnation of Europe in the period between the two world wars.[42]

The stock of knowledge and technological progress

These factors too have been considered above (chapter 3, section 5). Gains in "tested knowledge" rely on the existence of ingenious individuals who "invent" new knowledge. The number of these inventors may be proportionate to population size. In any case, the invention of new knowledge is favored by economies of scale (for example, the number of research or scientific institutes, the frequency of contacts between scholars) and so, all things being equal, should enjoy increasing returns as population grows. As Kuznets,[43] a convinced proponent of this theory, admits, this point of view suggests that we cannot fully compensate for a potentially smaller number of inventors or institutions by greater investment in education and research: a large community will always have an advantage relative to a small one. It is certainly the case that technical progress – the true motor of development – must be ascribed to new "knowledge," applied with sufficient capital. If, then, the production of knowledge is favored by economies of scale resulting from demographic growth, we can conclude that the latter contributes to economic growth. While this position is theoretically plausible, it is more difficult to establish historically, especially when we consider the technical progress of demographically small countries like England or Holland, which for long periods significantly exceeded that of much more populous nations.

It is possible, then, that during the past two centuries demographic growth acted more as an incentive than a check to economic development (though more for the reasons given above in discussing purely demographic factors than those of scale and dimensional factors in general, and even less for those pertaining to the stock of knowledge and technological progress).

---

[42] J. M. Keynes, "Some Economic Consequences of a Declining Population," *Eugenics Review*, 29 (April 1937), pp. 13–17. These same ideas were stated much more explicitly in J. R. Hicks's review of Keynes, "Mr. Keynes' Theory of Employment," cited in Spengler, *Facing Zero Population Growth*, p. 62: "Expectation of a continually expanding market, made possible by increasing population, is a fine thing for keeping up the spirit of entrepreneurs. With increasing population investment can go roaring ahead, even if invention is rather stupid; increasing population is therefore actually favorable to employment."

[43] S. Kuznets, "Population Change and Aggregate Output" (NBER report), in *Demographic and Economic Change in Developed Countries* (Princeton University Press, Princeton, 1960), pp. 329–30.

For the opposite reasons we can expect that in the coming decades demographic decline and aging may have the reverse effect. However, the measure of past positive effects and future negative ones is a difficult quantity to assess.

7 More on the Relationship between Demographic and Economic Growth: Empirical Observations

Uncertainty about the nature and causal direction of the relationship between economy and population does not prevent us from observing the progress of these forces during the past two centuries, centuries characterized by vigorous expansion of both total and per capita production. Total production, as expressed by GDP (gross domestic product), measures the value of all goods and services produced, excluding foreign trade, and is expressed in constant prices. The series used here, constructed according to a standardized method, are taken from a comparative study of 16 developed countries for the period 1870–1987 (for some countries the reconstruction extends back to 1820).[44] The accuracy of this reconstruction can only partially compensate for the problems of inadequate statistics (especially for the period prior to the First World War) and of conversion to constant prices and a single currency. Consequently, the results should be considered with caution.

The case of the United Kingdom is the most well known. Table 4.7 covers a time span of two centuries, and from it we can derive the principal aggregate characteristics of modern demo-economic evolution: an increase in population and employment by a factor of four or five; a halving during the last century of the average number of hours worked per worker; an elevenfold increase in per capita production and still greater jump (20 times) in productivity per hour worked. Demographic evolution has fueled population and employment increase; social evolution has freed up a large chunk of what was once work time; and economic evolution has multiplied the returns from labor.

Table 4.8 lists a number of indices for the 16 countries at the beginning and end of the comparative study (1870–1987) together with annual rates of

---

[44] These series, in 1970 international dollars, are found in A. Maddison, *Phases of Capitalist Development* (Oxford University Press, Oxford, 1982), pp. 158–60. The successive revision used here extends the series to 1987 (in 1980 international dollars). See Maddison, *The World Economy.*

Table 4.7 Population, number of employed, production, and productivity in the United Kingdom (1785–1987)

Year	GDP in millions of 1970 $	Population (in thousands)	Employed (in thousands)	Hours worked per year per person	GDP per hour worked (1970 $)	Per capita GDP (1970 $)
1785	4,959	12,681	4,915	3,000	0.34	391
1820	9,052	19,434	6,884	3,000	0.44	466
1870	29,254	29,365	12,285	2,984	0.8	996
1913	65,591	42,886	18,566	2,624	1.35	1,529
1950	105,471	50,363	22,400	1,958	2.4	2,094
1987	254,872	56,687	24,542	1,511	6.87	4,496

Source: Adapted from A. Maddison, *Phases of Capitalist Development* (Oxford University Press, Oxford, 1982)

change for each of these. In spite of a degree of fundamental similarity, the performance of these countries varied considerably during the period considered. Annual population growth averaged between 1.5 and 2 percent for the transoceanic countries of immigration, while that for European countries normally ranged between 0.6 and 0.9 percent, with a few notable exceptions (France at 0.3 percent, Austria at 0.4, and the Netherlands at 1.2), which led to far-from-uniform demographic evolution within the European continent. Also significant were the different rates of increase in per capita GDP and productivity – per capita GDP ranged from 1.1 percent in Australia to 2.7 in Japan. We should keep in mind that seemingly small differences in growth rates result over time in enormous differences in absolute levels: German (post-World War II boundaries) per capita GDP, for example, grew at a rate of 2 percent per year during the period 1870–1987 and so multiplied by a factor of 10, while that of the Netherlands, growing at a rate "barely" a half point less, multiplied by 6.

The question arises whether the rate of population increase had an effect on economic development as measured by the growth of per capita production or productivity (admittedly approximate measures). Approaching the problem this way, we assume that demographic growth itself is not influenced by economic factors, and yet we have already seen that the phases of the demographic transition were profoundly affected by economic developments. Figure 4.12 charts the relationship between population increase and annual per capita GDP increase for the period 1870–1987.

Table 4. 8   Population, GDP, and productivity in 16 more-developed
countries (1870 and 1987; 1980 international $)

	Population (in thousands)			Gross Domestic Product (GDP)		
	1870	1987	% change	1870	1987	% change
Australia	1,620	16,196	2.0	4,184	154,398	3.1
Austria	4,520	7,562	0.4	4,822	66,488	2.2
Belgium	5,096	9,862	0.6	7,838	86,479	2.1
Canada	3,736	25,922	1.7	3,920	329,525	3.8
Denmark	1,888	5,108	0.9	2,170	50,818	2.7
Finland	1,754	4,952	0.9	1,227	47,049	3.1
France	38,440	55,685	0.3	40,237	527,602	2.2
Germany	24,870	60,858	0.8	23,671	606,404	2.8
Italy	27,238	57,094	0.6	34,275	515,158	2.3
Japan	34,437	122,897	1.1	14,468	1,198,943	3.8
The Netherlands	3,607	14,616	1.2	5,637	134,420	2.7
Norway	1,735	4,180	0.8	1,562	48,711	2.9
Sweden	4,169	8,366	0.6	4,022	86,403	2.6
Switzerland	2,664	6,593	0.8	3,202	78,268	2.7
United Kingdom	29,185	56,687	0.6	58,258	520,270	1.9
United States	40,061	244,171	1.5	63,687	3,308,401	3.4
Total	225,020	700,749	1.0	273,180	7,759,337	2.9

	GDP per capita			Productivity per hour worked (1980 $)		
	1870	1987	% change	1870	1987	% change
Australia	2,583	9,533	1.1	2.41	13.50	1.5
Austria	1,067	8,792	1.8	0.79	12.72	2.4
Belgium	1,538	8,769	1.5	1.24	16.41	2.2
Canada	1,049	12,712	2.1	1.04	16.51	2.4
Denmark	1,150	9,949	1.8	0.90	11.19	2.2
Finland	700	9,501	2.2	0.53	11.99	2.7
France	1,047	9,475	1.9	0.70	16.18	2.7
Germany	952	9,964	2.0	0.78	14.47	2.5
Italy	1,258	9,023	1.7	0.93	13.70	2.3
Japan	420	9,756	2.7	0.28	9.62	3.0
The Netherlands	1,563	9,197	1.5	1.38	15.34	2.1
Norway	900	11,653	2.2	0.75	15.25	2.6
Sweden	965	10,328	2.0	0.71	13.89	2.5
Switzerland	1,202	11,871	2.0	0.84	13.46	2.4
United Kingdom	1,996	9,178	1.3	1.59	14.03	1.9
United States	1,590	13,550	1.8	1.46	18.47	2.2
Total	1,214	11,073	1.9	0.93	14.70	2.4

Source: Adapted from A. Maddison, *The World Economy in the 20th Century* (Development Center, OECD, Paris, 1989).

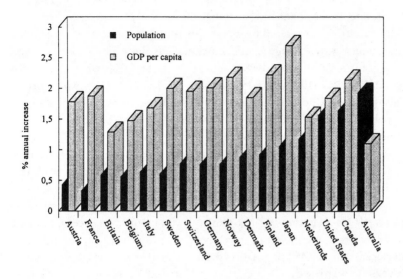

Figure 4.12 Annual rate of increase of population and per capita GDP for
16 industrialized countries (1870–1987)

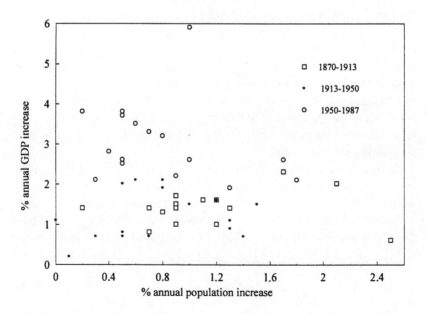

Figure 4.13 Annual rate of increase in population and per capita GDP for
16 industrialized countries (1870–1913, 1913–50, 1950–87)

The 16 countries are listed in ascending order according to population growth rates, from France to Australia. Clearly the economic performance of the countries considered bears no apparent relation to the intensity of demographic growth. Figure 4.13, which depicts the same relationship in a different form for the periods 1870–1913, 1913–50, and 1950–87 (each country appears three times), reinforces this impression. The long-term experience of wealthy nations, whose populations grew at different rates, does not allow us to attribute a particular economic role to demographic growth.[45]

One should not conclude based on the above analysis that there is no connection between demographic growth and economic development. Instead, this relationship is complicated by the interfering effects of other phenomena. Referring to the same period as that covered by Maddison and arriving at the same conclusion, Kuznets, founder of this school of aggregate analysis, observes: "Other factors – relative availability of natural resources, timing of the inception of the modern growth process, or institutional conditions – complicate the effects of population growth and prevent a simple association between it and growth in per capita product: and population growth itself may have both expansive and depressive effects on the increase in per capita product that differ in their weight in conjunction with other factors."[46]

Beyond these considerations there is a more general one which can only further complicate the relationship: population and economy are at the same time dependent and independent variables. Economic development, as we have seen, exercised a strong influence on the progress of mortality and fertility during the demographic transition, but, as described in the previous section, the reverse is also true. In an open and integrated system, characterized by significant currents of migration (which served as an important force for maintaining equilibrium in much of the period considered), the long-term effects of economic and demographic stimuli tend to mitigate and compensate for one another.

Remaining on an aggregate level, the large economic cycles of the modern era can provide us with a few more insights into the population-economy relationship. Keynes, for example, discussing the rate of capital formation in Great Britain between 1860 and 1913, stated: "Thus the increased demand for capital was primarily attributable to the increasing population and to the rising standard of life and only in a minor degree to technical changes of a

---

[45]　The lack of a clear relationship is evident even when examining separately the three subperiods. The correlation coefficients between the rates of variation for population and GDP are: 1870–1913, +0.003; 1913–50, +0.180; 1950–87, −0.220; 1970–1987, −0.119.

[46]　Kuznets, *Modern Economic Growth*, p. 68.

kind which called for an increasing capitalization per unit of consumption"; the demographic deceleration of the interwar period presumably influenced the level of demand, creating overproduction and unemployment.[47] Hansen was of a similar opinion and attributed 40 percent of capital formation in Western Europe and 60 percent in the United States during the second half of the nineteenth century to demographic growth; conversely, he traced the economic crisis of the 1930s to the demographic deceleration of the early part of the century and the consequent slowing of investment.[48] It was again Kuznets who attempted to detect a link between demographic and economic cycles in the United States. An increasing standard of living attracted immigration and encouraged nuptiality, accelerating demographic increase. Demographic increase in turn stimulated those investments particularly sensitive to population growth (housing, railroads), but at the expense of other investments in capital goods (machinery and industrial structures). The latter situation negatively affected production and consumption, and so demographic growth, and led to the beginning of another cycle.[49]

Figure 4.14 records changes (in relation to the previous decade) in population increase (in millions), in GNP increase (in billions of dollars), and in per capita income (in dollars) in the United States for each decade from 1875 to 1955. The trends of these three variables are surprisingly similar.

Returning to Europe, it is difficult to explain the phases of economic growth – expansion preceding the First World War, stagnation between the wars, and strong recovery in the past four decades (notably interrupted by the oil crisis of the 1970s) – in terms of demographic factors, which tend to act slowly. Nonetheless, this analysis would be incomplete if it did not take into account several significant demographic factors:

1   The first of these is the geo-demographic structure of the European continent (excluding the USSR) and its consequences for spatial politico-economic organization, indirectly connected with advantages or disadvantages of scale. Prior to the First World War, five large nations (Great Britain, France, Germany, Austria-Hungary, and Italy) dominated the European scene and contained more than

---

[47]   Keynes, "Some Economic Consequences," p. 15.
[48]   Cited in Spengler, *Facing Zero Population Growth*, p. 64.
[49]   S. Kuznets, *Economic Growth and Structure* (Norton, New York, 1965), pp. 345–9. For refinement and discussion of the Kuznets model see R. A. Easterlin, "Economic–Demographic Interactions and Long Swings in Economic Growth," *The American Economic Review*, 56 (1966).

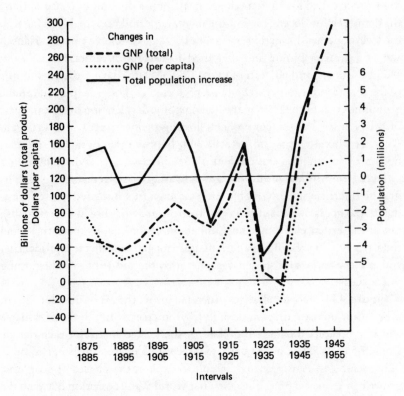

Figure 4.14 Changes in the population increase compared with changes in GNP, total and per capita, 1929 prices, overlapping decades, United States (1870–1955)

Source: S. Kuznets, *Economic Growth and Structure* (Norton, New York, 1965), p. 350.

three-quarters of the total European population. The rest of the population was scattered among a dozen small countries containing about 6 million inhabitants, plus Spain, of intermediate size. After the First World War and the Versailles Treaty Europe was divided into 22 nations, and the large states, with the dismemberment of Austria-Hungary, were reduced from five to four. The level of continental fragmentation increased, a situation that aggravated the effects of political barriers to the mobility of population and goods.[50] After the Second World War and the "separation" of Eastern Europe,

---

[50] I. Svennilson, *Growth and Stagnation in the European Economy* (United Nations Economic Commission for Europe, Geneva, 1954), pp. 67–8.

compartmentalization (which declined within Western Europe due to economic unification) became regional. This division collapsed as a result of the events of 1989–90 in the Soviet Union and the Soviet bloc nations and the unification of Germany, which now demographically (not to mention economically) dominates the center of Europe. Both the demographic and political aspects of these recent changes should be taken into account when evaluating subsequent European development, as they bear significantly on the obstacles to population mobility and therefore on the better utilization of human resources. These same factors have also changed economies of scale linked to the absolute and relative size of markets and economic space in general.

2   Another important aspect in determining the role of demographic growth in the expansion of demand is the growth of urban areas and above all of large cities, so often the catalysts of development. Urban growth requires large investments in construction and also frequently in high technology infrastructure. The 25 European cities that had populations above 500,000 in 1910 had grown in the period 1870–1910 at an annual rate of 1.9 percent; between 1910 and 1940 growth slowed to 0.9 percent and then to 0.3 between 1940 and 1970.[51] One could make similar observations regarding the non-European developed countries: while strong in the pre-World War I period, the driving role of urban growth rapidly declined afterward.

3   Mobility and migration measure the ability of a demo-economic system to efficiently distribute human resources. From this point of view, recent European history can be divided into three periods. The first ended with the imposition of immigration restrictions by overseas receiving countries in the early 1920s. It was characterized by strong redistribution processes which sent masses of primarily rural population to overseas destinations. At the same time migration between and within European states was also intense. Legislative barriers to migration were few, and the international labor market was relatively fluid and flexible, despite the difficulty and high cost of transportation. The second period, that between the two world wars, was characterized by the closure of extra-European outlets and the

[51]   The population of these 25 cities was 13.1 million in 1870, 28.4 million in 1910, 37.7 million in 1940, and 41.4 million in 1970. Data taken from B. R. Mitchell, *European Historical Statistics* (Macmillan, London, 1980).

progressive internal compartmentalization of the continent.[52] The labor market shrank and became fragmented. The third, post-World War II, phase has been characterized by the "natural" end of emigration outside of Europe, by considerable population redistribution within Western Europe (sharply divided from non-market economy Europe), and by the increasing availability of non-European labor. It is a phase that closes progressively in the 1970s and 1980s as the population reservoir of Mediterranean Europe gradually dries up and closed door policies are adopted. The importance of a mobile and plentiful labor force was underlined by economists like Kindleberger, who attributed to it the rapid economic recovery of Western Europe in the immediate postwar period.[53]

The conclusions to be drawn from this analysis, kept intentionally general, are fairly weak. If nothing else, we can assert that during the past two centuries demographic growth did not hinder economic development. In fact, there are indications that the reverse was true. And while maintaining a position of neutrality on the question of the relationship between economic and demographic growth, it is nonetheless the case that those nations that experienced the greatest demographic growth are those that have assumed a leading economic role. A final example may help to clarify this relationship. Between 1870 and 1987 the annual growth rate of per capita GDP in the United States and France was identical (1.9 percent), while the population growth rates were very different (1.5 percent in the United States, barely 0.3 percent in France). As a result, comparison of the economic dimensions of the two countries, as measured by GDP, has changed from a 1.6-to-1 ratio (in favor of the United States) in 1870 to 6.3-to-1 today. One cannot but ask the entirely rhetorical question: Would the United States be the leader of the Western world if it had experienced more modest demographic growth?

[52]   D. Kirk, *Europe's Population in the Interwar Years* (League of Nations, Princeton University Press, Princeton, 1946), pp. 97–125
[53]   C. P. Kindleberger, *Europe's Postwar Growth* (Harvard University Press, Cambridge, Mass., 1967).

5

The Populations of Poor Countries

1 An Extraordinary Phase

As the rich countries of the world complete a phase of population expansion, the poor countries have embarked upon an extraordinary and nonrepeatable one of their own. The characteristics of this growth cycle are well described by the arid figures charting recent demographic growth in the so-called less-developed countries – namely those countries whose populations live, by Western standards, in poverty.[1] The 1900 population of the poor countries, about one billion, had multiplied fourfold by 1990; by the year 2000 that factor will have increased to five. In about a century these countries have matched the expansion of the rich countries in the two centuries following the Industrial Revolution. That speed of growth is extraordinary. Between 1900 and 1920, we estimate the growth rate of the poor countries to have been about 0.6 percent per year; this rate doubled for the period 1920–50 (about 1.2 percent) and once again (almost) over the past 40 years (2.2 percent). In the 1960s a maximum rate of 2.5 percent was reached, followed by gradual decline in the last two decades (table 5.1). By contrast, the Western countries (Europe and its overseas projections) only rarely exceeded a rate of 1 percent during

[1]   In this chapter I shall use the term "poor countries" for those countries frequently described as "less developed" or "developing," and "rich countries" for those usually called "developed" or "more developed." Rich and poor countries are of course abstract categories and serve primarily as a scheme of definition. The rich countries include the countries of Europe and North America, Australia, New Zealand, and Japan; by a considerable stretch of imagination, the countries of Eastern Europe are also included. Occasionally I shall use the term "Western countries" to refer to the countries of Western Europe and their projections in North America and Oceania, excluding Japan, which has a distinct demographic history.

Table 5.1 World population, rich and poor countries (1900–2000)

Year	Population (in millions)			Annual increase (%)[a]			Percentage share (%)		
	Rich	Poor	World	Rich	Poor	World	Rich	Poor	World
1900	563	1071	1634	–	–	–	34.5	65.5	100
1920	654	1203	1857	0.76	0.58	0.64	35.2	64.8	100
1930	727	1309	2036	1.06	0.84	0.92	35.7	64.3	100
1940	794	1473	2267	0.88	1.18	1.07	35.0	65.0	100
1950	809	1711	2520	0.19	1.50	1.06	32.1	67.9	100
1960	911	2110	3021	1.19	2.10	1.81	30.2	69.8	100
1970	1003	2695	3698	0.96	2.46	2.02	27.1	72.9	100
1980	1080	3364	4444	0.74	2.22	1.84	24.3	75.7	100
1990	1143	4141	5285	0.67	2.08	1.73	21.6	78.4	100
2000	1186	4972	6158	0.37	1.83	1.53	19.3	80.7	100

[a] Compared with previous date.
Sources: United Nations estimates (1920–90); United Nations Projection (2000); author's estimate (1900)

their two centuries of expansion. During the past half century the poorer part of the world has grown at twice that rate.

The reasons for this difference are, on the surface, rather simple, though the underlying reality is complex. In the rich world the demographic transition came about slowly as a result of a gradual decline in mortality, accompanied by a similar decline in fertility. Slow mortality decline, as described in the previous chapter, was the result of an accumulation of knowledge, especially medical knowledge, which helped to bring infectious diseases under control beginning at the end of the eighteenth century. In the poor world mortality levels remained high until recently. In 1950, for example, average life expectancy in poor countries was still below 40. However, beginning in the mid-twentieth century, that knowledge slowly accumulated by the rich countries was rapidly transferred to the poor ones and mortality dropped dramatically. Fertility, largely dependent upon slowly changing cultural factors, either did not follow the trend in mortality or else did so slowly, and the two indices assumed widely divergent levels.

As mentioned above, the apparent simplicity of this process is misleading. The poor world is divided into societies characterized by vastly different environmental, cultural, and political settings, and these differences are reflected in the demographic behavior of individual populations. Nor has the poor world been isolated from the rich, so that a degree of knowledge and technology transfer took place prior to the last half century. Still, taking these factors into account, the fact remains that demographic change in the poor world in recent decades has on average proceeded rapidly as compared to the path previously followed by the rich (figure 5.1).

Table 5.2 describes global demographic diversity as measured by a number of now-familiar indices (for 1950–5 and 1985–90) for poor and rich, for large continental areas, and for India and China – these last two contain half the total population of the poor world. These data permit us to make three general observations regarding: the distinctive characteristics of rich and poor countries, the changing demography of the poor countries during recent decades, and interregional differences.

The differences between poor and rich populations are enormous: life expectancy today (1990–95) for the poor populations is 63 years, for the rich 74; the average number of children per woman is 3.5 as compared to 1.7; and the poor population rate of increase is quadruple that of the rich populations (1.9 percent as compared to 0.4), though the gap between mortality and

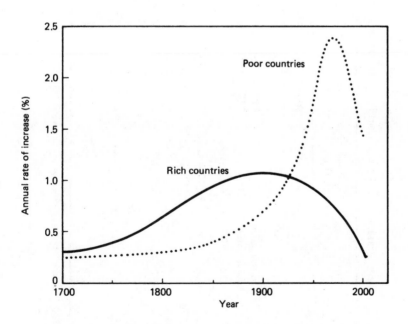

Figure 5.1 Comparison of demographic transitions: rates of increase for poor and rich populations (1700–2000)

Table 5.2 Demographic indicators of world population (1950–95)

Region	Population (in millions)		Annual rate of growth (%)			Birth rate (per 1000)		Death rate (per 1000)		Total fertility rate		Life expectancy at birth	
	1950	1995	1950–95	1950–5	1990–5	1950–5	1990–5	1950–5	1990–5	1950–5	1990–5	1950–5	1990–5
World	2520	5717	1.82	1.78	1.57	37.4	25.0	19.8	9.3	4.97	3.10	46.4	64.7
More developed countries	809	1167	0.81	1.20	0.40	22.0	12.6	10.2	10.1	2.77	1.70	66.5	74.3
Less developed countries	1711	4550	2.17	2.05	1.88	44.5	28.3	24.2	9.1	6.13	3.48	40.9	62.9
Africa	224	728	2.62	2.23	2.81	49.2	41.9	26.8	13.7	6.64	5.80	37.8	52.8
North America	166	293	1.26	1.80	1.05	24.6	15.8	9.4	8.7	3.47	2.06	69.0	76.2
South America	166	482	2.37	2.69	1.84	42.1	26.0	15.5	6.8	5.87	3.09	51.4	69.0
Eastern Asia	671	1424	1.67	1.75	1.04	40.8	17.8	23.3	7.2	5.61	1.91	42.9	70.8
Southeast Asia	182	484	2.17	1.92	1.81	44.3	27.2	24.7	8.1	6.03	3.29	40.5	53.0
Southern Asia	499	1381	2.26	2.03	2.10	44.7	31.4	24.8	9.9	6.08	4.12	39.3	61.3
Western Asia	50	168	2.69	2.59	2.43	45.2	31.9	21.7	7.3	6.37	4.41	45.2	68.3
Europe	549	727	0.62	1.96	0.15	20.9	11.6	10.6	11.2	2.56	1.56	66.1	72.9
Oceania	13	29	1.78	2.21	1.54	27.7	19.2	12.3	7.8	3.84	2.51	60.8	73.0
China	555	1221	1.75	1.87	1.11	43.6	18.5	25.0	7.2	6.11	1.95	40.8	68.5
India	358	936	2.14	2.00	1.91	44.1	29.1	25.0	10.0	5.97	3.75	38.7	60.4

Source: World Population Prospects: The 1994 Revision (New York, 1995)

fertility levels was greater 30 years ago than it is today. It is also worth noting that around 1950, at the beginning of developing country demographic transition, mortality levels for these countries corresponded more or less to European rates of the mid-nineteenth century (life expectancy at birth about 40 years); not so for fertility, as the developing country level of 6.2 children per woman considerably exceeds Western levels of a century before (generally below 5). The difference lies in the effectiveness with which the European populations exercised the Malthusian check on marriage (late marriage and high rates of the never married), a check only rarely encountered among the poor populations.

If we compare the situation at the beginning and the end of the 40-year period considered, we find that the poor country growth rate is little changed, since mortality and fertility have experienced similar amounts of absolute decline. However, in relative terms, the drop in mortality (62 percent) has been much greater than that in birth rate (36 percent). And though the level of detail in table 5.2 is not very fine, it nonetheless reveals great disparities within the developing world, a world which includes both the African (transition barely initiated) and Chinese (transition nearly complete) populations: while these populations had similar total fertility rates and life expectancies in 1950–5, the respective values 40 years later were 5.8 as compared to 2 children per woman and 53 as compared to 69 years of life expectancy. In the various continental areas, and even more so in the various populations that inhabit them, we find a gamut of intermediate situations.

This diversity is better displayed by examining these same indices for the 25 demographically largest nations of the several continents that make up the developing world (and contain over 80 percent of its population).[2] Figures

---

[2]   The 25 countries considered are not in absolute terms the 25 most populous countries of the poor world, but rather the most populous from each continent (excepting several, like Vietnam or Iran, for which demographic estimates are not available): 8 in Africa (Egypt, Ethiopia, Kenya, Morocco, Nigeria, Sudan, Tanzania, and Zaire), 9 in Asia (Bangladesh, China, India, Indonesia, Pakistan, the Philippines, South Korea, Thailand, and Turkey), and 8 in America (Argentina, Brazil, Chile, Colombia, Ecuador, Mexico, Peru, and Venezuela). The combined population of these countries – 1.405 billion in 1950 and 2.980 billion in 1985 – represents respectively 83.5 and 81 percent of the total population of the poor countries. From the point of view of their history and demographic growth, Argentina and Chile have more in common with the European countries (of which they are "projections") than with other Latin American countries. The exclusion of small countries – like Hong Kong, Singapore, Mauritius, Costa Rica, and Taiwan – eliminates interesting cases of precocious transition, processes which, however, are in part favored by these very small dimensions.

5.2 and 5.3 (for 1950–5 and 1980–5) place each of these nations in the strategic space of growth defined by life expectancy (e_0) and number of children per woman (*TFR*), according to the scheme described in chapter 1 (section 5). The differences are obvious but require some interpretation. The space occupied in 1950–5 is more compact than that occupied in 1980–5; fertility and mortality vary little, and almost all the countries occupy the space between the isogrowth curves of 2 and 3 percent. In 1980–5 the populations occupied a larger space, and many fell between the 1 and 2 percent growth curves (and some between 0 and 1), a clear sign of the initiation of demographic transition. Extremes, however, endure: countries with "old regime" life expectancies (Ethiopia at barely 40 years) and others whose level approaches that of the developed countries (Argentina, Mexico, China, Korea); populations without birth control (Bangladesh, Pakistan) and others approaching a fertility level of two children per woman (China, Korea).

A final observation confirms the initiation of an irreversible transition. At the earlier date (figure 5.2) there appears to be no relation between mortality and fertility, since fertility is generally high throughout the poor countries (due to the limited spread of voluntary fertility limitation), regardless of the level of mortality. Mortality on the other hand had dropped in many countries as a result of the massive infusion of knowledge and technology begun in the 1940s. At the later date (figure 5.3) there is a clear and negative correlation between e_0 and *TFR*, as the high life expectancy countries are also those with reduced fertility. This came about in part because increased material well-being influences life expectancy and fertility in opposite directions, but also because improved survival has begun to have a direct influence on fertility, making high levels of the latter unnecessary and more expensive. Once this process has begun, it tends to perpetuate itself until mortality has completed its decline.

2 *The Conditions of Survival*

Reduced mortality and establishment of the chronological age-linked succession of death are prerequisites to development. Moreover, a reduction in infant and child mortality is one of the necessary conditions for fertility decline and the shift from a regime of demographic "waste" to one of demographic "economy." Beyond these fairly simple observations, we need to expand a bit our general discussion of poor world mortality decline. First,

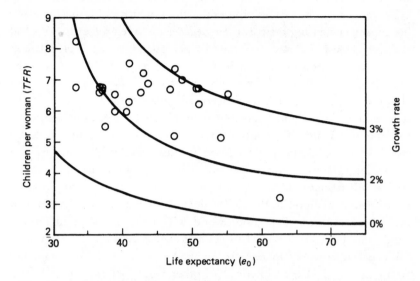

Figure 5.2 Relation between life expectancy (e_0) and average number of children per woman (*TFR*) for 25 large less-developed countries (1950–5)

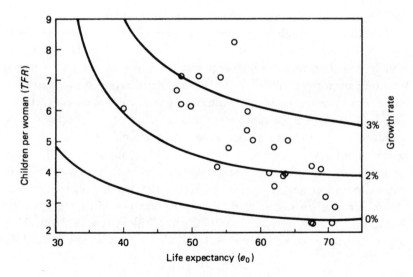

Figure 5.3 Relation between life expectancy (e_0) and average number of children per women (*TFR*) for 25 large less-developed countries (1980–5)

we should consider the reasons behind the different rates of survivorship improvement for the various poor populations, which as a whole increased life expectancy during the past three decades (between the early 1950s and the early 1980s) at a rate of 7 months per calendar year; regional rates ranged from 5 months per year in Africa to 11 months in China, and the differences are greater still if we consider smaller areas.

Survivorship improvement is achieved, first of all, by means of the reduction of infant and child mortality. The United Nations[3] estimates that the probability of a newborn dying before his or her fifth birthday was 134 per thousand in 1980–5 for the less-developed countries as a whole, but variation among these countries was great: 182 per thousand in Africa, 157 in southern Asia, 88 in Latin America, 50 in eastern Asia. By comparison, this level in the rich countries is barely 19 per thousand. If the other countries of the poor world were to reduce their infant and child mortality to the level of China and eastern Asia (50 per thousand), life expectancy would increase by eight years in Africa, six in southern Asia, and two in Latin America.[4] In other words, elimination of infant mortality differences would eliminate much of the disparity in life expectancy and so is a primary objective in the quest for improved survivorship: its reduction not only represents a considerable decline in general mortality, but also favors the modernization of reproductive behavior and improves the level of health at an age crucial to the development and subsequent efficiency of the survivors.

The causes of high infant mortality are many and complex: from infectious diseases typical of infancy (measles, diphtheria, whooping cough, polio, tetanus); to a high incidence of diarrhoea and gastroenteritis resulting from poor sanitation; to the combined action of malnutrition, poverty, and infection; to the existence of vast malarial areas. There are solutions to all of these problems: the diseases typical of infancy can be combated with programs of vaccination and immunization; diarrhoea and gastroenteritis with improved environmental conditions and hygiene; malaria with disinfestation; and malnutrition with programs of diet supplementation and, in many areas, by discouraging early weaning. When illnesses do occur, medical intervention can often prevent their lethalness; in many instances diarrhoea, which kills by repeatedly attacking and dehydrating the infant, can be cured by simple rehydration methods

---

[3]   United Nations, *Mortality of Children under Age 5* (New York, 1988).
[4]   These figures are calculated assuming that mortality beyond the age of five for these "new survivors" is that of the respective areas.

administered by family members.[5] There are solutions, but only providing that the material resources, technical knowledge, and collective and individual awareness necessary to implement them – that is to say, education and development – exist.

A clear, if summary, picture of the conditions accompanying infant mortality is provided by table 5.3, which records several health indices for

Table 5.3 Infant and child mortality and health indices (1990)

Region	Year of survey	Infant mortality	Child mortality	% of births attended by trained health personnel	Months breastfed	Children with stunted growth (%)	Children fully immunized (%)	Population with access to safe water (%)
Sub-Saharan Africa								
Ghana	1993	66	119	86	21	26	55	39
Kenya	1993	62	96	95	21	31	79	
Nigeria	1990	87	192	57	20	37	30	22
Tanzania	1991–2	92	141	53	22	38	71	46
Uganda	1988–9	101	180	38	19	44	31	30
North Africa and Middle East								
Egypt	1992	62	85	53	19	26	67	86
Morocco	1992	57	76	31	16	21	76	18
Sudan[a]	1989–90	70	123	69	19		52	20
Tunisia	1988	50	65	69	15	18	78	31
Turkey	1993	53	61	76	12	16	65	70
Asia								
Bangladesh	1993–4	87	133	10	36		59	89
Pakistan	1990–1	91	117	19	20	43	35	42
Philippines	1993	34	54	53	14		72	72
Sri Lanka	1987	25	35	87	20	27	65	55
Thailand	1987	35	45	66	15	22	37	85
Latin America								
Bolivia	1994	75	116	47	18	28	39	30
Brazil[a]	1991	75	86	70	4		56	61
Colombia	1990	27	35	81	9		68	82
Mexico	1987	47	61	70	8		22	49
Peru	1991–2	55	78	53	17	29	58	24

[a] Sudan, only northern region; Brazil only north eastern region
Source: *Demographic and Health Surveys: Newsletter*, vol. 7, no. 2 (1995), except statistics on drinking water, drawn from World Resources Institute, *World Resources* (Oxford University Press, New York, 1994).

5   ORT, or oral rehydration therapy. These are simple packets, the contents of which are soluble in water and contain the essential salts lost by the infant suffering attacks of diarrhoea; the afflicted baby, by drinking this solution, is able to make up for these losses. It is a therapy easily administered by the child's mother or another family member.

selected countries. High infant and child mortality go hand in hand with lack of professional assistance at delivery, lack of access to safe water, low immunization, and high stunting. Figure 5.4 shows the relationship, for 55 poor countries, between mortality ages 0–4 and the availability of adequate sewage systems; the inverse correlation is clear.

The complexity of the causes of high infant mortality make intervention difficult when attempting to pass from a "medium" level (the result of initial progress) to a low one like that of the developed countries. I shall return to this question after having discussed the general mortality situation for the various populations, which is most concisely expressed by life expectancy (e_0). In figure 5.5 life expectancy for 1990–95 is compared with the classic index of well-being – per capita GDP (1993, calculated in 1980 international dollars) – for 25 poor countries.[6] As can be seen from the figure, this

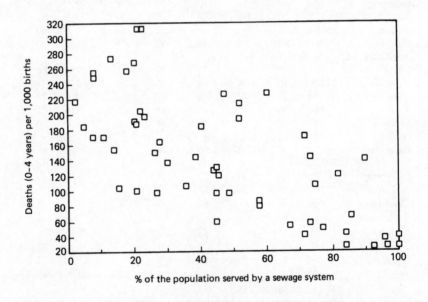

% of the population served by a sewage system

Figure 5.4 Relation between percentage of the population served by a sewage system and 0- to 4-year-old mortality in 55 poor countries (early 1980s)

[6] The countries represented in figure 5.5, as in figures 5.9 and 5.16, are: Egypt, Ethiopia, Kenya, Morocco, Nigeria, Sudan, Tanzania, Zaire, Bangladesh, China, India, Indonesia, Pakistan, the Philippines, South Korea, Thailand, Turkey, Argentina, Brazil, Chile, Colombia, Ecuador, Mexico, Peru and Venezuela.

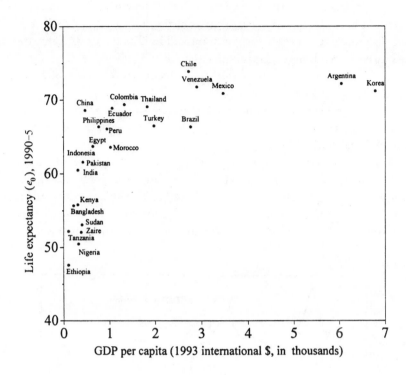

Figure 5.5 Per capita GDP (1993) and life expectancy (e_0) in 25 less-developed countries of Asia and Latin America (1990–5)

relationship is similar to that for the Western countries over the years 1870–1987 (see chapter 4, figure 4.4): there is a big increase in life expectancy as per capita GDP increases from very low levels, but a gradual attenuation of survivorship improvement with subsequent increases in production. In other words, the growth of material well-being is progressively less effective at increasing life expectancy. This relationship is in keeping with an initial phase of considerable mortality reduction linked to the introduction of relatively inexpensive and large-scale technology: antibiotics, DDT disinfestation, certain vaccines.[7] Sri Lanka provides an example of this initial rapid

[7]   These include not only the smallpox vaccine – smallpox virtually disappeared at the end of the 1970s – but also vaccines against measles (responsible for 2 million infant deaths per year), whooping cough (0.6 million deaths), neonatal tetanus contracted at birth as a result of umbilical cord infection (0.8 million deaths), and polio, tuberculosis, and diphtheria, which claim an undetermined number of victims. See "Immunizing the World's Children," in *Population Reports*, series L (March–April 1986).

phase of mortality decline:[8] largely due to DDT spraying begun in the late
1940s and the reduced incidence of malaria, the crude death rate fell from
21.5 per thousand in 1945 to 12.6 per thousand in 1950. Figure 5.6 compares
the mortality trends in two areas of the island having the highest and lowest
incidence of malaria; the effect of the 1946–7 disinfestation on the otherwise
gradual rate of decline is obvious.

Further improvements in survivorship are not so easily achieved. In the
1970s, as poor country mortality decline showed signs of slacking, criticism
mounted against the creation in these countries of health programs which
emulated rich country models and so depended upon the development of
sophisticated and expensive hospitals, clinics, and schools. It was argued
that these programs often were unable to serve the whole population and
that, while good at diagnosis and cure, they did not attack the causes of high
mortality.[9] At the end of the 1970s, the international health organizations

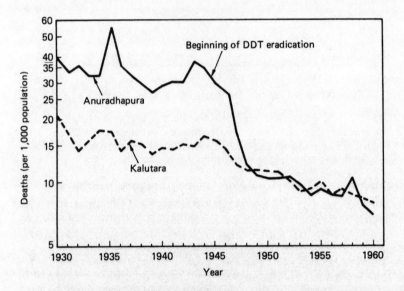

Figure 5.6   Mortality in the most malarial (Anuradhapura) and least
malarial (Kalutara) zones of Sri Lanka (1930–60)

---

[8]   S. A. Meegama, "The Mortality Transition in Sri Lanka," in *Determinants of Mortality
Change and Differentials in Developing Countries* (United Nations, New York, 1986).
[9]   W. H. Mosley, "Will Primary Health Care Reduce Infant and Child Mortality? A
Critique of Some Current Strategies with Special Reference to Africa and Asia," in
Health Policy, Social Policy and Mortality Prospects, ed. J. Vallin and A. D. Lopez (INED and
IUSSP, Ordina, Liège, 1985).

(WHO and UNICEF) embarked upon a new strategy (called Primary Health Care, or PHC) which involved active community participation and used paramedical personnel (more easily trained) together with simple but effective technology.[10] In addition to services of disease prevention and cure, this strategy includes educational programs, water and sanitation systemization, and the encouragement of appropriate agricultural technology. It is a strategy aimed at the greater spread of effective, nonsophisticated techniques and the development of individual and community awareness, which is the basis of that behavior indispensable to the reduction of mortality. Unfortunately, the application of these strategies, while theoretically appropriate, is difficult, since these strategies require changes in individual and family behavior and they must operate through various channels of social activity, including schools, public health programs, and so on.

In order to complete this discussion we should return to figure 5.5 for a moment. We can see that some countries lie considerably above the theoretical GDP–e_0 curve – that is to say, they enjoy a life expectancy considerably longer than we would expect given their level of well-being – while others lie below and so have lower than expected life expectancy. The first category includes China and Chile, the second Brazil and Turkey. Other examples (not included in figure 5.5) further emphasize the differences between indices of well-being and indices of life expectancy in the early 1990s. The countries with a 1993 per capita income between $300 and $400 include some (Niger, Bukina-Faso) with a life expectancy below 50 while India enjoys a life expectancy of 61 and Nicaragua 67. A few steps higher on the well-being scale (1993 per capita income of $600) we find Sri Lanka and Ivory Coast with life expectancies of 72 and 51. Higher still (at $2000) survival rates in Costa Rica ($e_0 = 76$) are well above those of Namibia (59).[11] China and Sri Lanka, among the poorest countries in the world, enjoy lower mortality than many countries well on the way to economic development, while many other countries, wealthy thanks to petroleum exports, have mortality levels near to those of countries lacking in the most basic necessities.

These huge disparities (which manifest themselves if we use other development indices as well) are proof of the fact that the accumulation of material wealth does not by itself guarantee improved health conditions, and not only because of its unequal distribution among the population. Often the

[10]   WHO – UNICEF, *Alma Ata 1978: Primary Health Care* (WHO, Geneva, 1978).
[11]   The values of per capita GNP and of e_0 refer to 1993 and are World Bank estimates. See World Bank, *World Development Report 1995. Workers in an Integrating World* (Oxford University Press, New York, 1995).

problem lies with the levels of individual, family, and community awareness, which do not necessarily increase with economic development. They
are instead the product of deep-rooted cultural inheritance or of deliberate
social and political action. Improved education, and especially female
education (because of the woman's decisive role in childrearing, domestic
hygiene, and food preparation), appears to be a necessary prerequisite to
improved sanitary conditions. The fact that certain Islamic countries still
have high levels of mortality in spite of considerable economic development has been explained by the subordinate status of women and the limited
instruction they receive.[12]

Moreover, those countries which have had particular success in combating death are those in which government policy has allocated sufficient
human and economic resources to the health sector. The examples of
China, Sri Lanka, Cuba, and Costa Rica – politically diverse countries
which have made considerable efforts in this area – show that low mortality
is within reach of even the poorest populations.[13]

High mortality and high incidence of disease cost years of life and, for
those who survive in poor health, years of healthy life. And healthy
survival is a prerequisite for many, indeed most, of the ingredients of
development: the acquisition of physical efficiency, the achievement of
intellectual ability and skills, and the extension of individual time horizons to allow planning for the future. It is also a prerequisite for
changing the demand for children and, therefore, for fertility control. In
order to assess improvements and make comparisons in this regard, it is
important to combine survival measures and measures of incidence of
disease. Survival indicators alone may reveal only part of the picture:
reliance on medicine may prolong a life made miserable by inadequate
nutrition and the absence of elementary hygiene. An important improvement over survival measures, for the purpose of our argument, is the
calculation, for a given population, of the years of healthy life lost because
of premature death or because of disabilities produced by disease and
accident. In practice two quantities are calculated: (a) the number of years
of life lost – obtained for each death as the difference between the age at
death and the expectation of life at the same age in a low mortality
population; (b) the number of years of healthy life lost because of disease
or accident – estimated as the difference between the inception of the

---

[12]   This is the point of view expressed in J. C. Caldwell, "Routes to Low Mortality in
Poor Countries," *Population and Development Review*, 12 (1986).
[13]   Ibid., pp. 209–11.

condition and its remission (or death). These years are not counted in full (as they are in the case of death) but each condition or disease is assigned a certain weight (between 0 and 1) according to the severity of the disability.

The combination of the future years lost in full because of premature death and of the future years lost partially because of disability give the total number of lost years (the World Bank has labeled these DALY or disability-adjusted life years). Table 5.4 reports some of these: deaths, diseases, and accidents in 1990 will deprive the 5.3 billion inhabitants of the world of 1.362 billion DALY (or 1.362 billion healthy years) which amounts to 259 per 1,000 population. The maximum incidence is in Sub-Saharan Africa (575 DALY per 1,000 population), the minimum incidence in the rich countries (117 per 1,000). The inequalities between regions (a factor of 5) are large and mask still larger inequalities between individual countries, social groups, etc.

3   A Brief Geography of Fertility

During the past few decades the fertility of the poor world has been changing, and signs of the spread of voluntary control are ever more frequent. Areas which still conform to traditional procreational patterns now exist side by side with others which resemble instead the more developed world. In order to obtain an initial impression of the changes which have taken place in the poor countries as a whole over the past 40 years, we should return for a moment to table 5.2. The average number of children per woman has declined by more than 2, from 6.2 to 3.9, though China, which has reduced fertility to replacement levels (from 6.1 to 2.1), is responsible for a good half of this decline. Fertility in the other large areas of the poor world differs widely: African fertility has undergone a modest decline from 6.6 to 5.8 children per woman, and birth control is still rare;[14] the change in

---

[14]   In fact, in some countries of sub-Saharan Africa there is a clear evidence of an increase in fertility – an increase explained by shorter breast-feeding, and so reduced birth intervals (see below in this section), and by improved sanitary conditions, which have reduced the incidence of certain infectious disease causing sterility or reduced fecundity. The United Nations, for example, estimates that the TFR for western Africa has increased from 6.7 to 6.9 between 1950–5 and 1975–80 and that of eastern Africa from 6.7 to 7.

Table 5.4 Estimates of the burden of premature death and disease (1990)

Region	Population (millions)	DALYs (millions)	DALYs by cause (%) Communicable disease	DALYs by cause (%) Non-commu-nicable disease	DALYs by cause (%) Injuries and accidents	DALYs by cause (%) Total	DALYs per 1000 population	Equivalent infant deaths (millions)
Sub-Saharan Africa	510	293	71.3	19.4	9.3	100	575	9
India	850	292	50.5	40.4	9.1	100	344	9
China	1134	201	25.3	58	16.7	100	178	6.2
Rest of Asia	683	177	48.5	40.1	11.3	100	260	5.5
Latin America	444	103	42.2	42.8	15	100	233	3.2
North Africa and Middle East	503	144	51	36	13	100	286	4.4
Former Soviet socialist republics	346	58	8.6	74.8	16.6	100	168	1.8
Developed market economies	298	94	9.7	78.4	11.9	100	117	2.9
World	5267	1362	45.8	42.2	11.9	100	259	42

Source: The World Bank, World Development Report, 1983: Investing in Health (Oxford University Press, Oxford, 1993).

southern Asia has been larger still with a reduction from 6.1 to 4.1, and this decline is due almost exclusively to lower Indian fertility; Southeast Asia (6 to 3.3) and Latin America (5.9 to 3.1) have registered larger declines. Taking into account the different scale of present-day poor world demography, the current situation resembles that of the Western world at the beginning of this century when areas where fertility control was widely practiced (like France) coexisted with others where "natural" fertility still prevailed (like certain areas of Mediterranean Europe or the northern and eastern peripheries of the continent).[15]

Fertility decline seems to have accelerated in recent years, an observation supported by the recent Demographic and Health Surveys (DHS) of 25 developing countries carried out in 1985–9.[16] These surveys measure fertility levels directly, rather than by means of indirect estimates, and monitor the most recent trends. In particular, it is possible to compare partial *TFR* levels (summing fertility coefficients for ages 15 to 34 – TFR_{15-34}) for the 3 years preceding the survey with those for the period 12 to 15 years earlier (so a 1989 survey would measure 1986–9 and 1975–8 fertility).[17] In nine sub-Saharan African countries the decline was slight: TFR_{15-34} dropped on average from 5.4 to 4.7 (− 12 percent); in addition to small countries where a change is underway (Botswana, Zimbabwe), there are others where little or nothing has changed (Mali, Liberia, Burundi, Uganda). The situation is a little better in North Africa (Egypt, Morocco, Tunisia: TFR_{15-34} from 4.8 to 3.5, −27 percent) and in nine Latin American and Caribbean countries (including Brazil, Mexico, and Colombia: TFR_{15-34} from 4.4 to 3.3, −25 percent), where fertility decline seems to be proceeding

---

[15]   Naturally, this analogy is only applicable in a general sense, and the attendant circumstances were very different. Mortality decline in Europe came about more gradually and so allowed a gradual adjustment of fertility. Moreover, even in high fertility areas birth control was practiced by a significant sector of society, such as the urban classes and the well educated.

[16]   The first phase of the DHS, completed in 1990, includes 34 studies on groups of reproductive-age women ranging in size from 3,000 to 12,000. The survey questionnaire includes questions on demographic characteristics, fertility history, contraceptive use, the health of the woman and her children, and many other socioeconomic variables.

[17]   F. Arnold and A. K. Blanc, *Fertility Levels and Trends*, DHS Comparative Studies no. 2 (Institute for Resources Development, Columbia, 1990). More recent DHS surveys show that in some countries the downward trend goes unchecked: in Bangladesh TFR has declined astonishingly from 4.3 to 3.4 between 1989–91 and 1991–3; in Kenya TFR has declined from 6.7 in 1981–3 to 5.4 in 1990–2. See DHS, *Newsletter*, vol. 7, nos 1 and 2, 1995.

at a rate faster than was imagined possible. Finally, three Asian countries (Indonesia, Thailand, and Sri Lanka: TFR_{15-34} from 3.7 to 2.9, -22 percent) confirm the speed of the transition (from which, however, the Indian sub-continent is largely excluded).

Explanation of these trends requires analysis of the principal components of human fertility, discussed in chapter 1 (section 4). Recall that the average number of children per woman (TFR) is determined by a combination of factors, predominantly biological, which determine natural fertility (birth intervals linked to the duration of breast-feeding, waiting time linked primarily to the frequency of sexual relations, fetal mortality); by marital patterns (age at marriage and percentage unmarried); and by the level of birth control.

I have already made reference to the fact that the "initial" fertility level of the poor countries – over six children per woman – was considerably higher than that of the West prior to the demographic transition (less than five). This is due primarily to higher levels of nuptiality: poor country age at marriage (or the age at which a stable reproductive union is established) has traditionally been low, with almost no one remaining unmarried, unlike the situation in the West. The World Fertility Survey (WFS)[18] revealed, for the late 1970s, an average age at first marriage of 19.8 years in 12 African countries (from a minimum of 17.5 in Cameroon to a maximum of 23.9 in Tunisia); of 21 in 13 Asian and Pacific countries (from 16.3 in Bangladesh to 24.5 in the Philippines); and of 21.5 in 13 Latin American and Caribbean countries (from 19.2 in Jamaica to 23.2 in Peru). These levels, considerably below the Western average of about 24, are already 1 to 1.5 years above the levels of 15 years earlier.[19] Estimates for the early 1980s indicate that age at marriage continues to increase in Asia (21.4) and Latin America (22.1), but not in Africa (19.5).[20] In these same countries, and again according to the WFS, the percentage of unmarried women at the end of the reproductive period was barely 1 in Africa and

---

[18]   On the general characteristics and principal results of the World Fertility Survey, see WFS, *Major Findings and Implications* (London, 1984). The surveys, normally carried out on groups of 3,000 to 10,000 reproductive-age women, comprised 41 developing countries and 21 developed countries; most were conducted in the second half of the 1970s.

[19]   United Nations, *Fertility Behavior in the Context of Development. Evidence from the World Fertility Survey* (New York, 1987), pp. 78, 82.

[20]   United Nations, *First Marriage: Patterns and Determinants* (New York, 1988).

Asia and 4 in Latin America (as compared to levels often over 10 percent in the West).[21]

Although the general trend is toward higher ages at marriage, there is still ample room in which the Malthusian preventive check might act. Several countries, China being the most notable, have passed legislation to this end. In 1950 the Chinese government set the minimum age at marriage at 18 for women and 20 for men, and subsequently (1980) raised it to 20 and 22, while a massive propaganda campaign advocated 23 and 25.[22]

However, although the Malthusian check does reduce fertility, its effectiveness is limited. For example, in the absence of voluntary fertility control, an increase in age at marriage from 18 to 23 (a radical change in nuptial behavior) will result in a reduction of the number of children per woman of 1.5 to 2. Clearly this reduction is too small to bring fertility down to levels compatible with moderate rates of population growth.

The DHS results confirm an increase in the average age of the mother at the birth of her first child – in part a result of increased age at marriage – and so an effective reduction of the fecund period in the countries of North Africa and Asia. This tendency, however, is only sporadically evident in the countries of sub-Saharan Africa and Latin America, where marriage does not necessarily mark the beginning of the reproductive period and non-marital unions are frequent.[23]

The decisive check to fertility, however, is its voluntary control. A simple measure of its "prevalence" is the percentage of reproductive age women who in a given period use some methods of birth control. This percentage in turn can be broken down according to method used ("traditional" and less efficient methods, like coitus interruptus or periodic abstinence (rhythm), or "modern," more efficient methods, like the pill, IUDs, and sterilization). Contraceptive prevalence of about 70 percent and above indicates low levels of fertility like those found in the rich countries.[24] The WFS (for 38

---

[21] The World Bank, *World Development Report 1984* (Oxford University Press, New York, 1984), pp. 115–16.
[22] Arnold and Blanc, *Fertility Levels and Trends.*
[23] W. P. Mauldin and S. J. Segal, "Prevalence of Contraceptive Use: Trends and Issues," *Studies in Family Planning,* 19 (1988), p. 340. Of course these measures only give a very general picture, as the effectiveness of the various contraceptive methods depends in part on the method itself (the pill or IUD are highly effective while coitus interruptus or rhythm are not) and in part on the motivation and assiduousness of the couple.
[24] United Nations, *Fertility Behavior,* p. 133.

developing countries in the late 1970s) found levels of contraceptive prevalence of 10 percent in Africa, 23 percent in Asia, and 40 percent in Latin America and the Caribbean. About three out of four of the women practicing some form of birth control used the so-called "modern" methods.[25] The 46 countries investigated by the DHS between 1986 and 1994 show an increase of contraceptive prevalence. The level for Sub-Saharan Africa (mean of 22 countries) stands at 15 percent, while it reaches 44 percent in Asia/North Africa (average of 12 countries) and 52 percent in Latin America (average of 12 countries).[26]

Figure 5.7, borrowed from a World Bank survey, depicts a model of the factors responsible for reducing the average number of children per woman from traditional levels to replacement levels in a number of poor countries. The model shows the contributions, positive or negative, to *TFR* reduction (from a maximum of 7 to a minimum of 2.1 children per woman) made by changes in: age at marriage, duration of breast-feeding, contraceptive prevalence, the frequency of abortion, and a series of other residual factors. One of these factors – the declining duration of breast-feeding – has in fact contributed to fertility increase. The demographic transition in these countries has entailed a shorter period of breast-feeding which, all things being equal, would have led to shorter birth intervals and a 31 percent increase in *TFR* (equal to 1.5 children). All things, however, were not equal, and the other factors led to an overall reduction. First among these factors was increased contraception (-93 percent $= -4.5$ children), followed by a higher age at marriage (-28 percent $= -1.4$ children) and higher frequency of abortions (-10 percent $= -0.5$ children).

We can conclude this discussion of poor world fertility by considering figures 5.8 and 5.9, the first of which compares per capita GDP and *TFR* in 23 large developing countries in the 1990s. The relationship resembles that revealed by the analogous comparison for the rich countries (see figure 4.8): as income increases, fertility decreases, but the amount of decline is progressively less. Naturally, this relationship is obtained only by drastically simplifying a complicated and diverse reality. Deviation from the abstract income-fertility curve of figure 5.8 may be considerable. The fertility of some countries (like Mexico and Venezuela) is higher than would be expected based on their income levels, while that of others (like China and Thailand) is a good deal lower. In other words, economic development as approximated by per capita GDP has been accompanied by very different fertility levels. In the

---

25   DHS, *Newsletter*, vol. 7, no. 2, 1995.
26   Ibid.

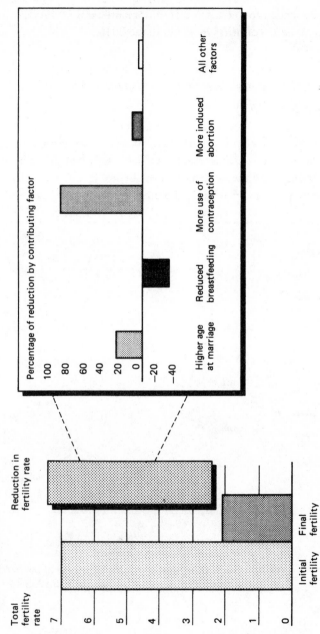

Figure 5.7 Model of the contributions of various factors in reducing fertility from natural to replacement levels
Source: The World Bank, *World Development Report 1984* (Oxford University Press, New York, 1984), p. 115.

pages that follow we shall seek to understand why. An initial clue is provided by figure 5.9 which reveals a strong correlation between illiteracy – not necessarily dependent on economic development – and fertility at the end of the 1980s in the 25 countries included in the DHS.[27]

4 The Conditions and Prospects for Fertility Decline and Demographic Policy

Confronted with the rapid growth rates of poor populations in recent decades, scholars and social workers have debated at length the causes of high fertility and the factors that might bring about its decline, the prerequisite to moderate growth. In the previous section we have discussed

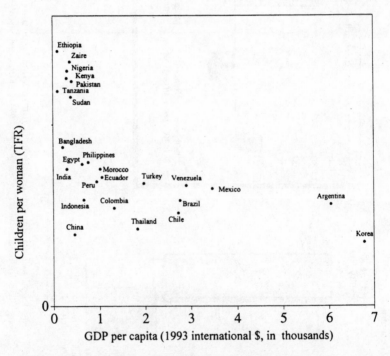

Figure 5.8   Per capita GDP (1993) and average number of children per woman (TFR) in 23 less-developed countries of Asia and Latin America (1990–5)

[27]   The correlation between TFR and adult illiteracy is $r = 0.77$, between TFR and per capita GDP -0.57, and between per capita GDP and adult illiteracy -0.58.

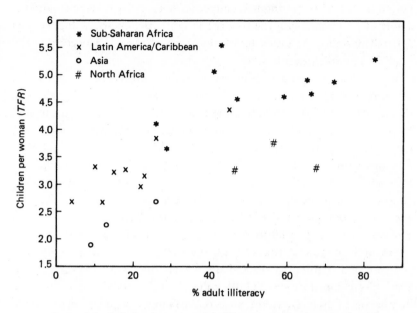

Figure 5.9 Relation between adult illiteracy and average number of children per woman (TFR) in 25 less-developed countries (late 1980s)

the mechanics of fertility, analyzing its various biological and social compo-nents. We have seen that increased age at marriage and, above all, the spread of birth control are the instruments of fertility decline. However, in order for decline to occur, a change in the reproductive plans of couples is neces-sary. We must therefore understand what determines these plans and what can be done to change them. To borrow the economist's terminology, we must understand what determines the "demand" for children on the part of parents – still high in the poor countries – and what the factors are that might change it.[28]

In the first place, we may take for granted that preservation and survival (of the individual, the family group, or the collectivity to which they belong) are innate values of the human species, just as they are for other animal species. Fertility therefore must compensate for mortality; when the latter is high, the former must be so as well. From this point of view, five or six children per woman is compatible with normal pretransition mortality levels. Often the

[28] R. D. Lee and R. A. Bulatao, "The Demand for Children: A Critical Essay," in *Determinants of Fertility in Developing Countries*, vol. 1, ed. R. D. Lee and R. A. Bulatao (Academic Press, New York, 1983).

risk of having no surviving heir induces couples to have many children as a sort of insurance, with the result that aggregate fertility is higher than general mortality. As stated above, mortality decline is a necessary prerequisite to fertility decline.

In almost all poor countries mortality, but not fertility, has declined considerably. Why does fertility remain high? Why has the "demand" for children by parents not slacked off? First, the cost of raising children remains low. In rural areas and under certain conditions, children may constitute a net gain for their parents. The work performed by children and adolescents may offset the costs sustained by the family, which in any case are low in a poor economy.[29] Second, in many social contexts parents consider children a guarantee of economic and material assistance, not to mention affection, in old age. Studies in Indonesia, Korea, Thailand, Turkey, and the Philippines reveal that 80 to 90 percent of parents interviewed count on receiving economic assistance from their children in old age.[30] And in any case, it is natural to depend upon help from one's children in the event of great misfortune.[31] Third, cultural context often demands a large number of children: as an affirmation of the family, as a guarantee of generational continuation, or as the expression of deep-rooted religious principles. Finally, ignorance of birth control methods, unavailability of contraceptives, and inadequate medical and health services contribute to inadequate fertility control or increased recourse to abortion. Legislation controlling the spread of contraceptives can reinforce these barriers to fertility decline.

If these are the causes of high fertility, then it is necessarily by means of their modification that the birth rate might decline. Above all, mortality must decline. Figure 5.3 (in which fertility and mortality are compared) indicates that in 1980–5 all the countries with a life expectancy over 60 had a relatively low *TFR*, the result of a certain degree of fertility control independent of socioeconomic conditions.

The increasing "relative cost" of childrearing also appears to be a factor in fertility decline. This increase may, for example, come about as the result of expanded female education, so that women are less willing to give up the

[29]   For differing interpretations regarding the cost of children, see J. C. Caldwell, "Direct Economic Costs and Benefits of Children" and P. H. Lindert, "The Changing Economic Costs and Benefits of Having Children," both in Lee and Bulatao, *Determinants of Fertility*.
[30]   The World Bank, *World Development Report 1984*, p. 52.
[31]   M. Cain, "Risk and Insurance: Perspectives on Fertility and Agrarian Change in India and Bangladesh," *Population and Development Review*, 7 (1981), pp. 435–74.

possibility of wage-earning employment in favor of housework and raising children. Other factors might include compulsory childhood schooling, which delays the beginning of a child's work life, or a general increase in well-being and the attendant requirements for greater investments in children. The creation of institutional mechanisms of social protection reduces the need of aging parents for support from their children, and so another incentive to high fertility is undermined. Other elements that tend to hasten fertility decline include the elimination of legislative obstacles to birth control, a policy actively supporting family planning, the spread of contraceptive knowledge and techniques and the fact of their being both affordable and psychologically acceptable.

None of the above factors can on its own bring about the transition from high to low fertility levels, and the proper combination of factors is difficult to determine, since it depends upon many characteristics of the society in question. The elements discussed entail improvements in medical and health services, economic development, and social change (changes in values, free-dom for women, secularization of behavior) – essentially all the aspects of societal development. No one aspect will effect change, and each country will have to find the appropriate mix.

Nonetheless, certain forms of intervention are simpler or more contained than others and so are more likely instruments of policy. Since the 1950s, for example, family planning has been a preferred approach and, generally speaking, it is unlikely that fertility decline will occur without an adequate network of these services.[32] Today, the political acceptability of this sort of intervention is taken for granted, but this was not always the case. In the 1950s and 1960s, family planning programs – often naively and even clumsily introduced – were opposed in much of the poor world. In those countries embracing a socialist political system or ideology, for example, it was claimed that economic development would spontaneously regulate fertility. In others, ruling nationalists viewed birth control policies as an attack on the numerical strengthening of the nation, while these policies were opposed on moral grounds in countries where religious fundamentalism played an important role. The support given by rich countries – especially the United States – to these programs, often of dubious motivation, was considered a subtle form of capitalist imperialism. Still in 1974, at the United Nations

---

[32]   This really only applies to developing countries. In the West almost the entire fertility transition took place by means of traditional methods like coitus interruptus. In fact, in most of the West the distribution and advertisement of birth control methods was illegal until after World War II.

World Population Conference in Bucharest[33] (a conference restricted to official national delegations), China, Algeria, Brazil, and Argentina headed a large group of nations opposed to policies aimed at lowering population growth rates. On the other hand, many Asian countries, especially those of the Indian subcontinent, were in favor of such policies. A memorable slogan from that conference claimed that "the best contraceptive is economic development." Ten years later in Mexico City, again at a UN conference,[34] opposition had disappeared; all nations agreed that demographic growth should be curbed by the application of specific policies not necessarily linked to other development policies. In 1994, at the Cairo United Nations Conference on Population and Development, this point was reaffirmed and unanimously endorsed.[35]

What have the results of demographic policy (understood in the restricted sense of family planning programs) been? (We shall for the moment leave aside the special case of China, whose coercive policy is unique.) The answer to this question contains important implications for future policies aimed at reducing fertility and slowing down the speed of population growth. According to one conventional view, a large part of the variation of fertility in poor countries derives from the fact that a large proportion of women who would like to limit their fertility are unable to do so because they are unaware of the existence of contraception or because contraception is either not available or access to it (in some cases because of cost) is restricted. Making contraception easily available then – or as is often said, satisfying the "unmet need" for contraception – will accelerate fertility decline. Satisfying that need is the goal of population policies, one they have gone some way to achieving in the past decades.[36] The existence of an "unmet need" is attested to by the fact that a percentage of pregnancies are unwanted, or mistimed (therefore not wanted at that particular moment), and that a share of women who do not use contraception want either to avoid or postpone pregnancies.[37] The role

[33]   United Nations, *Report of the United Nations World Population Conference* (New York, 1975).
[34]   United Nations, *Report of the International Conference on Population, 1984* (New York, 1984).
[35]   United Nations, International Conference on Population and Development, *Programme of Action*, Cairo, 1994.
[36]   J. Bongaarts, "The Role of Family Planning Programs in Contemporary Fertility Transition," *Working Paper*, no. 71, The Population Council, 1995.
[37]   On unmet need, see J. Bongaarts and J. Bruce, "The Causes of Unmet Need for Contraception and the Social Content of Services," *Working Paper*, no. 69, The Population Council, 1994; C. F. Westoff and A. Bankole, "Unmet Need: 1990–94," *DHS Comparative Studies*, no. 16 (Macro International Inc., Calverton, Maryland, 1995).

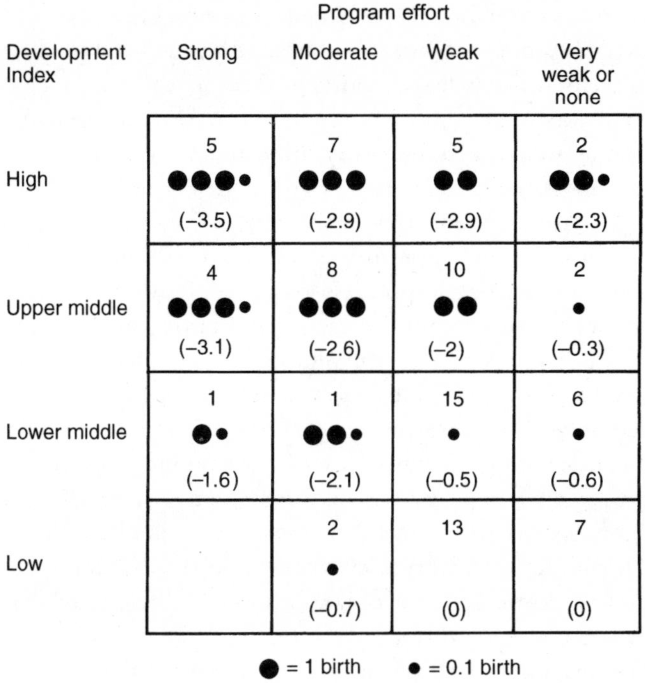

Program effort

Development Index	Strong	Moderate	Weak	Very weak or none
High	5 ●●●• (–3.5)	7 ●●● (–2.9)	5 ●● (–2.9)	2 ●●• (–2.3)
Upper middle	4 ●●●• (–3.1)	8 ●●● (–2.6)	10 ●● (–2)	2 • (–0.3)
Lower middle	1 ●• (–1.6)	1 ●●• (–2.1)	15 • (–0.5)	6 • (–0.6)
Low		2 • (–0.7)	13 (0)	7 (0)

● = 1 birth   • = 0.1 birth

Figure 5.10   Absolute decline in total fertility rate (1960–5 to 1990), by level
of development in 1985 and average program effort level in 1982–9
Note: in each square: top figure = number of countries: bottom figure (in
brackets) = decline of TFR (or children per woman) between 1960–5 and 1990.

of family planning programs can be assessed from Figure 5.10. This is a
classification of 88 poor countries according to the average fertility (TFR)
decline between 1960–5 and 1990 as a function of two variables: (1) a
development index (a synthesis, for 1985, of various indicators of education,
mortality, income, occupation, and urbanization); and (2) an index of family
planning program effort for 1982–9 (based on a variety of factors including
measures of policies, resources, "stage setting," services, record keeping,
and availability of fertility regulation supplies and services).[38] The results
are as expected: the greatest fertility decline occurred in countries where
both these indices were in the upper to middle range. Conversely, fertility
remained high in countries where development was low and programs weak
or nonexistent. Less easily predicted, decline was minimal in those countries

[38]   P. W. Mauldin and J. A. Ross, "Family Planning Programs: Efforts and Results,"
Studies in Family Planning, 22, no. 6 (1991).

enjoying relatively high levels of development but lacking much in the way of family planning programs. Development without appropriate programs slows down the process of fertility decline, while the combined action of these two factors speeds it up. Efforts to measure the "net" ("net" of the effects of development) contribution to fertility decline of the family planning programs are plagued with difficulties, and results vary from next to nothing to almost one-half.[39]

Less sophisticated supporters of the conventional view observe that contraceptive prevalence (the proportion of reproductive-age women currently employing contraception) is low where fertility is high and vice versa, and a close correlation of these variables is revealed in figure 5.11c (based on the findings of DHS surveys in the late 1980s and early 1990s in 44 developing countries).[40] It follows that policies that increase contraceptive supply will increase contraceptive prevalence and bring about a proportional decline in fertility. This sort of argument, however, is like saying that building new schools will bring about an increase in primary education, irrespective of the fact that parents might not be willing to send their children to school or that teachers might be missing and so on. In the case of fertility, contraception is only an instrument through which desires and aspirations may be realized.

A mirror-image approach as compared to the conventional "supply-side" view focuses instead on "demand," where demand refers to the children effectively wanted by parents.[41] Simply put, the theory states that fertility is driven by the desires of women or couples. Populations with high fertility then also have a high demand for children. Even if the supply of family planning services is high and they are efficiently run, they will be little used and fertility will remain high. This situation is particularly frequent in sub-Saharan countries and among many Islamic populations. Conversely, low demand for children coincides with low fertility even in the absence of family planning programs. Indeed in Western countries fertility declined in the first two-thirds of this century in spite of legislation hostile to family planning and a limited supply of contraceptives (advertising contraceptives

[39]   J. Bongaarts, *The Fertility Impact of Family Planning Programs* (The Population Council, New York, 1993), p. 4.

[40]   Of the 44 countries, 21 are from sub-Saharan Africa, 12 from Asia and North Africa, 11 from Latin America; the earliest survey was taken in 1986, the latest in 1994. See DHS, *Newsletter*, vol. 7, no. 2, 1995, p.12.

[41]   For an effective criticism of the conventional view and a demand-oriented approach, see L. H. Pritchett, "Desired Fertility and the Impact of Population Policies," *Population and Development Review*, 20 (1994), no. 1.

was illegal in many countries until the 1950s and 1960s). The level of fertility then is dictated by motivations, expectations, and desires. If these change, so will fertility. Figure 5.11 lends some support to this view. Indeed panel c – as we have seen – shows the close inverse relation between fertility and contraceptive prevalence, but the same association can also be seen between wanted fertility and contraceptive prevalence (panel d).[42] The close similarity of the two figures implies a very close association between actual and wanted fertility, as is indeed shown by panel a. In other words, variation in actual fertility is almost completely explained by variation in wanted fertility. When fertility is high, wanted fertility is also high. Panels b and e of figure 5.11 are still more interesting. In panel b, actual fertility is compared to the proportion of fertility that is unwanted.[43] As we can see, there is no correlation between the two variables: indeed, with the decline of fertility towards small family norms there is no attendant decline of unwanted fertility. On the contrary, unwanted fertility seems to increase in the intermediate stages of the fertility transition. Similar observation can be made regarding panel e, where the proportion of unwanted fertility is compared to the prevalence of contraception. One would think that increased prevalence of contraception should reduce unwanted fertility but such is not the case. A recent study suggests instead that the variation of fertility across countries (holding desires constant) is explained only in minimal part (1 or 2 percent) by variation in contraceptive prevalence.[44]

---

[42]   Prevalence of contraception is defined as the percentage of currently-married women, 15 to 49 years old, currently using any method. Wanted fertility (WTFR) is close, but not identical, to the concept of "desired fertility." This can be assessed on the basis of answers to the DHS survey question: "If you could go back to the time you did not have any children and could choose exactly the number of children to have in your whole life, how many would that be?" Subtracting from the number of actual births those births in excess of each woman's desires, a desired total fertility rate (DTFR) is computed. Answers to the question on desired fertility are obviously influenced by the mothers' rationalization of past behavior. Alternatively, wanted fertility can be estimated indirectly using answers to the question about desires for future births. This answer refers to the future and not to the past and is not biased by ex-post rationalization. Past births to women who want another child are classified as wanted and, with other adjustments, a measure of total wanted fertility is estimated (WTFR). For desired fertility, see C. Westoff, "Reproductive Preferences: A Comparative View," *Demographic and Health Surveys, Comparative Studies*, no. 3 (IRD/Macro Systems, Columbia, Maryland, 1991). For the concept of wanted fertility, see J. Bongaarts, "The Measurement of Wanted Fertility," *Population and Development Review*, 16 (1990), no. 3. For a discussion of the various measures, see L. Pritchett, "Desired Fertility."

[43]   Defined as $(TFR - WTFR)/TFR \times 100$.

[44]   L. H. Pritchett, "Desired Fertility," p. 15.

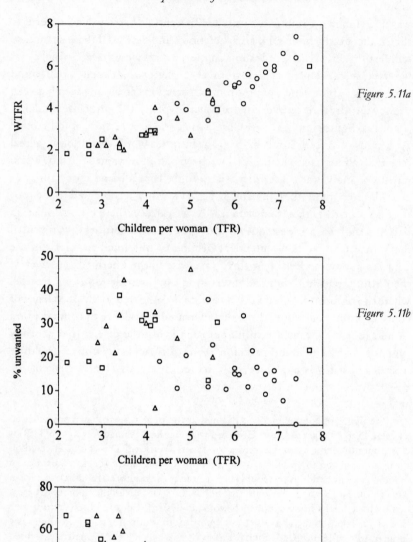

Figure 5.11a

Figure 5.11b

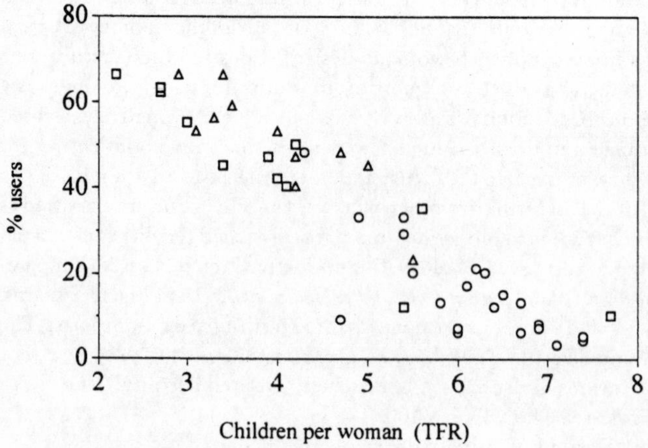

Figure 5.11c

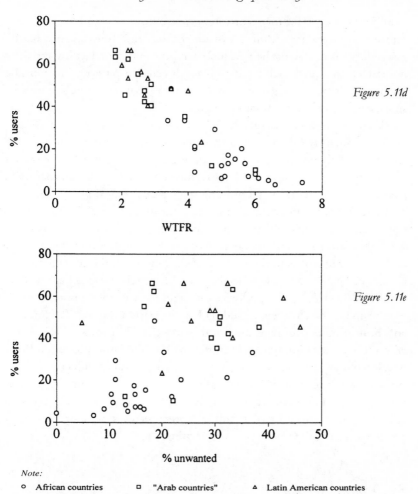

Figure 5.11d

Figure 5.11e

Note:

○ African countries   □ "Arab countries"   △ Latin American countries

African countries: Botswana, Burkina, Burundi, Cameroon, Ghana, Kenya, Liberia, Madagascar, Malawi, Mali, Namibia, Niger, Nigeria, Rwanda, Senegal, Sudan, Tanzania, Togo, Uganda, Zambia, Zimbabwe

Arab countries: Bangladesh, Egypt, Indonesia, Jordan, Morocco, Pakistan, Philippines, Sri Lanka, Thailand, Tunisia, Turkey, Yemen

Latin American countries: Bolivia, Brazil, Colombia, Dominican Republic, Ecuador, El Salvador, Guatemala, Mexico, Paraguay, Peru, Trinidad

TFR = Total Fertility Rate
WTFR = Total Wanted Fertility Rate
% users = Population of woman 15 to 49 practicing some method of contraception
% unwanted = Difference between TFR and WTFR as percentage of TFR

Figure 5.11   Relation between the average number of children per woman (TFR) and the percentage of undesired fertility for 44 populations (late 1980s)

Summing up: (1) fertility is driven by motivations and desires; (2) contraception is a necessary technical instrument for controlling fertility, but its availability – other factors being equal – has little impact on fertility and does not reduce unwanted fertility; (3) policies directed to lower fertility must be "demand" oriented, trying to influence the factors that determine the propensities, desires, and motivations of couples.

This debate has been useful in providing better guidelines for policies. It is clear that small family norms, well-rooted in society, cannot be brought about by family planning programs alone, no matter how well-conceived and aggressive they might be. Paul Demeny has identified four factors as particularly important in determining the fertility transition: (a) the direct cost parents must incur in raising and educating their children; (b) the opportunity costs of children to parents (or the earnings that a couple – in general the woman – forgoes because of children); (c) the contribution that children's labor makes to the income of the family; (d) the contribution of children to parents' economic security in old age relative to other forms of security.[45] Therefore, those policies that tend to favor the responsibility of parents in raising children, including bearing part of the cost of education and health; that encourage women to enter the labor force; that enforce compulsory education of children; that make child labor illegal; and that develop old-age private or public insurance schemes are conducive to fertility decline. The combination of these policies with well-balanced programs for family planning and reproductive health – which increase access to contraception, reduce its cost, and compress recourse to abortion – may accelerate a smooth transition to low fertility.

5   India and China

By the mid-1980s almost all the governments of the world officially supported family planning to some degree; the United Nations announced that this was the case for 127 countries comprising 94 percent of the world's population.[46] However, behind these encouraging figures are both successes and failures, as well as combinations of the two. The cases of India and China are representative and merit attention if only by virtue of the demographic

---

[45]   P. Demeny, "Policies Seeking a Reduction of High Fertility," in United Nations, *Population Policies and Programmes* (New York, 1993).

[46]   "Law and Policy Affecting Fertility: A Decade of Change," *Population Reports*, series E (Nov. 1984), p. E–117.

dimensions of these two countries: together they account for 38 percent of the world's population, about half the total for the developing countries.

Demographic data for the two countries are listed in table 5.5 and require little commentary. Between the early 1950s and the early 1990s Chinese fertility has been reduced by two-thirds, while that of India has declined by little more than one-third. Chinese life expectancy at birth, at the same level as India's at mid-century, is now 8 years longer. Today, Chinese fertility is at replacement level, and if it remains there the population will become stationary. By contrast, Indian fertility – almost two children per woman more – ensures continued rapid population growth.

In order to understand these great differences we must consider the demographic policies adopted by these two countries and their results. The Indian government has pursued slower demographic growth since 1952. The first two five-year plans (1951–6 and 1956–61) called for the creation of family planning centers; the fifth plan (1971–6) called for a crude birth rate of 25 per thousand by 1984 (clearly a goal not met, as the 1980–5 birth rate was 10 points higher).[47] Accomplishments have been few and fertility decline minimal: in 1970 the percentage of couples (woman of reproductive age) using birth control was very low (14 percent). (For both males and females the method most often used was sterilization.[48]) Success has been limited to a few states, the upper classes, and the urban population. Confronted with these poor results – caused by insufficient investment but also discontinuities and the difficulty of administering a program in a country characterized by a variety of languages, religions, and customs – Indira Gandhi's government decided in 1976 to speed up the program. With the declaration of April 16, 1976, the government implemented a series of measures (including strengthening of the existing program and increased financial incentives for the participants) and encouraged the state legislatures to pass laws making sterilization obligatory after the birth of the third child (only the state of Maharastra passed such a law, and it was not enforced).[49] This coercive line inspired violent protests that were among the causes of the defeat of Gandhi's Congress party in the March 1977 elections.[50] As a result, the Indian program suffered a notable setback. Indira Gandhi's return to power in 1980 and the unexpected

---

[47] A. Mitra, "National Population Policy in Relation to National Planning in India," *Population and Development Review*, 3 (1977); A. J. Coale, "Population Trends in India and China," *Proceedings of the National Academy of Sciences*, 80 (1983), p. 1759.

[48] Mauldin and Segal, "Prevalence of Contraceptive Use," table A.3.

[49] "National Population Policy: A Statement of the Government of India," *Population and Development Review*, 2 (1976).

[50] Mitra, "National Population Policy in India," p. 207.

Table 5.5 Demographic indices for India and China, 1950–90

(Population in millions)

Year	India	China
1950	358	555
1960	442	657
1970	555	831
1980	689	999
1990	851	1155
2000	1022	1285
Index 1990 = 100	285	232

Year	Birth rate (per 1000)		Death rate (per 1000)		Children per woman (TFR)		Life expectancy (e₀)		Annual growth rate	
	India	China	India	China	India	China	India	China	India	China
1950–55	44.1	43.6	25	25	5.97	6.11	38.7	40.8	2	1.87
1955–60	43.6	35.9	21.7	20.6	5.92	5.38	42.6	44.6	2.26	1.53
1960–65	42	37.8	19.4	17.1	5.81	5.61	45.4	49.5	2.26	2.07
1965–70	40.2	36.9	17.5	10.9	5.69	5.94	48	59.6	2.28	2.61
1970–75	38.2	28.8	15.8	6.3	5.43	4.76	50.3	63.2	2.24	2.21
1975–80	34.7	21.5	13.9	6.7	4.83	3.26	52.9	65.3	2.08	1.48
1980–85	33.8	20.6	12.6	6.6	4.47	2.5	55.4	66.6	2.18	1.38
1985–90	31.3	22.2	11.2	6.7	4.07	2.41	57.9	67.1	2.04	1.53
1990–95	29.1	18.5	10	7.2	3.75	1.95	60.4	68.5	1.91	1.11
Index 1950–5=100	66	42	40	29	63	32	156	168	96	59

Note: Figures for 1990–5 are estimates based on partial information.
Source: United Nations, *World Population Prospects: The 1994 Revision* (New York 1995).

results of the 1981 census (which revealed a population considerably larger than expected) led to renewal of the demographic policy. The seventh five-year plan (1986–90) calls for the achievement of replacement fertility by the year 2000. This is probably an unrealistic goal as it would require a fertility decline similar to that experienced in China during the 1970s under exceptional and perhaps nonrepeatable conditions. The Indian plan calls for greater investment in the family planning program; increased financial incentives for its participants; a big increase in sterilization and more widespread use of the IUD, not to mention other forms of birth control; and combining family planning services with maternal and infant services.[51]

"Despite official support (for 30 years) of family planning, the government of India has not been able to organize a birth control program that regularly provides adequately staffed services to most of the population. At different times the responsible central agency . . . has promoted different methods of contraception and tried different organizational approaches. At first, when modern contraceptives were not widely used anywhere in the world, there was a hope, soon disappointed, that periodic continence (the rhythm method) would reduce the birth rate in India, where it seemed to conform so well with Gandhian principles. Later there was primary reliance on the intrauterine device, but the health and family planning network never developed the capacity for skillful insertion, proper monitoring, and adequate counseling to counter exaggerated reports about the dangers of the device, to reassure patients about the side effects, or overall to obtain sustained high rates of insertion and retention. For various reasons, oral contraceptives have never been authorized for use in India." This is the harsh judgment of Ansley Coale, an expert on the Indian demographic situation.[52] The only aspect of the program which enjoyed a degree of success was sterilization, the frequency of which increased dramatically in 1976–7 (8 million sterilizations in two years as compared to an average of 2 million per year in the period just before). After Gandhi's defeat, however, the sterilization program came to a violent halt and has only shown signs of recovery in recent years.

The 1980s should have signaled a new strategy, concentrating not only on family planning but also on those aspects of social and economic development which favor fertility decline: increasing age at marriage, raising the status of women, improving female literacy, enhancing child survival,

[51] United Nations, *Population Policy Briefs: The Current Situation in Developing Countries, 1985* (New York, 1986).
[52] Coale, "Population Trends," p. 1760.

alleviating poverty, and providing for old age security.[53] These good intentions, however, have had little effect. In spite of increased resources, the 1980s witnessed "a steep decline in the quality of family planning and public health practice" due to the increasing role played by bureaucrats as opposed to specialists.[54] At the end of his term as prime minister, Rajiv Gandhi issued sharp criticism of population policy failure in India, citing excessive bureaucratic centralization of the program which allows little flexibility in a country characterized by vastly differing needs.[55] In recent years, the Government seems to have adopted a more diversified approach: couples are provided with information on a broad range of family planning methods, and the family planning targets set in various districts have been eliminated in order to dispel fears of coercion. A recent survey (1992–3) estimated a total fertility rate of 3.4 for all India; 4 women out of 10 were currently using contraception and two-thirds of these were sterilized; about four-fifths of all contraceptives were obtained from public sources. New steps then have been made in spite of the uncertain role of government actions. [56]

The history of government family planning programs in China differs considerably from that of India.[57] In 1949 Mao declared: "China's vast population should be viewed as a positive asset. Even if it should multiply many times, it will be fully able to resolve the problems created by this

[53]   United Nations, *Review of Recent Demographic Target-Setting* (New York, 1989), pp. 96–108.

[54]   D. Banrji, "Population Policies and Programmes in India during the Last Ten Years," in *Population Transition in India*, vol. 1, ed. S. N. Singh, M. K. Premi, P. S. Bhatia, and A. Bose (B. R. Publishing, New Delhi, 1989), p. 49.

[55]   Speech of Rajiv Gandhi inaugurating the 21st General Conference of the International Union for the Scientific Study of Population (IUSSP), New Delhi, September 20, 1989: "Yet, to a large extent, our family planning programs are more or less uniform throughout the country. Virtually the same package is delivered to the high population growth areas as to the low population growth areas . . . each couple's perception, especially the woman's perception, of the desired family size . . . is most influenced by the desires and ethos of the local community or neighborhood. How could this be determined monolithically by a central agency?"

[56]   *Populi*, 22 (1995), no. 4, p. 2; East–West Center, "New Survey Finds Fertility Decline in India," *Asia-Pacific Population Policy*, 32, January–February 1995.

[57]   On Chinese population policy I have used M. Aglietti, "La politica di pianificazione familiare in Cina dalla fondazione della Repubblica a oggi," degree thesis in demography, political science faculty, University of Florence, 1986–7. See also "Population and Birth Planning in the People's Republic of China," *Population Reports*, series J (Jan.–Feb. 1982); J. Banister, *China's Changing Population* (Stanford University Press, Stanford, 1987).

growth. The solution lies in production . . . Revolution and production can resolve the problem of feeding the population."[58] However, as the revolution was consolidated and the results of the 1953 census became known, concern over the population problem began to emerge. At the Eighth Party Congress in 1956 Zhou Enlai's speech included these remarks: "We all agree on the desirability of adopting measures favoring birth control, both for the protection of women and children and to ensure that the younger generations are brought up and educated in such a way as to guarantee national health and prosperity."[59] This first birth control program required the creation of an assistance network, the production of contraceptives, and a plan to encourage the population to use these birth control services and devices. However, demographic prudence was not in keeping with the ambitious socioeconomic program of 1958/9 – the Great Leap Forward – and the attendant blind faith in gigantic productivity goals. As a result the program came to a sudden halt; but after the failure of the Great Leap Forward, poor harvests, famine, and the high mortality of 1959–61, a second campaign was launched with the creation of a Department of Family Planning. This second campaign, which among other things introduced the IUD and advocated later marriage, was essentially suspended during the Cultural Revolution. It was only with the return to normality in 1971 that the third campaign began, based on the three principles of later marriage, longer birth intervals, and fewer children. Later marriage meant, for women, 23 years of age in rural areas and 25 in the city; longer intervals meant four years between the first and second child; and fewer children meant no more than two children in the city or three in the country. In 1977 the latter limit was lowered to two for both city and country. The unquestioned success of this program in the 1970s was due to a system of birth quotas: "According to this system, the Chinese government began to establish annual numerical objectives for the natural rate of population increase in each province . . . Provincial authorities and prefects, in turn, translated their assigned rate into a birth quota, distributing this quota among the prefectures and counties under their jurisdiction. This process continued on down until it reached the work team or its urban equivalent."[60] Within these groups, couples planning to have children met with group leaders to determine which were entitled to have a child the following year. About half of the couples practicing birth control

---

[58]   Aglietti, "La politica," p. 20.
[59]   Ibid., p. 28.
[60]   Ibid., pp. 152–3.

used an IUD, about a third used sterilization, and the remainder chose a variety of other methods, including a considerable proportion using steroids.[61] Abortion also became widespread and easily obtainable, free of charge, and did not require the husband's consent.

After Mao's death and the defeat of the Gang of Four, demographic objectives became both more explicit and more ambitious. During the second session of the Fifth National People's Assembly in 1979, Hua Guofeng affirmed that a large reduction in demographic growth was one of the essential conditions for the success of the "four modernizations" (of agriculture, defense, industry, and science and technology). Initially, the aim was to reduce the rate of natural increase to 0.5 percent in 1985 and zero in the year 2000. In September 1980, Hua updated these objectives, the new goal being to not exceed 1.2 billion in 2000. In order to accomplish this a birth limit of one child per couple was established in 1979, with exceptions for ethnic minorities, border areas, and couples in special situations. A series of incentives and disincentives has been introduced in order to meet this difficult goal. The primary tool has been the one-child certificate, issued by local authorities, which guarantees a series of benefits for couples and their children in exchange for the commitment not to have more than one child. The benefits include wage and pension increases, larger dwellings, free medical care, and priority in schools for the child. Couples who refuse to cooperate and give birth to a second, or worse, a third, child are penalized in the form of wage cuts, revocation of privileges, and other disincentives.[62]

The Chinese one-child policy has been pursued with varying intensity. Until 1983, pressure increased as coercive methods were implemented on a vast scale. The resulting protests and discontent, however, led to a period of uncertainty. On the one hand, recognition of the growing number of women of reproductive age born during the period of fertility increase which followed the catastrophic Great Leap Forward (between 1983 and 1993 the number of women aged 21 to 30 has increased from 80 to 125 million), argues for maintaining the policy;[63] on the other hand, the protest and resistance of a population denied one of the most basic of human rights urges its relaxation. The 1990 census counted 1.134 billion Chinese and reveals that the official goals will not be easily realized. Until 1985, government policy continued to target a population not over 1.2 billion by

---

[61]   "Population and Birth Planning in China," p. 590.
[62]   Aglietti, "La politica," p. 217.
[63]   K. Hardee-Cleaveland and J. Banister, "Fertility Policy and Implementation in China," *Population and Development Review*, 14 (1988), p. 247.

the year 2000, but this formula has since been made more elastic, calling for "about 1.2 billion," which in practice means that the ceiling has been lifted to 1.25 billion. This limit too has been recently officially revised to 1.3 billion.[64] The 1980s were indeed characterized by several examples of the relaxation of the policy: the progressive extension of the right of rural couples to have a second child when the firstborn is a girl, or permission granted on special, probably discretionary, grounds or because the family lived in a remote area or had special characteristics.[65] Fertility decline stopped in the first part of the 1980s and fertility even increased between 1985 and 1987 (TFR grew from 2.3 to 2.5). The dismantling of the socialist collectives, which were an essential tool of family planning policies, "led to an erosion of cadre power and a breakdown of the system of economic incentives and disincentives on which policy enforcement had been largely based."[66] Moreover, the process of economic liberalization and the general attenuation of public control over individual behavior increased the obstacles to full implementation of the policy. Nonetheless, at the beginning of the 1990s the Chinese leadership renewed its commitment to the one-child policy, leaving the regulations intact and strengthening their implementation: a nationwide fertility survey put total fertility at 1.9 for 1992, well below the average level of the 1980s. Apparently this new party-led drive is enjoying success, reinforcing commitment to family planning at all levels and responsibility systems, strengthening economic incentives and penalties, introducing old-age insurance schemes, etc.[67] Continuing rapid economic growth and associated social change have also influenced

---

[64] "China's Experience in Population Matters: an Official Statement," *Population and Development Review*, 20 (1994), no. 2; text read before the 27th Session of the United Nations Population Commission on March 28, 1994, by Peng Yu, China's representative to the Commission. The text refers also to the official population policy guidelines. The medium variant projection of the United Nations (1994 revision) predicts a population of 1.285 billion for the year 2000.

[65] Jiali Li, "China's Family Planning Program: How, and How Well, Did it Work?," The Population Council, *Working Paper*, no. 65, 1994. Out of a sample of permissions granted to rural couples for second or higher order births in the province of Hebei in 1983–8, 33 percent were granted because the first child had died or was disabled; 7 percent because of remarriage; 25 percent because the couple lived in a remote area or had special characteristics (belonged to a minority or one member worked as a miner, was disabled, etc.); 14 percent because a "special permit" was granted; 21 percent because of the desire to have a male child who could carry on the family line.

[66] S. Greenhalgh, Z. Chuzhu and L. Nan, "Restraining Population Growth in Three Chinese Villages," *Population and Development Review*, 20 (1994), no. 2, p. 366.

[67] Ibid., pp. 382–9.

reproductive norms and values thus facilitating the task of policymakers.

In spite of great difficulties, Chinese demographic policy has clearly realized goals not even approached by the other Asian population giant. The reasons for this success are many, but may be summarized by the following four points:

1   Chinese social transformation has proceeded more quickly and efficiently in the area of public health care. Mortality as a result has declined more rapidly than in India, favoring fertility decline.
2   In the Chinese political system, the authority of the Communist Party ruling group extends through all levels of the administrative hierarchy down to the production squads. This system has allowed for the quick execution of demographic policy directives, a task facilitated by effective propaganda and indoctrination.[68]
3   An efficient distribution and assistance network has been established employing a variety of birth control methods, including abortion.
4   Chinese society may be more receptive to fertility limitation. Other East Asian societies, linked to some degree to Chinese society, have experienced rapid fertility decline in a variety of socioeconomic contexts; these include Japan, Taiwan, South Korea, Singapore, and Hong Kong.[69]

The age structures for China and India in 1950 and 2025 (the latter according to the United Nations projections which, incidentally, do not predict full realization of Chinese goals) are compared in figures 5.12a and 5.12b. In 1950 the shape of these structures is similar and China has a larger population in each age group: 555 million total in China as opposed to 358 million in India, a difference of almost 200 million (+55 percent). In 2025 the population of China will be smaller than that of India in each age group up to age 35 as a result of more rapid fertility decline since 1970. Only at the older ages will Chinese population be much greater than that of India. The difference between the total population in the two countries will decline considerably (1.526 billion in China, 1.392 in India: + 10 percent). Between 1950 and 2025 the population of India will almost quadruple while that of China will increase by a factor of less than three.

[68]   Aglietti, "La politica," p. 328.
[69]   Coale, "Population Trends," p. 1761.

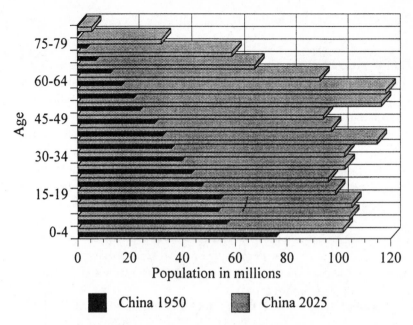

Figure 5.12a   Age structure in China (1950 and 2025)

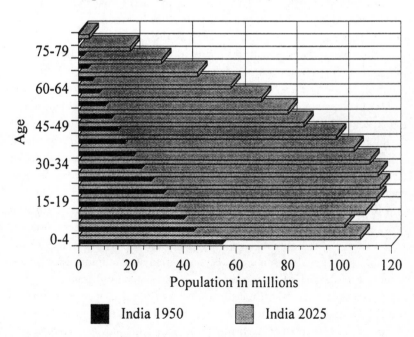

Figure 5.12b   Age structure in India (1950 and 2025)

6   *Fertilia and Sterilia*

"In the tropical region of a large continent lie the two bordering lands of
Fertilia and Sterilia, which have in common a primarily agricultural economy pursued in the more temperate highlands. Sterilia has an outlet on the
sea where its principal city is found. It has for centuries been a center of
maritime commerce and trades with countries near and far, including a
former colonial power. Sterilia's population is, especially in the coastal
region, ethnically mixed as a result of the several currents of immigration
which have peopled its shores. Fertilia, on the other hand, landlocked and
extending to the interior of the continent, is characterized by ethnic
homogeneity and a traditional culture. Politically it is dominated by an
upper class of large landowners, and contact with the outside world is
minimal. At the time of decolonization, which occurred contempora-
neously in the two countries, the two populations were about the same size
and had similar demographic characteristics: fertility was high and
uncontrolled and mortality, though high by Western standards, had nonetheless declined considerably thanks to the introduction of penicillin and
the elimination of malaria by DDT spraying in the colonial era. As a result,
both of the countries had high rates of growth, between 2 and 3 percent.
Independence brought a coalition backed by the large landowners to power
in Fertilia, while the merchant class gained hegemony in Sterilia. In addition to trade liberalization, one of the first political acts in Sterilia was the
initiation of a vigorous family planning program, spread throughout the
country by a system of internal communications and supported by foreign
investment. A trained corps of personnel and a mobile network of
consultants were quickly established. Other measures included liberalized
abortion and sterilization, subsidies for contraceptives, and incentives for
participation in the program. We shall probably never be able to determine
whether this program was actually the cause of the profound changes in
reproductive behavior which followed or else simply accelerated a transition
already on the verge of initiation. In either case, fertility declined quickly,
soon reaching replacement levels. By comparison, the more traditional
government of Fertilia, influenced by fundamentalist religious groups and
ruling a population little exposed to foreign contact and trade, only for-
mally recognized the UN directive to respect the right of every couple to
decide how many children it wanted. In spite of pressure from the ex-colo-
nial power, which provided considerable economic aid, no active family
planning policy was initiated and, if anything, the government blocked

similar programs advanced by private concerns. Birth control spread slowly and, 30 years after independence, the women of Fertilia bore on average two children more than those of Sterilia.

These two policies have affected the demographic growth and economic development of these countries very differently. The demographic consequences include divergent rates of growth and age structures. Equally populous at the time of independence (which, however, was referred to as the Revolution in Sterilia), the ratio was 1.4-to-1 after 30 years (in favor of Fertilia naturally) and 2-to-1 after 60. In Sterilia, population under the age of 15 accounted for 42 percent of the total at the time of the revolution; after 30 years this figure had dropped to 27 and after 60 to 21 (at which time the growth rate was about zero). In Fertilia, on the other hand, the under 15 proportion, equal to that of Sterilia at the time of independence (42 percent), declined more slowly, representing 38 percent of the total after 30 years and 30 percent after 60. At the latter date population growth was still running about 1.5 percent per year. By contrast, 60 years after the Revolution the proportion of the population over 65 in Sterilia (12 percent) was double that in Fertilia.

Differences in economic development have been equally significant. The high rate of growth in Fertilia has led to the quadrupling of the working-age population with an attendant high level of agricultural underemployment. Strong currents of migration flow primarily toward the capital city, which has become a sprawling megalopolis crowded with improverished masses. Given the still large average family size, the average Fertilian's small income goes almost entirely to obtaining the necessities of survival, leaving little for savings; this is to the detriment of investments, which only barely keep pace with population growth. The meager financial resources commanded by the government have been insufficient to expand infrastructure and services. In particular, the spread of education has been slow: in spite of the (slow) fertility decline, the school-age population, between the ages of 5 and 15, has tripled in the 60 years considered. The combination of a slow rate of agricultural development and a high rate of urbanization has transformed the country from an exporter of tropical products to a net importer of foodstuffs. Lack of investment has inhibited the development of its fragile manufacturing industry, and the country has accumulated an enormous foreign debt. The growth of per capita income has been small, and the absolute number (if not the percentage) of the marginally poor and illiterate has increased dramatically.

Sterilia's recent history differs substantially from that of Fertilia. Fertility limitation has ensured that, during the 60 years since the revolution, the size of Sterilia's school-age population has remained constant (as opposed to its tripling in Fertilia), which has enabled public monies to be used for considerable expansion and improvement of the education system. As a result, succeeding generations entering the labor market have been both smaller in number and better trained than in Fertilia. Labor force efficiency has increased rapidly, fueling development in both the traditional and modern sectors of the economy. Birth control has also meant smaller families and so more rapid emancipation of women and the possibility for personal savings of those resources no longer completely absorbed by basic needs. Greater savings have allowed investments to outpace demographic growth, making infrastructure modernization, greater agricultural production, and economic diversification possible. Moreover, changes in age structure have notably reduced the dependency ratio (the number of nonproductive members of society – the old and the very young – per 100 productive members), and this too has favored economic development. This same process has proceeded much more slowly in Fertilia. Lower levels of population increase and urbanization and above all improved agricultural productivity have ensured that Sterilia remains a net exporter of foodstuffs, which has helped to finance the purchase of machinery for the development of the manufacturing industries. Per capita income has grown rapidly and, 60 years after the Revolution, Sterilia has half the population of Fertilia, a larger gross national product, and a standard of living envied by its neighbor."

The preceding passage is an invention on the part of the author, but might be taken from the work of an historian attempting to describe and interpret the recent past of these two countries, also purely imaginary.[70] Analyses of this sort have been frequent over the decades since the Second World War, during which the population growth rate of the developing countries has risen dramatically, making demographic increase a major contemporary concern. The contrast between Fertilia and Sterilia serves to illustrate the paths which the poorer nations have followed in recent decades or might follow in the near future. However, the above analysis, while fairly convincing in its general line of reasoning, is less so for the basic assumptions that it takes for granted.

[70] I am indebted to a well-known scholar both for the idea and the names of Fertilia and Sterilia. See J. E. Meade, "Population Explosion, the Standard of Living and Social Conflict," *The Economic Journal*, 77 (1967), pp. 233–55. The example of the two islands of Fertilia and Sterilia is found on pp. 239–42, together with many discerning observations about the relationship between demographic growth and economic development. My attempt to find alternative names to Fertilia and Sterilia and so avoid the above plagiarism met with no success.

The first of these assumptions is that rapidly growing population inevitably leads to diminishing returns from labor and other factors of production and so to that capital dilution which, all things being equal, increases poverty; according to this formula, the slower population growth of Sterilia is clearly an advantage. The second assumption is that smaller families lead to the creation of savings and so greater investments, another point in Sterilia's favor. The third is that slower population growth means greater work force efficiency and so greater productivity. And according to the fourth, factors of scale related to demographic size are of little relevance and so do not benefit the more rapidly growing population. Similarly, population increase is assumed to have no positive effect on technological progress. In short, success at limiting demographic growth must be a determining factor of economic development. It should follow, then, that demographic growth and economic development over the past 30 or 40 years relate inversely to one another.

This final point, which sums up the previous ones, can be put to a first-order test. It is a fairly crude test, analogous to that made in chapter 4 (section 7) for the Western countries, comparing population growth rates and per capita income for 57 poor countries.[71] I need not repeat here the cautions I have already expressed at some length regarding this exercise. Figure 5.13 plots the population growth rate against the per capita GNP growth rate for the period 1965–86. The correlation between these two variables is nonexistent and the points on the graph are spread about in complete disorder. In figure 5.14 the population rate is for the period 1950–70, 15 years earlier than that used for the GNP rate (1965–86), in keeping with the hypothesis that the intensity of demographic growth is reflected in GNP growth only after a certain delay (here taken as the approximate time between birth and entry into the work force). Again there is no apparent correlation between the two variables. Finally, figure 5.15 compares demographic and economic performance during the entire period 1950–87 for 15 Asian and Latin American countries, reinforcing the impression that there is no correlation between these two variables. Taiwan and Bangladesh, for example, have had the same rate of population growth but respectively the highest and lowest rates of economic growth of the group. Similar contrasts exist between China and Argentina and between Korea and Chile.

This test does not of course prove that there is no connection between

[71] Not included among the 57 are the large petroleum exporters, very small nations, and those severely affected by war or revolution.

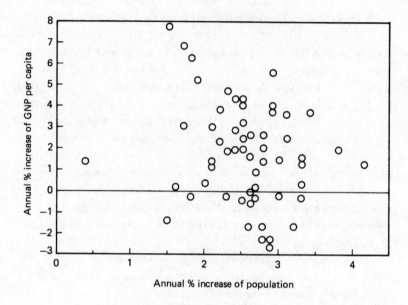

Figure 5.13   Annual percent increase of population and per capita GNP in
57 less-developed countries (1965–86)

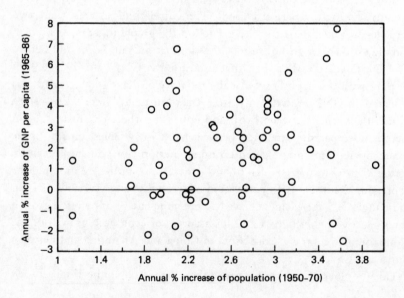

Figure 5.14   Annual percent increase of population (1950–70) and per
capita GNP (1965–86) in 57 less-developed countries

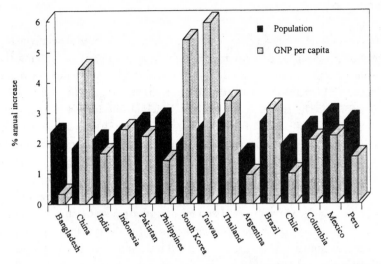

Figure 5.15   Annual percent increase of per capita GDP and population in
15 less-developed countries (1950–87)

the phenomena of population growth and economic development. It only
indicates that this connection is blurred by a series of factors which probably cancel one another. It also indicates that demographic growth has
probably not been an insurmountable obstacle to increasing well-being
and that, for diverse and complicated reasons, those factors which seemed
so clearly at work in Fertilia and Sterilia have in fact operated in a much
less clear fashion in recent decades.[72] I shall turn to this problem in the
pages that follow.

[72]   In a recent overview of the relationship between population and development,
Robert Cassen writes: "Altogether simple economics seems to suggest that countries
with faster population growth will in the long run end up with lower per capita
income . . . But neither theory nor econometrics has so far been able to demonstrate this relationship beyond doubt." See R. Cassen, "Overview," in *Population and
Development: Old Debates, New Conclusions*, ed. R. Cassen (Transaction Publishers, New
Brunswick, USA, 1994), pp. 10–11. For Ansley Coale, the lack of association between
population and economic growth is due to the banal fact that population growth is
(migration aside) the difference between birth and death rates, and both of these
have strong inverse relations with the gradient of development. As a consequence,
the same rate of population growth can occur at different levels of development
blurring any visible relation with the speed of economic growth. See A. Coale,
"Population Trends and Economic Development," in *World Population and the U.S.
Policy: The Choices Ahead*, ed. J. Menken (W. W. Norton, New York, 1986).

7 Explaining a Paradox

Considerable debate has arisen over the fact that the model relationship between demographic growth and economic development underlying the examples of Fertilia and Sterilia cannot be verified (as crudely demonstrated by figures 5.13–5.15). As a result, scholars have sought both empirical verification for the theoretical premises on which the model is based and explanations for the lack of confirmation.[73] Ironically, it was at just that moment when it became universally accepted that population growth must be controlled – at the 1984 United Nations Conference in Mexico – and that fertility growth was considered a goal in and of itself and not subordinate to others, that the existence of an unambiguous relationship between the phenomena of demographic and economic growth also began to be questioned. This is not surprising, however, since the idea of limiting growth has been accepted as a worthy goal in and of itself, independent of empirical verification.

Returning to the heart of the problem, faster demographic growth – that of Fertilia as compared to Sterilia – is considered harmful to economic growth for a series of reasons. In simplified form they are:

1   The stock of physical capital (that is, capital goods such as tools, machinery, infrastructure, and buildings) per worker declines, or is "diluted," by the addition of new units of population. As a result, per capita production also declines.[74] Fertilia, growing more quickly than Sterilia, suffers from this handicap, which could be overcome if its rate of investment (the proportion of GDP dedicated to investment) were to increase. This increase, however, can only come about if a smaller proportion of income is devoted to consumption, which in turn is linked to the standard of living. Table 5.6 reports absolute values of gross investment for a number of countries as well as investment as a percentage of GDP and per capita investment

---

[73]   There is considerable literature on this topic. I shall cite several works that seem to me fundamental both for their broad scope and systematic approach: The World Bank, *World Development Report 1984*, esp. chaps. 5 and 6; G. McNicoll, "Consequences of Rapid Population Growth: An Overview and Assessment," *Population and Development Review*, 10 (1984), pp. 177–740; E. Hammel et al., *Population Growth and Economic Development: Policy Questions* (National Academy Press, Washington, D.C., 1986); A. C. Kelley, "Economic Consequences of Population Change in the Third World," *Journal of Economic Literature*, 26 (1988), pp. 1685–728; R. Cassen, *Population and Development*.

[74]   On this and the following points, see the classic work of A. J. Coale and E. M. Hoover, *Population Growth and Economic Development in Low-Income Countries* (Princeton University Press, Princeton, 1958), pp. 19–20.

Table 5.6 Gross investment and working age population, selected less-developed countries and five major economies

Country	Gross domestic investment		Annual increase of working age population (in millions) 1985–90	Gross investment per potential additional worker (thousands $)	% increase of working age population (1990–2000)
	% of GDP	Millions $			
China	38	136,435	15.8	8.6	12
India	24	66,586	10.8	6.2	25
Bangladesh	12	2,224	2.28	1.0	34
South Korea	30	45,360	0.58	78.2	11
Thailand	28	15,400	0.84	18.3	23
Nigeria	13	4,147	1.52	2.7	40
Ethiopia	16	902	0.58	1.6	33
Egypt	20	6,600	0.66	10.0	32
Brazil	23	71,539	1.90	37.7	25
Mexico	20	29,568	1.58	18.7	28
Bolivia	11	439	0.18	2.4	35
Major 5[a]	21	2,195,052	1.90	1,155.3	3

[a] United States, Japan, Germany, France, and Italy.
Source: Data on population derived from United Nations, The Sex and Age Distribution of Population (New York, 1991); data on gross investment derived from World Bank, World Development Report 1990 (Oxford University Press, New York, 1990)

per each potential additional worker between 1985 and 1990. Investment available per each additional worker in poor countries varies from a minimum of $1,000 in Bangladesh to $78,000 in South Korea, but even the latter is barely one-fifth the available investment in rich countries. The problem for the poor countries (especially those with high rates of natural increase) is made worse by the fact that over the next decades their work forces will expand at rates far above those of the rich countries and so, in order to reduce the gap between them, they must not only match but exceed the rich country rate of investment increase. However, as far as variation of the labor force is concerned, prospects in less developed countries vary considerably. Figure 5.16 compares the annual rate of increase of the labor force in Asia and sub-Saharan Africa during the past 30 years with the same rate estimated for the next 30 years. For the majority of Asian countries (panel a) future rates are well below past rates, while the reverse is true for sub-Saharan Africa. In this latter group of countries available investment will encounter an accelerating supply of labor (in many cases with rates of increase exceeding 3 percent a year), while in Asian countries the labor force supply will decelerate (many countries with rates below 1 percent).

2   When natural resources – especially land and the water necessary to make it productive – are scarce or expensive, they too are affected by excessive population growth, suffering the progressively diminishing returns which we have already discussed at length (see chapter 3, section 1). During the decade 1990–2000 the working-age agricultural population will continue to increase rapidly in many Asian countries already characterized by very high agricultural population densities, a high level of landlessness, and small average holdings among the landed. As rural population increases, "the implications will be grim. Arable land per farmer will decline even further, lowering labor productivity and income, increasing the incidence of rural poverty and exacerbating inequality."[75]

3   Human capital, as expressed by the physical and technical efficiency of the population, is subject to rules similar to those applying to physical capital. If, for example, Fertilia and Sterilia invest the same percentage of GDP in social programs (education, but also public health) at the beginning of their demographic transitions, then the subsequent and growing difference in the size of the school-age populations will be such that while in Sterilia education can expand and improve without increasing this percentage, the same can only occur in Fertilia if the percentage increases

[75]   J. Bauer, "Demographic Change and Asian Labor Markets in the 1990s," *Population and Development Review*, 16 (1990), p. 631.

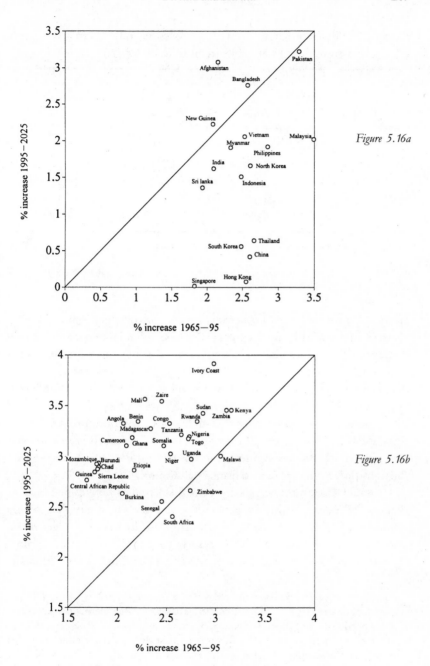

Figure 5.16a

Figure 5.16b

Figure 5.16   Past and future labour-force growth in (a) Asia, and
(b) Sub-Saharan Africa

Table 5.7 Malawi: projected primary school costs under alternative fertility
assumptions (1980–2015, in millions of dollars)

Year	Modest fertility decline	Rapid fertility decline	Savings with rapid fertility decline (%)
1980	9.8	9.8	–
1995	26.9	25.1	7
2000	34.6	27.1	22
2005	40.9	27.0	34
2010	47.8	26.6	44
2015	54.3	23.5	57

Enrollment increasing from 65% in 1980 to 100% in 2000.

Source: The World Bank, *World Development Report 1984* (Oxford University Press, New York, 1984),
p. 85

(at the expense naturally of other investments or consumption).[76] Table 5.7,
again from the World Bank Report, reveals the potential impact of differing
demographic trends in Malawi, taking universal elementary education by the
year 2000 as a goal. The country would spend much less should fertility
decline more quickly than the current trend suggests: 27 million dollars as
opposed to 48 million (44 percent less) in the year 2010. The money saved
might be put to use improving the quality of instruction, prolonging the
time spent in school, or for other purposes. Increased education has
beneficial effects on development, and this effect is particularly strong with
the transition from illiteracy to primary education.[77]

4   Rapid growth may create a general distortion of public spending. As
literacy and public health are generally given priority, a rapidly growing
population may require that a larger portion of the overall budget be set
aside for these needs than is the case for a population growing more
slowly.[78] Fewer resources remain for investment in fixed capital, generally

[76]   Coale and Hoover, *Population Growth*, p. 25.
[77]   A study of a group of developing countries has shown that increasing the average
amount of education of the labor force by one year raises GDP by 9 percent; this rate
of improvement, however, only holds for the first three years of education after
which the return for an additional year of education diminishes to about 4 percent.
See The World Bank, *World Development Report 1991* (Oxford University Press, New
York, 1991), p. 43.
[78]   Ibid., p. 285.

considered more profitable in the short or medium run, and so growth is less than it would otherwise be.

5   Rapid demographic growth also inhibits the creation of family savings. These in turn represent a significant portion of the private savings which determine the resources available for investment.[79] Rapid growth implies high fertility and large families. As a result family income is devoted primarily to satisfying basic needs, leaving only a few cents for savings. As the number of children per family declines, a larger percentage of family resources becomes available for savings, and so for investments. The link to economic growth is clear.

6   Several of the previous points suggest that population increase (or increase of the absolute dimensions of the economy) does not generate positive factors of scale. In other words, a larger population would not create better conditions for the use of the factors of production (natural resources, capital, labor).[80]

In order to verify the above points (which are simplifications of much more complex theories), we should be able to detect a negative relationship between demographic growth and economic development over the past decades. If we have been unable to do so, it is because the diverse situations of the poor countries and their often stormy political, economic, and social histories have altered, often in unexpected ways, the above mechanisms.

Consider the investments in fixed capital that make an important contribution to development in poor countries: for the period 1960–87 it has been estimated that about two-thirds of output growth was the result of increased inputs of capital as compared to one-fourth due to labor and one-seventh to total factor productivity or technical progress. In industrial countries, the contribution of fixed capital in the same period was much lower and estimated at between one-fourth and one-third of total growth.[81] All things being equal, there should in principle exist a thinning effect on

[79]   Ibid., p. 25.

[80]   With regard to the minimal relevance of factors of scale in the manufacturing industries, see National Research Council, *Population Growth*, p. 52.

[81]   The World Bank, *World Development Report 1991* (Oxford University Press, New York, 1991), p. 45. See also E. F. Denison, *Trends in American Economic Growth* (Brookings Institution, Washington, D.C., 1985), who estimates that the contribution of capital accumulation to US GNP growth between 1929 and 1982 was less than one-fifth. See also A. Maddison, *Phases of Capitalism Development* (Oxford University Press, Oxford, 1982), pp. 23–4; A. C. Kelley, "Economic Consequences of Population Change", pp. 1704–5.

capital per worker in more rapidly growing populations.[82] Many countries, particularly the poorest ones, have managed just the same to increase the percentage of their GNP devoted to investment: According to the World Bank, low-income economies increased this share from 20 to 30 percent between 1970 and 1993.[83] In this way the "thinning effect" on capital exerted by rapid population growth has been at least partially neutralized.

With regard to fixed natural resources, especially land, the agricultural expansion that has enabled the developing countries as a whole to increase agricultural production at a greater rate than population is primarily due to increasing yields (the "green revolution"), rather than the cultivation of new lands.[84] In fact, the introduction of green revolution technology in many areas has been aided by high population density, which favors infrastructure development and technology transfer.[85] In other areas, however, the scarcity of land and its high cost have created serious obstacles.[86]

Recent studies have also cast doubt on the theory that rapid demographic growth alters the proportions of public spending, favoring "social investments," especially education, at the expense of investments in fixed capital. According to some, poor country rates of demographic growth have not affected the progress of literacy and education, nor have they distorted public spending to the detriment of investments in fixed capital. More economical use of available resources (for example, limiting teachers' salaries) has allowed for the realization of goals in spite of high demographic pressure.[87] During the past 25 years, an increased proportion of

[82]   National Research Council, *Population Growth*, pp. 40–6.

[83]   The World Bank, *World Development Report 1995* (Oxford University Press, New York, 1995), table 9.

[84]   Y. Hayami and V. W. Ruttan, "The Green Revolution: Inducement and Distribution," *Pakistan Development Review*, 23 (1984), pp. 38–63; see also The World Bank, *World Development Report 1993*, p. 135 for regional estimates of the contribution of variation of areas and yields to cereal production.

[85]   P. L. Pingali and H. R. Binswangen, "Population Density and Agriculture Intensification: A Study of the Evolution of Technologies in Tropical Agriculture," in *Population Growth and Economic Development*, ed. D. G. Johnson and R. D. Lee (The University of Wisconsin Press, Madison, 1987).

[86]   Kelley, "Economic Consequences of Population Change," pp. 1712–15.

[87]   T. P. Schultz, "School Expenditures and Enrollments, 1960–1980: The Effects of Income, Prices and Population Growth," in Johnson and Lee, *Population Growth*; see also J. G. Williamson, "Human Capital Deepening, Inequality and Demographic Events along the Asia-Pacific Rim," in *Human Resources in Development along the Asia-Pacific Rim*, eds. N. Ogawa, G. W. Jones, and J. G. Williamson (Oxford University Press, Singapore, 1993).

production in many countries has been channeled to education.[88]

With regard to the creation of savings, both theoretical and empirical considerations challenge the assumption that rapidly growing population necessarily implies a lower rate of saving due to larger family size. Several possible mechanisms seem to neutralize this effect. The first is that adult labor intensity within the family does not remain fixed, but changes in response to changes in family size. A larger number of dependent children leads to intensification of productive activity (particularly in rural areas), an increase in resources and so perhaps also of savings.[89] In his classic study of peasant economies, Chayanov noted a clear relationship between the number of dependents per worker and labor intensity in peasant families of Tsarist Russia. Intensity increased as families grew and declined as they shrank.[90] In the second place, there is a higher ratio of young workers (who save) to old or retired workers (who have negative savings) in a rapidly growing population, and this effect tends to balance out the negative impact on savings of a large number of dependent children.[91] Finally, family savings in poor countries come primarily from a few very rich families and so are little influenced by family size. As things stand, the numerous tests of the relationship between demographic growth (not to mention age structure, dependency ratio, and so forth) and the rate of savings have not yielded significant results. Opposing forces seem to neutralize one another, and it may also be the case that insufficient data play an important role in the inconclusiveness of results.[92]

The final point concerns possible economies of scale, which I have already discussed (see chapter 3, section 5). Those who support the hypothesis of a negative correlation between demographic growth and economic development believe these to be nonexistent or at least irrelevant. Others, however, hold that population growth and increasing density have fueled the development of infrastructure (especially communications and transportation)

---

[88] A. Cammelli, "La qualità del capitale umano," in *Le risorse umane del Mediterraneo*, ed. M. Livi-Bacci and F. Veronesi Martuzzi (Il Mulino, Bologna, 1990).

[89] For a review of the relationship between demographic growth and savings, see A. Mason, "Saving, Economic Growth, and Demographic Change," *Population and Development Review*, 14 (1988), pp. 113–44; Kelley, "Economic Consequences of Population Change," pp. 1706–8; The World Bank, *World Development*, pp. 82–4.

[90] A. V. Chayanov, *The Theory of Peasant Economy* (Irwin, Homewood, Ill., 1966). For a more systematic and up-to-date treatment see J. Simon, *The Economics of Population Growth* (Princeton University Press, Princeton, 1977), pp. 185–95.

[91] National Research Council., *Population Growth*, p. 43.

[92] Ibid., pp. 43–5; Kelley, "Economic Consequences of Population Change," pp. 1706–7.

necessary to economic development.[93] As mentioned above, in many countries agricultural development and the green revolution seem to be helped
rather than hindered by higher demographic density, and so factors of scale,
in a broad sense, seem to exercise a significant positive influence.

The problems raised by consideration of the relationship between population and economy are intricate and involve variables whose interaction and
causal relationship with other factors are neither stable nor well understood.
The above discussion may help to explain why the evolution of the relationship between population and economy in recent decades escapes simple
theoretical schemes. The extreme adaptability of human behavior, both
demographic and economic, in the face of external limitations confounds
the simplifications of those who would like to translate this behavior into
simple formulas for the sake of easy analysis. In addition, the helter-skelter
progress of technology blunts, expands, and distorts relationships often
taken for granted.

Nonetheless, the fact that a clear and direct relationship between demographic growth and economic development is not readily discerned does not
mean that it does not exist nor that it is ultimately unmeasurable. The
conclusions reached by A. C. Kelley in his in-depth study of this problem
are relevant: "Economic growth (as measured by per capita output) in many
developing countries would have been more rapid in an environment of
slower population growth, although in a number of countries the impact
of population was probably negligible, and in some it may have been
positive. Population's adverse impact has most likely occurred where arable
land and water are particularly scarce or costly to acquire, where property
rights to land and natural resources are poorly defined and where
government policies are biased against the most abundant factor of
production – labor. Population's positive impact most likely occurred where
natural resources are abundant, where the possibilities for scale economies
are substantial, and where markets and other institutions (especially government) allocate resources in a reasonably efficient way over time and space."[94]

Therefore, between the demographic paths taken by Fertilia and Sterilia,
the choice will generally be for that of Sterilia, though we should keep in
mind that this choice may not always be a successful one.

---

[93]   Simon, *Economics of Population Growth*, pp. 262–77.
[94]   Kelley, "Economic Consequences of Population Change," p. 1715. See also A. C.
Kelley and W. P. McGreevey, "Population and Development in Historical Perspective," in Cassen, *Population and Development*.

6

The Future

1 Population and Self-Regulation

Two centuries ago, in the process of achieving greater demographic order and efficiency, human population embarked upon an unprecedented cycle of growth. And while this cycle is now coming to an end in the rich countries, it is still in full swing in the poor. World population hit the one billion mark as steam engines began to revolutionize transportation; the second billion was reached after the First World War, as airplanes became an ever more common means of transportation; the third billion was achieved at the beginning of the aerospace era. The fourth and fifth billion marks did not wait for similar revolutionary epochs and were reached in 1973 and 1987; and the sixth will be reached a couple of years before 2000. Many demographers, sure of winning, would be willing to bet that the seventh billion will not be reached before 2010, and that the eighth will come after 2020. The combination of current young age structures and high fertility ensures that these levels will be easily reached within this time frame. Longer-term prediction rapidly loses certainty, becoming eventually a purely mathematical exercise. This uncertainty, however, will not deter us from considering potential population growth well into the next century.

Many view this growth process like a spring that is ever more tightly compressed, ready at the first jolt to unload an accumulation of devastating force. From an economic point of view diminishing returns must sooner or later lower living standards, since land, water, air, and minerals are all fixed and limited resources, allowing only partial substitution and so bound to place a limit on growth. The link between demographic growth and environmental deterioration also seems clear, judging from the pollution caused by industrial expansion and the general ecological degradation associated with the increase of agricultural, industrial, residential, and other human activity. And demographic growth is also a threat to health and social order, given the impossibility of indefinitely expanding food production and the inevitability of competition and conflict between individuals, groups, and peoples in search of a higher standard of living.

Another camp, instead, has complete faith in the ability of populations to adjust to larger numbers. Technological progress, they point out, allows for the substitution of primary resources and leads to increasing agricultural production. In addition, the relative prices of energy, primary resources, and food are at historically low levels and, in any case, the market would react to scarcity by increasing prices and so stimulating technological progress, guaranteeing increased productivity and the possibility of resource substitution. With regard to the costs of unregulated production, currently paid for by humanity at large in the form of environmental deterioration, population optimists maintain that these costs can be "internalized" – that is, paid for by those responsible. Their final argument is that the physical and economic well-being of world population is constantly improving as a result of scientific and economic progress and there is no reason to fear that this situation might change.

It is difficult, if not impossible, to choose between these two modes of foreseeing the future. Once again we return to the Malthusian model and, with regard to the more radical versions of the above arguments, what seems to be a revival of the catastrophist versus optimist debate. However, perhaps the debate itself misses the point and the problem can be better understood by employing an alternative approach, referred to in earlier chapters. I have presented the history of population as a continual compromise between the forces of constraint and the forces of choice. Constraints have been imposed by a hostile environment, by disease, by the limitations of available food and energy, and now by an environment in danger. Choices have included flexible strategies of marriage and reproduction, of mobility, migration, and settlement, and of defense from disease. This interaction between the forces of constraint and choice has continually altered the point of population equilibrium and generated long cycles of growth as well as phases of stagnation and regression. The repeated reestablishment of equilibrium should not be seen as the product of spontaneous self-regulating mechanisms which minimize suffering and loss, but rather as a difficult process of adaptation which rewards more flexible populations while penalizing those more fragile and rigid. Many populations have succeeded at self-regulation, while others either have not or have done so too late, paying a hard price in the form of increased mortality, demographic regression, or in some cases disappearance. In the case of still other populations, mistaken decisions have impaired defensive ability in the face of catastrophe, increasing demographic vulner-ability.[1]

Looking to the future, we should reflect not only on the certain numerical growth of the coming decades (and the conjectural growth of the longer run), but also on the mechanisms of "choice" available to humanity and whether or not they are adequate in the face of external constraints and more or less efficient than in the past.

2 The Numbers of the Future

I have already mentioned that present-day populations are characterized by considerable momentum and so demographic projections for the next couple of decades are fairly plausible. For example, in 2015 the population over 20 years of age will have come from generations born before 1995, which is to say from generations already born and counted; one need only subtract mortality, which is fairly stable over time. On the other hand, the size of the population under 20 years of age, which will be born between 1995 and 2015, is an unknown and depends upon two variables. The first of these variables, the size of the reproductive-age population, is not a mystery, as, again, almost all of those who will enter their fecund period in the next 20 years are already born. The second, unknown, variable is the propensity of this population to bear children, and on this point we can at best make a good guess.

Population momentum can be measured in several ways. One of these consists of imagining that population, say from 1990, adopt (and not subsequently abandon) replacement fertility – which, as we know, will eventually lead to a stationary population (zero growth). Nonetheless, if the population in question has had until recently a high level of fertility and so a young age structure (as in all developing countries), then it will continue to grow for a certain period of time. In the following decades the many recently

---

[1] Examples can be found even in the present century. Consider the disastrous effects of forced collectivization during the Chinese Great Leap Forward of 1958–62 (30 million more deaths than normal in four years) or the similar effects of the 1932–3 crisis in the Soviet Union, certainly worsened by collectivization carried out in the countryside. See B. Ashton et al., "Famine in China 1956–81," *Population and Development Review*, 10 (1984); A. Blum, "Redécouverte de l'histoire de l'URSS (1930–1945)," *Population et Société*, 253 (Jan. 1991); A. Graziosi, ed., *Lettere da Kharkov* (Einaudi, Torino, 1991); M. Livi-Bacci, "On the Human Costs of Collectivization in the USSR," *Population and Development Review*, 19 (1993), n.4.

born will enter reproductive age and, even if each of them bears few children, being numerous they will nonetheless produce a large total number of births. These births in turn will far outnumber deaths, as the latter will come primarily from the elderly, who belong to the smaller generations born many decades ago when population was far less than today. As those born under the new fertility regime begin to enter reproductive age, the number of births will gradually decline until it is approximately equal to the number of deaths. The ratio between the "final" stationary population and the "initial" population is a measure of demographic momentum. In 1990 the population of India numbered 851 million. Imagining that from that date population suddenly achieved replacement level fertility, its final stationary population would be 1,450 million and the measure of momentum (1,450:851) equal to 1.7. Applying this calculation to the populations of other large countries,[2] we obtain values of 1.6 for China; 1.8 for Bangladesh, Pakistan, Indonesia, and Brazil; 1.9 for Mexico; and 2 for Nigeria. European populations have almost no momentum and coefficients are about 1–1.1.

In the upcoming decades demographic momentum alone will lead to the doubling of many populations. In order to suppress this momentum, China has resorted to the one-child law – that is, to a fertility level well below replacement. However, as we know, the fertility of the vast majority of populations is far above replacement level and so the force of high fertility must be added to that of momentum. The United Nations has for some time made accurate projections, periodically revised, of the evolution of world population.[3] Table 6.1 includes some of the principal results of retrospective estimates and so-called medium variant projections through 2025. The latter are based on the fertility and mortality evolution considered most plausible, namely that the fertility of the less-developed countries will continue to decline, from 3.83 children per woman in 1985–90 to 2.38 in 2020–25, and life expectancy at birth will increase in the same period from 60.5 to 71.3 years; for the developed countries a mild fertility recovery is predicted (from 1.83 to 1.93) and a further increase in life expectancy (from 74 to 78.6).

The most interesting results of this projection are the following:

1   World population will reach 6 billion in 1998, 7 billion in 2010, and 8 billion in 2022.

2   The world rate of population increase, equal to 1.7 percent in 1985–90, will gradually decline to 1 percent in 2020–25.

[2]   The World Bank, *World Development Report 1986* (Oxford University Press, New York, 1986), pp. 252–3.
[3]   United Nations, *World Population Prospects: The 1994 Revision* (New York, 1995).

Table 6.1 Global and continental populations (1950–2025) according to the estimates and projections of the United Nations

Area	1950	1975	2000	2025
	Population in millions			
World	2520	4077	6158	8294
More-Developed Countries	809	1044	1186	1238
Less-Developed Countries	1711	3033	4973	7036
Africa	224	414	832	1496
North America	166	239	306	370
Latin America and Caribbean	166	320	524	710
Asia	1403	2406	3736	4960
Europe	549	676	730	718
Oceania	13	21	31	41
	Percentage distribution			
World	100	100	100	100
More-Developed Countries	32.1	25.6	19.3	14.9
Less-Developed Countries	67.9	74.4	80.8	85.1
Africa	8.9	10.2	13.5	6.0
North America	6.6	5.9	5.0	4.5
Latin America and Caribbean	6.6	7.8	8.5	8.6
Asia	55.7	59.0	60.7	59.8
Europe	21.8	16.6	11.9	8.7
Oceania	0.5	0.5	0.5	0.5
	Average annual increase (%)			
World		1.9	1.6	1.2
More-Developed Countries		1.0	0.5	0.2
Less-Developed Countries		2.3	2.0	1.4
Africa		2.5	2.8	2.1
North America		1.5	1.0	0.8
Latin America and Caribbean		2.6	2.0	1.2
Asia		2.2	1.8	1.1
Europe		0.8	0.3	−0.1
Oceania		2.1	1.6	1.1

Source: United Nations, *World Population Prospects: The 1994 Revision* (New York, 1995)

3   However, as this decreasing rate of increase nonetheless applies to an
     ever larger population, absolute annual increase will remain at 88 mil-
     lion (1985–90 level) until 2005–10 before declining to 81 million in the
     last period (2020–25).

4   The target population of 8.3 billion for the year 2025 depends on the
     projected decline of fertility that – for the world as a whole – should
     drop from an estimated TFR of 3.10 in 1990–5 to a projected 2.38 in
     2020–5. Any decimal fraction of TFR above or below the 2.38 target
     at the end of the period will imply roughly 150 million inhabitants
     more or less in 2025.

5   The developing countries will account for approximately 97 percent
     of world population increase in the period 1990–2025.

6   Geo-demographic changes will be considerable: between 1950 and
     2025 the developed country share of world population will decline
     from 33.1 percent to 14.9; Europe's share will decline still faster, from
     21.8 percent to 8.7.

7   The growth of the poor continents will not be even. Again for the
     period 1950–2025, percentage of world population will change: from
     6.6 to 8.6 in Latin America, from 55.7 to 59.8 in Asia, and from 8.9 to
     18.0 in Africa, where, as we know, fertility is extremely high.

The dramatic and variable demographic growth of the past 40 years, and
of the coming 35, will alter considerably the classification of the world's
most populous countries (table 6.2). Nigeria should move from 14th place
in 1950 to 4th in 2025, Pakistan from 13th to 7th, while Japan will fall from
5th to 11th. All of the seven European countries that were in the top 20 in
1950 except Germany will have disappeared from the classification in 2025,
while two new African countries (Ethiopia and Zaire) will have joined. In
1950 only four countries had populations larger than 100 million; in 2025,
they should number 16. As a result, the quantitative ratio between populations traditionally in conflict, or simply in contact, will change. And
though relations between countries are conditioned primarily by political,
cultural, and economic factors, large changes in their relative population
sizes are bound to have an effect. For example, the Rio Grande separates the
rich world of North America from the poor world of Mexico and Central
America. The population ratio between these two areas was 4.5:1 in 1950; in
2025 it will be 1.9:1. It is hard to imagine that something will not change as a
result of this fact alone. The rich countries on the northern shore of the Mediterranean numbered 2.1 times the population of the poor countries on the
southern and eastern shores in 1950; by 2025 this ratio will be 0.6:1. Should it

Table 6.2 The 20 most populous countries in the world (1950 and 2025, population in millions)

1950			2025		
Rank	*Country*	*Population*	*Rank*	*Country*	*Population*
1	China	555	1	China	1526
2	India	358	2	India	1392
3	United States	152	3	United States	331
4	Russian Federation	103	4	Pakistan	285
5	Japan	84	5	Indonesia	276
6	Indonesia	80	6	Nigeria	238
7	Germany	68	7	Brazil	230
8	Brazil	53	8	Bangladesh	196
9	United Kingdom	51	9	Russian Federation	139
10	Italy	47	10	Mexico	137
11	France	42	11	Ethiopia	127
12	Bangladesh	42	12	Iran	124
13	Pakistan	40	13	Japan	122
14	Ukraine	37	14	Vietnam	118
15	Nigeria	33	15	Zaire	105
16	Vietnam	30	16	Philippines	105
17	Mexico	28	17	Egypt	97
18	Spain	28	18	Turkey	91
19	Poland	25	19	Germany	76
20	Egypt	22	20	Myanmar	76

Source: United Nations, *World Population Prospects: The 1994 Revision* (New York, 1995).

be surprising if this reversal carries with it some consequences? And what of the changing numerical relationships between countries traditionally in conflict and growing at different rates: Turkey and Greece, Brazil and Argentina, Israel and the nearby Arab countries (or the Arab population within its borders)?

We might also approach our speculations from another angle, comparing the various continental populations (table 6.3) past, present, and future with two theoretical "stationary" populations. The first of these populations (stationary 1 in table 6.3) is obtained according to the formula discussed above, namely the permanent achievement of replacement fertility in 1990. The second (stationary 2) is obtained imagining that replacement fertility will be achieved at different dates according to current levels and trends:

Table 6.3 1950, 1990, and projected 2025 continental populations together with theoretical stationary populations according to two hypotheses

				Stationary	
Continent	1950	1990	2025	1	2
	Population in millions				
Africa	224	648	1,581	1,296	2,531
America	331	724	1,099	1,086	1,216
Asia	1,375	3,108	4,889	5,128	5,974
Europe, USSR, Oceania	586	812	902	1,037	929
World	2,515	5,292	8,466	8,547	10,650
	Population %				
Africa	8.9	12.2	18.7	15.2	23.8
America	13.2	13.7	13.0	12.7	11.4
Asia	54.7	58.7	57.7	60.0	56.1
Europe, USSR, Oceania	23.3	15.3	10.7	12.1	8.7
World	100.0	100.0	100.0	100.0	100.0

Stationary population 1 is based on the achievement of replacement fertility in 1990. Stationary population 2 is based on the achievement of replacement fertility at various dates; for some of the major countries these are: China (2000), India (2010), Indonesia (2005), Bangladesh (2030), Pakistan (2035), Nigeria (2035), Mexico (2010), Brazil (2015).

Sources: United Nations, *World Population Prospects: The 1994 Revision* (New York, 1995); for stationary populations 1 and 2: World Bank studies with author's adaptations

2000 in China (where it is currently below this level), 2010 in India, 2015 in Brazil, 2035 in Nigeria, and, in any case, by the middle of the next century in all the countries of the world.[4] Following stationary 1, world population would settle at about the level projected for 2025, but with a smaller proportion for Africa (in fact nowhere near replacement) and larger ones for Europe, the former USSR, Oceania, and Asia, where replacement level fertility from 1990 would represent a mild increase for several large populations (Europe, China, Japan). The more plausible stationary 2 would settle world population at a level below 11 billion at the end of the twenty-first

[4] K. C. Zachariah, *World Population Projections, 1987–88* (The Johns Hopkins University Press, Baltimore, 1988).

century (reaching 9 billion about 2040 and 10 billion about 2070). The relative weight of Africa – the last of the continents to achieve replacement fertility – would increase from its present-day 12 percent to 24; that of the other continents would decline.

These last numerical exercises have taken us into the realm of conjecture. We should keep in mind that the concepts of replacement fertility and stationary population are little more than convenient reference points. Nothing ensures that fertility will not remain for long periods either below replacement (as in the West) or far above it. In fact, it is likely that the future evolution of world population, as in the past, will be the sum of non-uniform regional rates of increase. These exercises serve to measure the potential growth of the various continents (highest in Africa) and alert us to the fact that world population, having exceeded 8 billion in the first quarter of the next century, may well reach 10–11 billion before its end.

3 The Moving Limits

The latter part of the next century will likely witness a population double its present size. It is difficult, however, to say whether growth of this sort will jeopardize economic and social progress since, as repeatedly noted, population is not an "independent variable" but reacts and adapts to the possibilities for expansion that it encounters. In recent centuries, many scholars have held firmly to the idea that there is a global "carrying capacity" or in any case a maximum sustainable size given the limits of space and technology and the need to both maintain quality of life and avoid environmental decay.[5] One can of course debate at length the question of quality of life for, like Giammaria Ortes, we do not want to see humanity "grow not only beyond the number of persons that could breathe on the earth, but to such a number as could not be contained on all its surface, from lowest valley to highest mountain, crowded and crammed together like dried dead herrings in their barrel,"[6] a condition which a certain type of technological progress might even make possible.

[5]   An exhaustive review of the definitions and concepts implicit in the expression "carrying capacity" can be found in J. E. Cohen, *How Many People Can the Earth Support?* (Norton, New York, 1995), pp. 419–25. Indeed the whole book is dedicated to an analysis and dissection of this concept.

[6]   G. Ortes, "Riflessioni sulla popolazione delle nazioni per rapporto all'economia nazionale" [1790], in *Scrittori classici italiani di economia politica* (G. G. Destefanis, Milan, 1804), vol. 24, p. 28.

The identification of a "carrying capacity" presents so many conceptual difficulties as to be virtually useless for practical purposes. It is an idea derived from biology and animal ecology designed to measure the capacity of a certain environment to sustain animal life. With the human species, however, we also need to take into account the development of technology, the elasticity of the concept of quality of life, and the ability to adapt and interact in a complex and not easily-modeled dynamic system. Nonetheless, we do live in a finite world and the question of where we place the boundary beyond which numbers and resources enter into conflict is important. Figure 6.1, taken from a recent work by the authors of *Limits to Growth*,[7] describes four possible modes of interaction between population and "carrying capacity." The first two modes (6.1a and 6.1b) represent an optimistic view in which the two forces do not come into conflict. In the first case, as population grows so does carrying capacity (CP), thanks to technological progress, and the two curves do not intersect; in the second, CP is constant but population growth slows as it approaches the limit imposed by the finite environment. The other two curves (Figures 6.1c and 6.1d) represent instead the conflictual modes. In the first (overshoot and oscillation), there is a continual adjustment. In the second (overshoot and collapse), population growth provokes an environmental collapse and demographic catastrophe. Which then describes the future? Will there be no conflict and unlimited expansion (6.1a)? An inevitable conflict resulting in more or less dramatic and painful oscillations (6.1c or 6.1d)? Or instead adaptation and a limitation of growth as population approaches an environmental limit (6.1b)?

The attempt to estimate the earth's carrying capacity is more than three centuries old. These estimates are based on a variety of criteria: from categoric and absolute pronouncements, to the adaptation and extrapolation of mathematical curves, to the extension of observed population densities to the entire terrestrial surface.[8] Other methods rely on the availability of a limited resource, usually food, to calculate a maximum possible population; and others still combine several limited resources, for example food and water. The most complex efforts seek to simulate the interaction between various factors, their substitutability, and the adaptation of lifestyles. Recently, Joel Cohen has critically reviewed all the well-known attempts to estimate carrying capacity, from the earliest estimates of the Dutchman Leeuwenhoek (1679), the Englishman Gregory King (1695), and the German

[7]   D. H. Meadows, D. L. Meadows, and J. Randers, *Beyond the Limits: Global Collapse or a Sustainable Future?* (Earthscan Publications, London, 1992).
[8]   J. E. Cohen, *How Many People*, pp. 216–21.

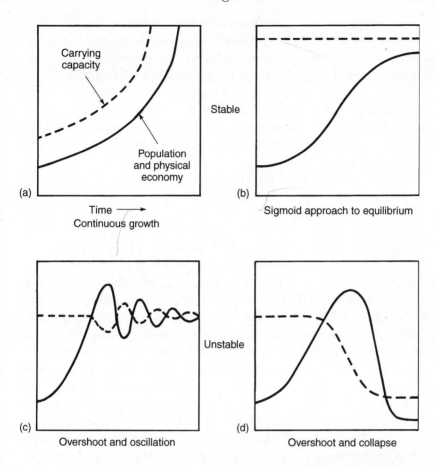

Figure 6.1 Possible modes of approach of a population to its carrying capacity

Note: Time is measured on the horizontal axis and increases from left to right. Carrying capacity (the dashed curve) and a combination of population size and the physical economy (the solid curve) are measured on the vertical axis; both increase upwards. (a) represents exponential or super-exponential growth; (b) represents logistic growth; (c) represents damped oscillations; and (d) represents overshoot or collapse

Source: D. H. Meadows, D. L. Meadows, and J. Randers, *Beyond the Limits: Global Collapse or a Sustainable Future?* (Earthscan Publications, London, 1992), p.108, figure 4.2.

Peter Süssmilch (1741 and 1765) – all within a relatively narrow range between 4 and 13.9 billion – to the most recent. Of the 93 estimates reviewed by Cohen, 17 give a carrying capacity below 5 billion; 28 between 5 and

10; 16 between 10 and 15; 8 between 15 and 25; 13 between 25 and 50; and 11 over 50.[9] The median is around 10 billion, a level that should be reached by about the year 2050 according to the latest UN projections. The differences depend on both the methods and the hypotheses used. Surprisingly, however, the "ceiling" does not increase as one moves from older to more recent estimates; instead it is the variability of the estimates that increases. But these figures are little more than statistics of statistics, good for satisfying one's curiosity but not much of a guide to the real carrying capacity of the earth.

Looking ahead to the future from our own vantage point in the present day, more recent estimates that take into account technological change and lifestyles and that are informed by contemporary and less hypothetical situations are of greater interest. A few merit our rapid consideration. One of the highest carrying capacities was calculated by De Wit (1967) on the supposition that the photosynthesis process would be the limiting factor and that neither water nor mineral resources would impose limits.[10] He divides an estimate of the productive potential of carbohydrates per hectare of cultivable land available in the various climatic regions of the world by per capita caloric consumption to come up with an estimated carrying capacity per hectare and so a maximum population should all possible land be devoted to cultivation (subtracting first for each individual a certain area for home, work, transportation, recreation and so on). In this way, he comes up with a maximum figure of 146 billion, allowing 750 square meters of non-productive land per person, or else 73 billion, allowing a double quota of 1500 m^2. Colin Clark (1967 and 1977) has obtained similar results by different means: estimating the surface area needed per person to feed and supply basic needs, he has come up with a maximum figure of 157 billion assuming Japanese levels of consumption (at the time) and a minimum of 47 billion assuming North American levels.[11] Roger Revelle instead has derived a lower estimate by multiplying available cultivable area (not including wet tropical areas and land needed for non-food production) by the productivity achievable with irrigation and present-day advanced technology to get a carrying capacity of 40 billion.[12]

[9]   Ibid., pp. 402–25.
[10]   C. T. De Wit, "Photosynthesis: Its Relation to Overpopulation," in *Harvesting the Sun: Photosynthesis in Plant Life*, ed. A. San Pietro, F. A. Greer, and T. J. Army (Academic Press, New York, 1967), pp. 315–20.
[11]   C. Clark, *Population Growth and Land Use* (Macmillan, London, 1977).
[12]   R. Revelle, "The Resources Available for Agriculture," *Scientific American*, Sept. 1976.

These estimates are all on the high end of the scale and rely on some difficult assumptions (for example, that all available land be cultivated with advanced techniques). By introducing more realistic hypotheses, the estimates rapidly decrease. Gilland (1983), for example, has employed a method similar to Revelle's but using less optimistic estimates with regard to cultivable area and productivity and derives a much lower estimate of 7.5 billion at comfortable levels of consumption.[13] A joint FAO-IIASA (1983) study takes a different approach. Based on a map of soil types prepared by FAO (and including all the developing world except China), various climatic regions were studied in relation to 15 basic crops and estimates of productive potential were arrived at according to three different hypotheses. The low hypothesis envisions unchanging cultivation and traditional methods employed without fertilizer, pesticides, or mechanization, while the high one foresees employment of the gamut of green revolution technology including full mechanization and use of pesticides and fertilizers. The middle hypothesis makes more realistic assumptions. The carrying capacity of this area which had a population of about 2 billion in 1975 (estimated to grow to about 3.5 by the year 2000) was put at 4 billion according to the low hypothesis, 13.7 according to the intermediate, and 32.8 according to the high.[14] Finally, in a recent and balanced study, Smil (1994) estimates that a realistic reduction in the inefficiencies, irrationality, and waste in the production, distribution, and consumption system could make possible the survival of another 2.5–3 billion people at current levels of consumption, and that additional productive inputs – leaving aside the possibility of revolutionary developments in bio-engineering – could feed another 2–2.5 billion.[15] It seems then realistic to think that the earth will be able to sustain 10 or 11 billion people during the upcoming century.

There are of course more restrictive hypotheses that incorporate higher levels of consumption and strict measures of conservation and environmental management and which estimate carrying capacities below the present-day population. The fact, however, that those limits have been exceeded in the context of declining real prices and increasing average levels of health and life expectancy casts them in some doubt. Moreover, during the past 20 years per-capita food production has been increasing at a rate of 0.5

---

[13] B. Gilland, "Considerations on World Population and Food Supply," *Population and Development Review*, 9 (1983).

[14] J. E. Cohen, *How Many People*, pp. 196–209.

[15] V. Smil, "How Many People can the Earth Feed?," *Population and Development Review*, 20 (1994), n. 2.

percent per year while the real level of food prices (in constant dollars) has been decreasing at about 4 percent per year.[16] A scissor effect of this sort would be inconceivable if the world productive system were in a state of serious tension. Summing up, then, one derives from these studies (and without entering into questions of distribution between countries or social groups) the abstract conviction that the earth's carrying capacity is considerably above the current level of population and that the economic system should be able for several decades to feed the world at average levels which exceed those of the present day.

For the near future, then, limits to population will not be imposed by the food supply. We should perhaps be looking elsewhere, for example at non-renewable resources necessary for the maintenance of production and standards of living. (Though we might at the same time remember the economist Jevons who in the nineteenth century feared that a scarcity of coal would compromise industrial production.) In this area, too, indications are that we shall not soon encounter limits, and for three closely-linked reasons. The first is that the ratio between reserves (not potential reserves but those that can be profitably extracted at current prices) and production (the reserve-to-production ratio or reserve-life index) has been increasing rather than decreasing over recent decades for the major minerals.[17] Secondly, as can be seen in figure 6.2 which compares real prices of primary resources and population, these prices have declined in spite of the growth of population and production. And thirdly, technological progress guarantees a high level of substitution for non-renewable resources. As one or another mineral becomes scarce, prices increase and so encourage the development of new technology to allow for this sort of substitution.

The reasoning above has been conducted on a global scale, and it is specifically about the planet as a whole that we are speaking. Differences in development, natural resources, political institutions, and natural or human-made disasters do not allow us to extend the same sort of discussion to local or regional levels.

---

[16]   Real world food prices have declined from 196 in 1975 to 85 in 1992 (1990 = 100). See World Resources Institute, *World Resources 1994–95* (Oxford University Press, New York, 1994), p. 262. For an analysis of food production, see T. Dyson, "Population Growth and Food Production: Recent Global and Regional Trends," *Population and Development Review*, 20 (1994), n. 2.

[17]   World Resources Institute, *World Resources*, pp. 5–6.

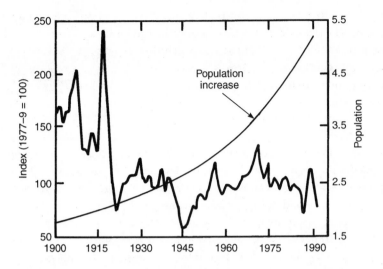

Figure 6.2 Long-run prices for non-ferrous metals (1900–91) plotted
against growth in population

Note: The index is based on the real prices of aluminum, copper, lead, tin, and zinc,
weighted by the value of developing country exports in 1979–81.
Source: World Bank data.

4 The Emerging Limits

The brief review above of the various estimates of the earth's carrying
capacity and the potential limiting factors on population growth – food
production, availability of primary resources – suggests that we are still
far from those limits and that in any case those key symptoms which ought
to announce their approach – reduction in reserves, increasing prices – are
nowhere in sight. If instead we take into consideration a larger context that
includes not only the availability of a certain quantity of goods per person
but also lifestyles, quality of the environment, availability of space, and all
those things which are valued in a particular historical and cultural period,
then the problem becomes much more complicated. It becomes in fact
insoluble, for there is a legitimate and ultimately unbridgeable philosophical
gap between those who believe in the need for the greatest possible
availability of open space and of silence and those instead who favor
lifestyles closely linked to large and dense populations. Nonetheless,
between the attempt to quantify these sentiments and simply refusing to
comment on them, there is an intermediate path. Over the next century,

population growth will effect important if as yet indeterminate changes in human lifestyles. In particular, it will have a profound impact on the environment, and, though the relationships are complex, we can at least make out their general nature.

Let us begin with the following identity proposed by Ehrlich:

$$I = P \times A \times T,$$

according to which the impact on the environment (I) is a function of population size (P) multiplied by the stream of goods per person (A) – expressed by per-capita consumption or income as proxies – multiplied by a factor that embodies the level of technology (T) – expressed by indices that measure the content of each unit of production in terms of inputs of material resources such as energy, commodities, space etc. If we want the impact on environment (I) to be stable or to decline while affluence, or the standard of living, (A) remains stable or increases, than we must obviously act on population size (P) and technology (T). Let us also assume that there is no interrelation between the variables (or that, for instance, variations in population do not affect A or T and vice versa), an hypothesis which I have argued against in this book. The only well-defined variable of the equation is P, for which we know the size with good precision as well as many other interesting characteristics such as location, sex, age, activity, etc. Of P we may also venture to predict future variation with relatively good chances of success. But what about A, or affluence? The addition of 10,000 dollars worth of motorcycle seems to increase individual affluence much more than the addition of 1,000 dollars worth of sophisticated bicycle or of 100 dollars worth of a good pair of shoes; but the calculation is not so straightforward if the motorcyclist is forced to operate in risky, polluted, and trafficky urban streets; the cyclist in a safe network of well-paved roads; and the pedestrian in a pleasant and green environment. So our A variable, or affluence, is not only a matter of economy, material resources, and the organization of society, but also of immaterial lifestyles, or better, philosophy of life, the nature of which varies in time and space. With T, or technology, things are more complicated still: while affluence, given certain hypotheses and approximations, can be measured by means of a monetary yardstick, there is no reliable metric to quantify technology and its change, particularly when applied to such different processes as the production of food or of energy, the manufacturing of a great variety of goods, or the performance of services.

In this context, the relation between population and environment can be

seen under different profiles, of which I will look at four. The first is the
inevitable growth of the consumption of non-renewable resources over
the coming decades and, therefore, the non-sustainability of development
for a more or less long period. The second is the impact of population
growth on the demand for food, on production, and on the environment.
The third concerns the changing allocation of space, with particular
emphasis on fragile environments. And the fourth examines the possible
contribution of population growth to atmospheric pollution and so to
global warming. The four points have an element in common: over the
next two generations the actual "momentum" built in to the young age
structure of poor populations will generate an inevitable increase; in fact,
the medium variant of the United Nations projection, extended up to the
year 2050, implies a near doubling of population by that year (the population of the less developed regions will increase from 4,550 million to
8,626). More population – and with it a greater degree of affluence – will
imply more human activity and a growing impact on the environment
unless their combined effect is offset by technological advance.

Let us examine the first point. It is well known that the per-capita
levels of consumption of commodities and energy for the rich economies
is several times that for the poor ones. The ratio is 20 times for aluminum
consumption, 17 for copper, 10 for iron ore, 9 for fossil fuel, and 3 for
roundwood, just to give a few examples.[18] Rich countries then contribute
disproportionately to the depletion of resource reserves. However, the
future outlook is less bleak than the present situation because substitution, recycling, and changes in consumption patterns are determining a
decline in the energy and commodity content of each additional dollar's
worth of rich-country production.[19] Moreover, the rich populations will
grow slowly or not at all in future decades. Prospects then for the
stabilization or even decline over the long run of the consumption of
basic resources in the rich countries have some foundation. Prospects for
the poor countries are different. According to World Bank estimates for
1992,[20] the per-capita GNP of the poor economies (defined as "low" or
"low-middle" income and representing 76.5 percent of the population of
the world) was 656 dollars as compared to 11,574 for the rich economies
("upper-middle" and "high"). Growth over the next decades of the poor
economies will have to exceed that of the rich ones if the ratio (if not the

---

[18]   World Resources Institute, *World Resources*, pp. 8–11.
[19]   Ibid., p. 6.
[20]   The World Bank, *The World Bank Atlas 1994* (Washington, 1993).

absolute gap) between the affluence of the two worlds is to be reduced. Over the next generation the per-capita GNP of these economies will have to be multiplied by a factor of 2, 3, or more, which will imply more iron and minerals for tools, more fibers for clothing, more wood for building, more food for nutrition, more space for living, and more energy for all these activities. Since the standard of living of the poor populations is very low, this additional stream of goods per person will have to be obtained with high inputs of energy, commodities, and space for each dollar's worth of production. And these populations are of course asking for more food, tools, clothing, houses, and fuel. Considering that over the next two generations or so they will double in size and that the stream of per-capita goods will have to be multiplied several times, it is easy to understand that this indispensable growth will hardly be sustainable for a very long time.[21]

The second point relates to agriculture and the demand for food. Over the next 30 years, world population will increase by 45 percent and the population of the poor countries by 55 percent. This growth will imply at least a proportional increase in the production of food. About four-fifths of total consumption consists of grains, so that the increased demand for grain (together with demand for other foods, fibers, and fuel) "will add enormously to pressure on natural resources – not only on agricultural land but also on stocks of water, fish, and timber. Natural resources will have to be managed with great care. They will need protection from the inadequate stewardship that is the consequence of poverty, population pressure, ignorance, and corruption. Natural forests, wetlands, coastal areas, and grasslands – all of high ecological value – will have to be protected from overuse and degradation."[22] This is the assessment of the World Bank. Past trends suggest the options for the future. Between 1961 and 1990 grain production in poor countries increased 118 percent compared to a population increase of 93 percent so that per-capita production has substantially increased. About 92 percent of this increase is attributable to increased average yields and only 8 percent to an increase in cultivated area. Of course, the same options are open for the future: grain production may be obtained either by adding new land to cultivation or through an intensification of already cultivated

---

[21] P. Demeny, "Population and Development", in IUSSP, *Distinguished Lecture Series on Population and Development* (International Conference on Population and Development, Cairo, 1994).

[22] The World Bank, *World Development Report 1992: Population and Environment* (Oxford University Press, Oxford, 1992), p. 134.

areas. Both options have different potential impacts on the environment; citing again the World Bank: "If more food can be grown on the same land, that will ease pressure to cultivate new land and will permit the preservation of intact natural areas . . . But intensification can also produce problems. Raising yields by increasing the use of chemicals, diverting more water for irrigation, and changing land use can create problems elsewhere. Runoff of fertilizer and animal wastes can cause algal blooms and the eutrophication of lakes, coastal estuaries, and enclosed seas. Although these externalities are more common in Western Europe and North America, pollution from agricultural sources is becoming significant in Eastern Europe and other parts of the developing world as well; in the Punjab in India and Pakistan and in Java, Indonesia, the use of chemical inputs is almost as great as in industrial areas."[23] The alternative to intensification is bringing new areas under cultivation (extensification), but one does not need to quote Malthus to conclude that this process cannot go on forever; indeed in some countries – Bangladesh, for instance – the limits have already been reached.

The third point derives from the second. If increased demand for food implies extensification of agriculture, then land-use modification may endanger areas already in fragile equilibrium. Habitat alteration is not, of course, anything new in human history. The face of Europe since the Middle Ages has changed profoundly as forest has receded in favor of cropland. At the global level, it has been estimated that cropland between 1700 and 1980 increased by a factor of 6, an increase less than proportional to population growth.[24] In 1989–91 the world's 130.4 million square kilometers of land were divided as follows: 14.4 million square kilometers (11.0 percent) were devoted to cropland; 33.6 (25.8 percent) to permanent pasture; 39 (29.9 percent) to forest and woodland; and 43.4 (33.3 percent) were classified as "other land" (uncultivated land, grassland not devoted to pasture, wetlands, built-up areas etc.).[25] Over the period 1979–81 to 1989–91 cropland increased by 1.8 percent, pasture by 2.4 percent, and other land by 5.5 percent, while forestland decreased by 7.8 percent.[26] Changes of this nature, if sustained over a long period, would obviously bring about profound modifications of the earth's surface.

[23] Ibid.
[24] G. K. Heilig, "Neglected Dimensions of Global Land-Use Change: Reflections and Data," *Population and Development Review*, 20 (1994), n. 4, p. 833 table 1.
[25] World Resources Institute, *World Resources*, p. 284, table 17.1.
[26] Ibid.

The role of population change is more evident in the case of fragile environments such as forests. Although there is controversy about the rate of deforestation, there is general agreement that the main factor is the clearing of land for agricultural purposes – particularly in Africa and Latin America – and that this cause accounts for almost two-thirds of all deforestation.[27] This sort of clearing is a direct consequence of increased demand for food and fuelwood and, indirectly, of population growth. At the aggregate country level, there is in fact some evidence of a positive relation between the rate of population growth and the rate of deforestation,[28] but this relationship is relatively weak as there are other intermediate factors at work: opportunities for intensification, population density, and government regulations and institutions. Individual country studies, however have clearly described situations in which deforestation has taken place under demographic pressure in contexts as different as the Philippines – where migration from the densely-settled lowlands to the mountainous interior has led to rapid deforestation – Guatemala, Sudan, and Thailand.[29]

The growth of built-up areas for housing; for industrial, commercial, and recreational use; for communications and other purposes is another aspect of the transformation of land-use that cannot go on forever under the pressure of population change. A driving force in this regard is rapid urbanization. According to United Nations estimates and projections (figure 6.3), urban population grew from 29.3 percent of total population in 1950 to 45.2 percent in 1995 and will surpass rural population in 2005; moreover, by that time 2 urban dwellers out of 5 will live in urban agglomerations of 1 million inhabitants or more. Data relating to a group of European countries shows – as expected – a direct relation between population density and the proportion of built-up land: a minimum is found in Iceland (0.3 percent of total land built-up and a density of 1 inhabitant per square kilometer) and a maximum in the Netherlands (15.9 percent and a density of 450 – see figure 6.4). The concentration of population growth in coastal areas is another potential problem; it is estimated that by the end of this century about two-thirds of the world

[27]   The World Bank, *World Development Report 1992*, pp. 57–8.
[28]   Preston, "Population and Environment from Rio to Cairo," in IUSSP, *Distinguished Lecture Series on Population and Development* (International Conference on Population and Development, Cairo, 1994), p. 8; R. E. Bilsborrow, "Population, Development and Deforestation: Some Recent Evidence," in United Nations, *Population, Environment and Development* (New York, 1994).
[29]   R. E. Bilsborrow, *Population, Development and Deforestation*, pp. 129–31.

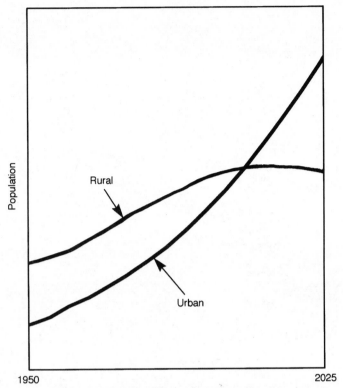

Figure 6.3   Rural and urban world populations (1950–2025)

population will live within 60 kilometers of the coast: "Consequently the environmental pressures upon coastal land and coastal waters – the whole coastal zone – are becoming evermore intense with ever expanding built environments, pollution and shallow seas, and depletion and exhaustion of marine fisheries . . . The environmental vulnerability of coastal areas has been highlighted in recent years by the recurrent natural hazards (e.g. typhoons, tidal waves) affecting the densely peopled deltaic areas of countries in South and South-East Asia, most notably Bangladesh, posing several problems of environmental management."[30]

The fourth and last point relates to the contribution of population

[30]   B. Zaba and J. I. Clarke, "Introduction: Current Directions in Population-Environment Research," in *Environment and Population Change*, ed. B. Zaba and J. I. Clarke (Ordina, Liège, n.d. [1994]), p.24.

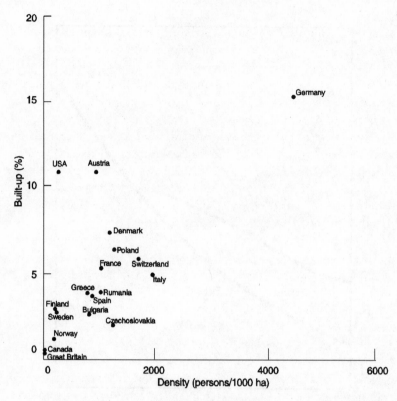

Figure 6.4   Population density and the proportion of built-up land in
Europe and North America, 1990

growth to atmospheric pollution. A growing volume of human activity,
and especially increased burning of fossil fuels, results in an increased
concentration of "greenhouse gases" in the atmosphere; by blocking
infrared radiation emitted from the earth's surface, these gases may cause
global warming with a variety of impacts on the environment and human
activities. Recent complex forecasts based on a "business-as-usual
hypothesis" estimate a doubling of CO_2 emissions before 2025 and a
quadrupling before the end of next century; this increase of emissions
would generate, in turn, a 1-degree Celsius increase of global temperature
by 2025 and a 3–4 degree increase by 2100.[31] It is worth noting, however,
that while the increase of emissions is an undeniable and relatively well-
measured phenomenon, inferences about the ensuing global warming are

[31]   The World Bank, *World Development Report 1992*, pp. 158–60.

subject to open debate. Finally, inferences about the economic and social consequences of (possible) global warming are based on speculation. Bongaarts recently estimated that population growth will account for about 50 percent of the net increase of emissions between 1985 and 2025; for the period 2025–2100, and under the hypothesis that population will reach 10.4 billion by the year 2100, the net contribution of population growth would be only 22 percent.[32] The role of technology in reducing future emissions is not incorporated into these estimates; and yet its present-day role is overwhelming in explaining why different countries – at different levels of income – have very different levels of emissions per capita and per GNP dollar produced.[33] Technology will certainly also be preponderant in determining emissions in the future, relegating population growth to a secondary role.

The above examples reveal the complexity of the relationship between population growth and the environment. This relationship is affected in multiple ways by the number of inhabitants and by the volume and nature of human activities (in symbols: P, A, and T). The inevitable population growth of the first half of the next century, together with an increasing degree of affluence, will determine an increased demand for commodities, food, and space; it will deplete some fixed resources and put increasing pressure on renewable ones. Technology may offset many undesirable effects, increasing substitution or abating pollution; and institutions may do the same, regulating land use, access to resources, and so on; while cultural changes may contribute to this end through modified consumption patterns and changes in behavior. In the end, the negative effects of population growth – at least for the next century – may be neutralized and the limits to growth pushed forward. But three points have to be recognized: the first is that population growth is not neutral; the second is that a slow-down of growth will ease the solution of many problems; and the third is that never before have the human forces that threaten the living system of the planet been so strong. It is prudent to lessen the risks, and restraint of population growth will contribute to this end.

---

[32] Bongaarts, "Population Growth and Global Warming," *Working Paper no. 37* (The Population Council, New York, 1992). See also W. Lutz, "Population and Environment – What Do We Need More Urgently: Better Data, Better Questions or Better Models?," in *Environment and Population*, ed. B. Zaba and J. I. Clarke.

[33] Preston, *Population and Environment*, pp. 13–14.

5   Calculations and Values

Our discussion does not conclude on the side of either the optimists or
the catastrophists. We can, however, attempt to understand whether the
mechanisms of "choice" available to population, which allow for the
regulation of growth as a function of perceived constraints, are weaker
or stronger than they were in the past. Our closing reflections consider
this question with regard to the perception of constraint and the functioning of mechanisms of choice and regulation.

Perception of the elements of constraint raises complex problems.
Given the strength of population momentum, corrections – for example,
a change in the supply of births – are only felt after a considerable delay.
Moreover, certain "danger" signs are only slowly recognized: environmental deterioration, for example, is only fully perceived after the damage has
been done. The slow deforestation of a valley will lead to disastrous
overflowing of the valley's river, but only long after the process has
begun. The "greenhouse effect," created by the accumulation of carbon
dioxide and other gases in the atmosphere, may only be felt after decades,
and an initial warming phase may even be erroneously interpreted as a
positive development.

In traditional rural societies, awareness of the problems created by
demographic growth was probably more immediate than it is in modern
society. The inhabitants of a village, valley, or region experienced directly
the negative effects of new settlement in an area already demographically
saturated, and, while less efficient than those of the present-day, regulating mechanisms could gradually bring about the necessary adjustments.
The expansion and integration of markets and the development of trade
have contributed to masking from individual perception the link between
natural resources (land, for example) and consumer goods. Hong Kong
can grow out of all measure, importing agricultural products from the
United States or Argentina, without any awareness of the connection
between the grain or beef consumed and the rural environment which
produces them. This sort of detachment is a necessary consequence of
economic development, but it should be pointed out that as a result the
direct link between the protagonist of demographic choice (the individual) and the producer of the forces of constraint (the environment) has
been broken. This link is slowly being reestablished as the minority of
individuals, institutions, and governments that now recognize the global
nature and interconnectedness of environmental phenomena increases.

On a more immediate, economic level, price fluctuations should provide "danger" signs, announcing the imminent shortage of fundamental goods and so the need to correct the situation by lowering demand (which may in the long run have demographic implications) when it is no longer feasible to increase supply. The price system, however, does not always send out the right signals and a policy of subsidies may distort this process. Often cited are the adverse (demographic) effects of developing country policies that keep basic food prices artificially low, compromising agricultural profits and further speeding migration to the already swollen cities. More generally, the noninclusion in prices of the expense of production-incurred environmental deterioration constitutes a serious distortion of the "signal" that prices should be sending.

I have already discussed at length the mechanisms of choice and growth regulation (see chapters 4 and 5), and clearly these have been enormously strengthened as a result of artificial methods of contraception. These relatively new and potent tools of regulation are spreading rapidly, making society more flexible in the face of the constraints it must face. In addition, even the Malthusian preventive check – access to reproduction, or marriage – seems to be in operation, judging from the increase in average age at marriage that most poor populations have experienced over the past few decades. I have also discussed mortality reduction. The improvements of the past two centuries have continued in recent decades as life expectancy has continued to increase even where it was already high. Nonetheless, we should not underestimate the fact that further mortality reduction may be blocked by the increasing costs of an unnatural lengthening of human life: the economic costs of medical technology and care, as well as the moral costs linked to the suffering involved in permanent therapeutic dependence or useless terminal treatment and to solitude. Furthermore, we must take into account the appearance of new diseases (AIDS) partly linked to new behavior patterns and the ability of viruses to transform over time; the continued toll taken by existing afflictions, like cancer, whose links to human-produced changes in the environment or food are difficult to eliminate; and the increasing importance of new and subtle forms of environmental constraint (stress, for example) accompanied by a series of negative consequences.

While modern society may be better equipped with regard to the regulation of mortality and fertility than societies of the past, the same cannot be said with regard to another mechanism of choice, namely migration. The peopling of the world has been accomplished by means of migration and settlement which has distributed population according to existing or potential resources. Emigration has also always been the principal route of escape from poverty and destitution.[34] This "freedom" of settlement, which in modern times has led to the Europeanization of temperate America and Australia, is today much impaired. In response to primarily political considerations, nations generally regard immigration as a marginal fact, acceptable only within a fairly rigid framework and in small numbers. Given the enormous national differences in wages and assets and the relative ease of mobility, perhaps it could not have been otherwise. Nonetheless, it is also the case that there exists no open and available territory to act as an outlet for demographic excess and to colonize with human population, plants, and animals.[35] In addition, greater economic integration (for example, the increased value of international trade in relation to production) is accompanied by greater separation of peoples and ethnic groups; the creation of new national states, often bounded by unnatural borders, has led to the redistribution of ethnic groups, previously mixed, within well-defined political units; and a tendency toward segregation between groups is also frequent within national borders. So the effectiveness of an important tool of "choice," migration, has declined as compared to the past.

Our balance sheet, then, has both credit and debit entries, and it is not easy to calculate the bottom line, though the ability to control fertility, when it becomes universal, will constitute the decisive factor for controlling growth.

More and more one hears that the control of population growth has been accepted as a positive value and so does not require demonstration or confirmation. All things considered, this is a fortunate development for demographers who will no longer be obliged to demonstrate the advantages of this or that trend. Our environment is certainly finite, even if its limits can be repeatedly expanded, and unlimited growth cannot continue without increasing risks. This observation should be sufficient to support the conviction that the human race must prepare itself for a long phase of demographic moderation, and in some cases reversal.

Another factor should be kept in mind: beyond certain limits, demographic growth creates diseconomies of scale, reversing a trend which seems to have dominated much of human history. Consider the

---

[34] J. K. Galbraith, The Nature of Mass Poverty (Penguin Books, Harmondsworth, 1980).
[35] A. W. Crosby, Ecological Imperialism. The Biological Expansion of Europe, 900–1900 (Cambridge University Press, London, 1986).

unrestrained growth of urban agglomerations in poor countries[36]: in 1970 only one exceeded a population of 10 million, in 1995 their number was 11, and in the year 2015 they should be 23 (with a total population of 378 million as opposed to 141 million in 1995). Social, sanitary, and environmental problems associated with this growth will involve management difficulties which increase at a greater rate than the aggregate they concern. Other diseconomies of scale will be encountered in the areas of poverty, nutrition, and illiteracy: even in the context of general economic progress, rapid demographic growth brings with it – in spite of a decrease in the overall frequency of these social blights (expressed as a percentage of total population) – an increase in the absolute numbers of the poor, malnourished, and illiterate. For example, the World Bank estimates that the frequency of poverty in sub-Saharan Africa will increase from 48 to 50 percent between 1990 and 2000, and the absolute number of the poor will increase from 216 to 304 million.[37] Relief programs forced to cope with a poor population that has increased by one-third will probably run into greater than proportional problems. The situation for malnutrition and education is analogous, given a large increase in the number of the hungry and illiterate. In many cases the elimination of a problem becomes proportionately more difficult as its dimensions grow; this is a diseconomy of scale.

It is therefore likely that we are entering an historical phase – of indeterminate length – during which population growth will cease to produce economies of scale and may well start producing overwhelming diseconomies. So there do exist justifications for the control of population growth; and as that control is becoming an accepted element in the strategy of global survival it tends to be less and less a matter of calculations and more and more one of values.

It is a common perception that current population growth is like a vehicle speeding on a dangerous road. The road represents resources that are believed to be limited (they are, but they are also very elastic). At the end of the road there is a ravine. Our vehicle covers the road at a fantastic speed approaching the ravine and disaster. There are two teams working on the problem. One tries to improve the road, either bypassing the ravine or building a bridge over it – that is human ingenuity trying to economize needed resources, substitute one with another, or invent new ones. The other team works on the vehicle, but there are disagreements. Some want

[36] United Nations, *World Urbanization Prospects* (New York, 1995)
[37] World Bank, *World Development Report 1992*, p. 30.

to reduce power and speed so that more time will elapse before the ravine is approached. Others want to improve steering, brakes, suspensions, so that the pilot is able to drive safely, adjusting to the characteristics of the road, accelerating, slowing down or coming to a halt if needed. This is the best vehicle, able to maneuver and to choose the safer course, with a responsible driver able to see the signs of danger.

Index